9/03

CHINA

A Global Studies Handbook

GLOBAL STUDIES: ASIA

CHINA

A Global Studies Handbook

Robert André LaFleur with

Warren Bruce Palmer

John A. Rapp

Shin Yong Robson

Tamara Hamlish

A B C CLIO

Santa Barbara, California • Denver, Colorado • Oxford, England

Library of Congress Cataloging-in-Publication Data

China : a global studies handbook / Robert André LaFleur ... [et al.].
    p. cm. — (Global studies, Asia)
Includes bibliographical references.
    ISBN 1-57607-284-3 (hardcover : alk. paper)
    ISBN 1-57607-736-5 (e-book)

1. China--Handbooks, manuals, etc. I. LaFleur, Robert André, 1959–
II. Series.
DS706.C4893 2003
951—dc21   2003004169

07 06 05 04 03   10 9 8 7 6 5 4 3 2 1

This book is also available on the World Wide Web as an e-book.
Visit abc-clio.com for details.

ABC-CLIO, Inc.
130 Cremona Drive, P.O. Box 1911
Santa Barbara, California 93116-1911

This book is printed on acid-free paper.
Manufactured in the United States of America

Contents

Series Editor's Foreword

It is imperative that as many Americans as possible develop a basic understanding of Asia. In an increasingly interconnected world, the fact that Asia contains almost 60 percent of all the planet's population is argument enough for increased knowledge of the continent on our parts. There are at least four other reasons, in addition to demography, that it is critical Americans become more familiar with Asia.

Americans of all ages, creeds, and colors are extensively involved economically with Asian countries. U.S.-Pacific two-way trade surpassed our trade with Europe in the 1970s. Japan, with the world's second-largest economy, is also the second-largest foreign investor in the United States.

American companies constitute the leading foreign investors in Japan.

The recent Asian economic crisis notwithstanding, since World War II East Asia has experienced the fastest rate of economic growth of all the world's regions. Recently, newly industrialized Southeast Asian countries such as Indonesia, Malaysia, and Thailand have joined the so-called Four Tigers—Hong Kong, the Republic of Korea, Singapore, and Taiwan—as leading areas for economic growth. In the past decade China has begun to realize its potential to be a world-influencing economic actor. Many Americans now depend upon Asians for their economic livelihoods and all of us consume products made in or by Asian companies.

It is impossible to be an informed American citizen without knowledge of Asia, a continent that directly impacts our national security.

America's war on terrorism is, as this foreword is composed, being conducted in an Asian country—Afghanistan. (What many Americans think of as the "Mideast" is, in actuality, Southwest Asia.) Both India and Pakistan now have nuclear weapons. The eventual reunification of the Korean Peninsula is fraught with the possibility of great promise or equally great peril. The question of U.S.-China relations is considered one of the world's major global geopolitical issues. Americans everywhere are affected by Asian political and military developments.

Asia and Asians have also become an important part of American culture.

Asian restaurants dot the American urban landscape. Buddhism is rapidly growing in the United States. Asian movies are becoming increasingly popular in the United States. Asian-Americans, while still a small percentage of the overall U.S. population, are one of the fastest-growing ethnic groups in the United States. Many Asian-Americans exert considerable economic and political influence in this country. Asian sports, pop music, and cinema stars are becoming household names in America. Even Chinese language characters are becoming visible in the United States on everything from baseball caps to t-shirts to license plates. Followers of the ongoing debate on American educational reform will constantly encounter references to Asian student achievement.

Americans should also better understand Asia for its own sake. Anyone who is considered an educated person needs a basic understanding of Asia. The continent has a long, complex, and rich history. Asia is the birthplace of all the world's major religions including Christianity and Judaism.

Asian civilizations are some of the world's oldest. Asian arts and literature rank as some of humankind's most impressive achievements.

Our objectives in developing the Global Studies: Asia series are to assist a wide variety of citizens to gain a basic understanding of Asian countries and to enable readers to be better positioned for more in-depth work. We envision the series being appropriate for libraries, educators, high school, introductory college and university students, businesspeople, would-be tourists, and anyone who is curious about an Asian country or countries. Although there is some variation in the handbooks—the diversity of the countries requires slight variations in treatment—each volume includes narrative chapters on history and geography, economics, institutions, and society and contemporary issues. Readers should obtain a sound general understanding of the particular Asian country about which they read.

Each handbook also contains an extensive reference section. Because our guess is that many of the readers of this series will actually be traveling to Asia or interacting with Asians in this country, introductions to language, food, and etiquette are included. The reference section of each handbook also contains extensive information—including Web sites when relevant—about business and economic, cultural, educational, exchange, government, and tourist organizations. The reference sections also include capsule descriptions of famous people, places, and events and a comprehensive annotated bibliography for further study.

—*Lucien Ellington*
Series Editor

Preface

Traveling on a freeway overpass in Shanghai late in the summer of 2002, I happened to see a large, bright billboard with the background formed by a ceremonial cauldron from early China. The English caption read, "Chinese Culture Flows Like a Great River." The Chinese phrase was even more telling, because it opened a small window into the ways that even today, in bustling Shanghai, many Chinese think about their past. "Five thousand years of Chinese culture," it began. Even without the multilayered meaning of the characters themselves (in which "culture" can mean something closer to bright, shining refinement), the billboard closely represented the image that I have gotten from Chinese friends and colleagues over the years—that of a continuous, building flow of tradition that, like the teeming, silty waters of the Yellow River, carves out a path that makes China unique.

Today's China—just as I saw traveling at sixty miles per hour on a freeway and grasping a connection to China's rich past—is filled with images of continuity and abrupt change. It has more than a billion people and a 3,000-year *written* history, not to mention the store of archaeological finds that are making the aforementioned 5,000-year claim seem more and more plausible. China's formidable population and long history, though, are only two reasons to take it seriously as an object of study for students, travelers, and businesspeople. Having just joined the World Trade Organization and been awarded the 2008 Olympic Games, China is sure to be on the international stage in the coming decades. With its barely tapped international economy and growing political power—within its region and beyond—it will undoubtedly be a major player in world affairs during the twenty-first century. But there is even more waiting for interested readers.

China remains, for all its size and strength, an enigma for many Westerners. With a language that is difficult to master, political institutions that often have roots in centuries-old practices, and social relationships grounded deeply in the cultivation of personal connections, China has long proven a formidable challenge for Western travelers. Even with China's increasing openness to foreign investment and travel, information is often difficult to find and even harder to interpret. What many students, travelers, and businesspeople lack is *context* for what they have learned from newspapers, travel, and anecdotes. Between serious scholarly studies and the daily or weekly press lies a confusion of materials that is often extremely difficult for even the most devoted generalist to evaluate.

This book is intended to fill that middle ground between the academic study of China and the array of reports and volumes one might find on any bookstore or library shelf. It is an introduction to China and the Chinese people for readers interested in a clear approach to the most important issues in China's history, economy, politics, society, and language. It assumes no previous knowledge of China, but it is written with the expectation that readers will be open to the challenges of learning about one of the world's greatest civilizations. The study of China is filled with such challenges, but it is important to show readers that it is accessible with the right tools, the right approach. China today is a vibrant society alive with change and connections to global issues that we all share. It is far too important to ignore, and far too important to marginalize by only looking at a narrow swath of contemporary issues. All the contributors to this volume share a deep interest in the study of contemporary China, but all appreciate (as will be clear from each chapter) the rich connections that China, in the early twenty-first century, has to a history that is thousands of years old.

I have written this volume with the help of four of my colleagues in the Asian Studies program at Beloit College. Warren Palmer, John Rapp, Tamara Hamlish, and Shin Yong Robson have my gratitude for producing their individual chapters and for reading the whole manuscript and making suggestions for revisions. I am just as indebted to Beloit College for its support of our teaching and writing on this project. I have used parts of the book in many of my classes, as have several of the contributors, and the feedback from students and colleagues has been invaluable.

This is a general book on China written by experienced college teachers, each with a decade or more of instruction in college classrooms. Our chapters thus have been written with the kind of understanding of beginning students that marks all of our introductory classes. Contrary to common assumptions, however, each of us knows that beginning students, and readers of this volume, are capable of learning a great deal if they are taught correctly, with each theme building upon others until the students attain a quite sophisticated understanding of the complex entity that is China. We have each seen the exhilarating changes in students' knowledge of Chinese history, culture, politics, economics, and language after a single semester.

We have also found that it is much easier to create that kind of deep understanding for beginning students *in the classroom*. I asked the contributors to give a sense of their introductory teaching as they wrote their chapters. We all found it to be one of the greatest challenges that we have faced. In my own experience, putting my teaching of Chinese history into a mere 20,000 words was harder than anything I have ever done. I have tried to convey the themes that I use in all of my teaching, but I have had to do so without the day-to-day interaction that I enjoy in the classroom. The contributors to this volume have voiced similar sentiments, but it is important to note that we have found the experience of writing these chapters to be a special version of our teaching. Each of our chapters is meant to reflect the way we convey ideas in the classroom but to an audience that is much wider than any we are likely to find there. Our intent is that the book mirror the freshness and pace of our own classes—to welcome those with little knowledge and leave them with a combination of analysis, stories, anecdotes, and information that will deepen their knowledge of this vast country.

Toward that end I have asked each contributor to keep two very clear examples of our audience in mind—one, a high school student writing a serious report on a country about which he or she knows little, and the other, an adult with no specific knowledge of China who is about to take a trip for business or pleasure. College students might end up reading parts of it, but it is addressed to general readers. We all wrote with specific examples of that audience in mind. I, for example, envisioned my nephew, a high school student, along with a good friend who was traveling to China for the first time on business. Neither speaks or reads Chinese, and neither is going to pursue the study of China at a professional level. These are the intelligent readers who often get lost in the flurry of publications in today's market.

This book was produced in that "teaching spirit," with a wide audience in mind. I have written the opening chapter, "China's Geography and History," with the goal of introducing readers to China's rich history and vast landscapes. Even though the chapter is arranged chronologically, from early myths and histories to the first decade of the twenty-first century, I have provided a number of core themes for readers that will help them better understand China's history. It will also help them read the subsequent chapters with a newfound appreciation for long-term changes in Chinese civilization. Chapter 2, "The Chinese Economy," was written by Warren Palmer, assistant professor of economics at Beloit, who has been almost a coauthor of this work. Warren not only wrote his chapter and contributed to the reference sections on Chinese economics but also read every chapter carefully and provided insightful comments. He also drafted a significant part of the geography section at the beginning of the volume. I am deeply indebted to him.

Chapter 3, "Chinese Politics and Government," was written by John Rapp, professor of political science at Beloit. John has inspired me and our students with his knowledge of and enthusiasm for Chinese politics and issues of comparative study. He has also been a trusted mentor for me ever since I came to Beloit. Tamara Hamlish, formerly associate professor of anthropology, provides perspectives on Chinese culture in Chapter 4 that come from her own field studies as well as personal experience that comes from a deep knowledge of the richly nuanced spoken language and the practice of calligraphy. Tamara and I were classmates at the University of Chicago and have taught together at Lake Forest and Beloit Colleges. She is one of the very best minds I have ever encountered, and one of my dearest friends.

These core chapters are followed by a reference section detailing major figures and events in China's history, from early times to the present. The final section of the book is comprised of reference materials on the Chinese language, organizations for students and travelers, and suggestions for further reading. This section begins with the work of my colleague Shin Yong Robson, who has used her teaching of the Chinese language to give a fascinating overview of the rich diversity of the written and spoken language in China. She has inspired me in the four years I have known her as a linguist and Chinese language professor with her high standards and good humor. She has created a superb Chinese language program at Beloit College, and her skills can be seen on each page of her section on Chinese language. That section is followed by pieces on Chinese cuisine, to which most of us contributed, and etiquette, which was written by Warren Palmer from presentations he has given on the subject with anecdotes added by several other contributors. All other sections—the key events, Significant People and Events section, the organizations, and recommended readings—have had input from all authors.

Many people beyond the contributors have helped with the production of this book. I would first like to thank the editors at ABC-CLIO. Alicia Merritt, Carol Smith, Michelle Asakawa, and Scott Horst have helped the project through numerous challenges since the autumn of 2000, when I took this project on. I would also like to thank the series editor, Lucien Ellington, who warmly entertained me in Chattanooga during one of my periods of doubt during the composition process. I want to thank Andrea Hugg, Beloit College class of 2002, for coordinating the acquisition of materials from the Beloit College museums and archives for use in this book. Paralleling what I have said of our Asian studies program, it is the very rare college that offers research and teaching resources directly relevant to a book such as ours, right from our own collections. One of the reasons I came to Beloit College five years ago was because it possessed a fine archival connection and two excellent museums. Fred Burwell, Bill Green, Nicolette Meister, Judy Newland, and Marcus Eckhardt have been enormously helpful to both Andrea and me in this process.

A number of people read portions of the manuscript, including all members of my History 291 classes at Beloit College in 2000 and 2001, as well as Warren Palmer's class on Chinese economics. My former student from Colby College, Adella Mikkelsen, read the entire manuscript and provided excellent advice on organizations and illustrations. Kai Wicker, Susannah Chang, and Amy Hilbert also read the volume and provided very useful comments. Ruby Marcello and Bogdan Stamoran helped enormously in the later stages of editing, since they have taken the courses on which four of the five major sections are based. Those who read parts of the manuscript are too numerous to name, but I deeply appreciate their help. Above all, Mara Naselli took the manuscript at a time when all of our collective energy was flagging, and brought a newfound crispness to our work. I thank her and all other readers for the enormous help they have given. Any mistakes or omissions that remain are the responsibility of myself and the contributors. All translations, unless otherwise noted, are my own.

Finally, I want to thank my students at Colby and Beloit Colleges, who during the past eight years have taught me a great deal about writing and speaking to very intelligent nonspecialists. All of the contributors have been blessed by an enormous display of goodwill and patience from our students, and they have kept us going through the challenges of teaching about a civilization and a language as vast and complex as China's. We dedicate this volume to them all.

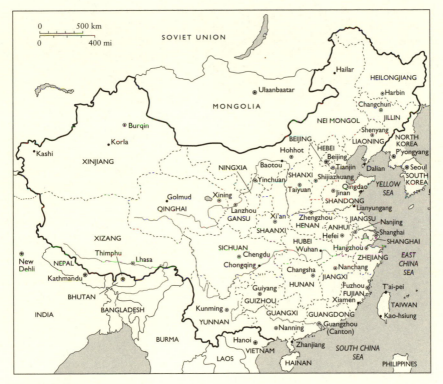

Map of China

PART ONE

NARRATIVE SECTION

CHAPTER ONE
China's Geography and History

Robert André LaFleur

THE PHYSICAL SETTING

To begin understanding China, let us start by comparing China to the United States. Both nations are continent-size countries, bigger than the Australian continent and slightly smaller than Europe. The surface area of the two countries is almost identical—only Russia and Canada cover greater areas. The northern tip of Heilongjiang province, the northernmost part of China, is farther north than Maine but south of Alaska. Hainan Island, the southernmost part of China, is far south of Key West, Florida, and slightly south of Hawaii, Puerto

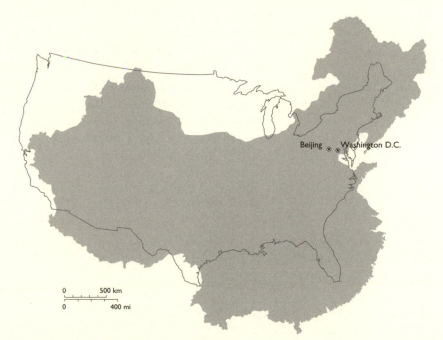

China superimposed on the United States

With 1.3 billion people, China is the most populous country on earth. (Bob Krist/CORBIS)

Rico, or Mexico City. Still, much of China lies within the same northern latitudes as most of the United States, except China has a much larger area in the far south. China is slightly wider than the contiguous forty-eight states.

One of the greatest contrasts between the two nations is population size. China is the most populous nation on earth, with 1.3 billion people, whereas the United States has 284 million people. To appreciate the difference in populations, imagine China with a billion fewer people—a number equal to its fifteen-and-under population. The remaining population would about match the United States population. Alternatively, imagine the United States as home to all of the people now living in North America, South America, and the European Union. Then the U.S. population would match China's population—but only after adding another 100 million people. Now take 70 percent of those people (about 900 million) and place them east of the Mississippi River—more than five people for every one now living in that area—then you have China Proper (the parts of the present-day People's Republic of China [PRC] having provincial status with the exclusion of Hainan and the provinces comprising Manchuria)—that is, those parts that have formed China for about 2,000 years.

Table 1.1 Population (1999) and Area of China's Provinces

Province	Population*	Area**	Province	Population	Area
North			**South-Central**		
Beijing	12.57	6.5	Henan	93.87	64.4
Tianjin	9.59	4.4	Hubei	59.38	72.4
Hebei	66.14	72.6	Hunan	65.32	81.1
Shanxi	32.04	60.3	Guangdong	72.70	68.7
Inner Mongolia	23.62	463.3	Guangxi	47.13	89.0
			Hainan	7.62	13.1
Northeast					
Liaoning	41.71	56.3	**Southwest**		
Jilin	26.58	53.3	Chongqing	30.75	31.8
Heilongjiang	37.92	182.8	Sichuan	85.50	218.8
			Guizhou	37.10	68.1
East			Yunnan	41.92	151.4
Shanghai	14.74	2.4	Xizang (Tibet)	2.56	456.6
Jiangsu	72.13	39.6			
Zhejiang	44.75	39.3	**Northwest**		
Anhui	62.37	53.9	Shaanxi	36.18	79.2
Fujian	33.16	46.9	Gansu	25.43	175.7
Jianxi	42.31	64.4	Qinghai	5.10	300.8
Shandong	88.83	59.1	Ningxia	5.43	25.5
*millions **1,000 square miles			Xinjiang	17.74	631.4

Source: China Energy Group. 2001. *China Energy Databook, Vol. 5.0.* Berkeley: Berkeley National Laboratory, table 10B.6. CD-ROM.

Both China and the United States are subdivided into smaller governmental units. China has twenty-two provinces, four large cities with provincial status, and five autonomous regions. Many of China's provinces, like U.S. states, have areas and populations that are as great or greater than most nations. For example, the areas of Texas and of Sichuan province are both more than 50 percent larger than that of Germany. In terms of population, however, Sichuan and Germany have about the same number of people, between 80 and 90 million, whereas Texas is home to about 21 million people. China's largest political unit, Xinjiang in the far west, has 20 percent more land area than Alaska and is bigger than Spain, Italy, and France combined. The four cities with provincial status, Beijing, Chongqing, Shanghai, and Tianjin, have populations greater than New York City, the largest city in the United States, and have land areas greater than that of our smaller states, such as Rhode Island, Delaware, and Connecticut.

Just as we conceptually divide the United States into geographical regions, China too can be usefully divided into regions (see table 1.1).

As in the United States, one of the most important regional distinctions in China is that between north and south. We will return to this north-south distinction many times in this book. In China the distinction is rooted in geography, climate, and history. From early times, distinct cultures have developed between north and south, and they have remained a lively topic of conversation for Chinese travelers for centuries. Regional differences are also of great interest to the Chinese, because each region has distinct customs, food, markets, and politics. Both China and the United States contain wide ranges of environments, from the frigid north to the sultry south, from high mountains to desert basins below sea level. However, of the two nations, China is more rugged and mountainous, with less arable land and a greater variability in rainfall. Unlike the United States, which has oceans to the east, west, and much of the south, China's climate is dominated by the vast bulk of Asia that surrounds it to the north, west, and southwest. The land to the west blocks all rain from that direction. The Tibetan plateau and the Himalayas on the southwest edge of the country block all moisture coming north from the Indian Ocean. Major storm systems form primarily in the seas to the southeast of China and move northwest across the country, and rainfall is more plentiful in the south than in the north. China also is subject to the monsoon weather patterns caused by the Asian continent, so that precipitation is not spread evenly throughout the year as it is in much of the United States. Instead, monsoons produce the heaviest rains in the summer months. The amount of rainfall decreases and its variability increases as we travel from the southeast to the northwest. The western interior of China is a parched land, most of which is ill-suited to agriculture, because of both inadequate moisture and high elevation.

From east to west China rises in a stair-step fashion to the Tibetan plateau. Almost 70 percent of the country is higher than 3,200 feet, more than 40 percent is higher than 6,000 feet, and a large part of the Tibetan plateau is higher than 16,000 feet above sea level. Even in the lower lying areas within 500 miles or so of the coast, China has much rugged terrain, especially in the southeastern provinces, such as Zhejiang, Jiangxi, Fujian, Hunan, Guangdong, and Guangxi. China's major rivers rise in Tibet and take an easterly course as they head to the sea, carving deep canyons as they descend the heights. Much of China's early history is closely connected with the geography of its rivers.

The home of early Chinese civilization lies in northern China, in the vast drainage area of the Yellow River valley. In fact, no other phys-

The Pudong area of Shanghai, near the mouth of the Yangzi River (Yang Liu/ CORBIS)

ical feature in early Chinese history played as prominent a role as the Yellow (or Huang) River, which serves to this day as a supporter of agricultural civilization. About 2,700 miles in length, the Yellow River has built a vast flood plain from centuries of silt deposits. In fact, the silty loess sediments of the Yellow River played a role in later Chinese history unlike any other physical feature on the Chinese landscape. The river's frequent flooding created a continuing problem for Chinese rulers, who had to build dikes and clear sediments in order to keep the river on course. Indeed, the river has jumped its banks, broken its dikes, and changed course many times in the past 2,000 years, causing great devastation as it surged to the sea, and giving the river its title as "China's Sorrow."

China's southern river, the Yangzi or Changjiang, is 3,200 miles long and less prone to flooding than the Yellow River. Even so, heavy rainfall on its vast watershed can quickly raise water levels to enormous heights. It, too, has caused frequent devastation throughout Chinese history. The Yangzi River represents the geographical features of the south in other ways as well. Its vast network of tributaries is reminiscent of what was called in early times the "marshy southland." In fact, one of the most powerful differences between northern and southern

China is the wetness of lands in the Yangzi River valley and southward. It creates the possibility of easy rice cultivation (grains such as wheat are far more prevalent in the arid north), fishing, and river trade.

One historian, examining Chinese dynastic histories over two millennia, noted that flooding or drought accounted for almost fifteen disasters a decade throughout Chinese history. Clearly, the geography of this complex land mass has played a significant role in the lives of its people. This is also the case in the matter of rainfall. We can draw a line from Manchuria in the northeast down to the far southwest of China Proper to mark the rather dramatic differences in rainfall from northwest to southeast. In fact, we can follow that diagonal line to see that the more arid northwest regions support a vastly different kind of economy than the more lush southeast. The peoples who lived for generations in the arid regions beyond the Great Wall were never closely, or continuously, connected to the people and territories most often covered in Chinese civilization narratives, yet these nomadic peoples played an enormously important role in later history. The wetter regions of the far south also were not fully integrated into Chinese culture until the beginning of the common era—indeed, some only within the past thousand years. Until relatively recently, exceedingly wet or dry regions had rather tenuous connections to the mainstream political and cultural life in China Proper, at least in its early history.

China is also known for its vast and complex mountain ranges, many of which have figured in political history and, for that matter, in thousands of pages of poetry written over three millennia. Most symbolic of all are what are called the "Five Cardinal Peaks" in the north, denoting each of the "five directions" so important to Chinese cosmological classification—north, west, south, east, and center. The major mountain ranges form great physical barriers that protected warring states such as the Qin in the third century B.C.E., gave respite to rebel groups harassed by government troops (as in the case of the White Lotus rebels in the late-eighteenth century), or even sheltered Mao's Long March in the 1930s.

Finally, there is China's coastline, which makes up 8,700 of miles of China's border. Until the nineteenth century the coast did not represent a significant vulnerability to external threat—in fact, coastal defenses were something of an afterthought throughout Chinese history. To be sure, Japanese and other travelers arrived at Chinese ports, and coastal trade was present from early times. Still, China scarcely worried about its coastal borders until the British arrived with opium in the eighteenth century and spent little effort exploring the possibilities beyond the coasts. Aside from a few missions initiated by the First Emperor of the Qin and a brief three decades of naval exploration as far as Africa in the fifteenth century, life beyond thirty miles of the coastline held little appeal to most prominent actors in Chinese history.

Rivers, mountains, coastlines, and other geographical features figure prominently in any narrative of China's past. It is important not to think of them as causes of historical change, in and of themselves. Yet their very structural significance, in terms of rainfall, flooding, mountainous respite, and coastal possibility, figured greatly in the choices historical figures made (or failed to make) in the light of these enormous geographical features.

ARCHAEOLOGY

Anyone fortunate to have visited the Shanghai Municipal Museum and the National Palace Museum outside of Taipei, Taiwan, surely has noted a great contrast. I placed this question to some of my students recently: *What is different about the two?* The items one sees in Taipei's National Palace Museum form the core of what most of us know as "Chinese culture." Room upon room showcases scrolls filled with paintings and calligraphy—a plethora of writing from almost every period of Chinese history—as well as beautifully crafted furniture, lacquer ware, vases, and the like. The collections in the National Palace Museum have been lovingly preserved, in many cases over an enormous span of time. A visit to the Shanghai Museum has a different, less refined, feel to it. There are coins, official seals, pots, urns, and sacrificial vessels. Most of the items on display have been recently unearthed. The pieces in the Shanghai Museum are newer—in that they were just recently discovered—and yet are in some cases the oldest known artifacts that deal with the history of China. Though it is not apparent at first, if one stands back, physically and intellectually, the difference between the two museums becomes clear: One shows a China represented in its written history, and the other represents materials that have been buried for much of the past two millennia.

As will be explained later in this chapter, when the Republican armies fled the mainland of China between 1947 and 1949, ultimately arriving on the island of Taiwan, they brought with them the carefully preserved artifacts of Chinese history. This is a very great sore point with the government of the People's Republic of China. The "great river" of Chinese culture, it feels, should be back on the mainland of

China. The charges and countercharges (which bring up matters of the Cultural Revolution in the 1960s and 1970s) do not matter here, although the disagreement remains fascinating. What is key is the point that history stops for no one. The National Palace Museum has the greatest collection of Chinese cultural artifacts in the world, but it has ceased to grow in any significant sense. The Shanghai Museum (and others in China) is benefiting from what can only be called a renaissance of archaeological work and scholarship. Most of what we know about early Chinese culture has come from digging. Occasionally, a scroll is found in a musty study, or, rarer still, a collection from an overseas collector is given back to a Chinese museum, as happened recently in Shanghai. Mostly, though, the freshest knowledge is coming from the ground.

In fact, what we know about China today, more than half a century since the establishment of the People's Republic of China in 1949, is breathtaking. Much of that excitement comes from archaeology. Although a deep knowledge of traditional sources of Chinese history and culture will never be outgrown, there is no doubt that the most dramatic changes in our understanding of China are coming from archaeological sites. This is not just true of ancient history, either. Even for relatively recent periods, such as the Ming and Qing dynasties, archaeological evidence is reshaping the way that we perceive urban life, attitudes toward the dead, and a plethora of assumptions that we have had about the practice of daily life. In fact, it is not an exaggeration to say that one cannot have a nuanced perspective on Chinese history and culture without having an understanding of the archaeological finds of the past half-century.

The discoveries are dizzying. Beginning more than a century ago, farmers began digging up what they often referred to as "dragon bones" while tilling their fields. This led to the discovery that the writing on these bones (which were ox scapulae—shoulder blades—and tortoise shells) was an early form of Chinese script, and that the inscriptions were divination made toward *tian,* or heaven. These early inscriptions have, over the past century, led to a much deeper knowledge of the practice of government in very early periods than we ever thought possible. Even "later" discoveries (tombs or sites dating to the first millennium B.C.E.) show us whole tombs, such as that of the relatively insignificant Lady Di, that are filled with items meant to accompany her in death. The yield there has provided so much information that one wonders at the possibilities for tombs of figures with important stations in early Chinese society.

As one moves through over two millennia of archaeological finds (many of which are shown in Beijing's and Shanghai's museums), one realizes that the treasures stored in the National Palace Museum in Taiwan are rich and vitally important, but represent only a part of the continuing desire to understand China's past. This book will seek a balance between these perspectives, showing the wonderful new perspectives we have gained from our knowledge of archaeological discoveries that continue to clarify assumptions about the origins of Chinese culture. It will not, however, like some recent works, dismiss the rich mythological and even magical narrative of China's past as outdated because of new discoveries. A vital balance should remain.

With all of the details that we have added to our knowledge of China's past with archaeological discoveries, the fact remains that much of the previous three millennia have been informed by earlier anecdotes, myths, and legends. Whether or not we have found new etymological or archaeological evidence about these things, they were spoken of *as true* for twenty centuries. To ignore that tradition would be as foolhardy as to accept it without reservation. In the remainder of this book we will seek to achieve that balance sought by the sage himself, Confucius, who taught that contemporary events were best understood through the lens of older, even ancient, ones.

FOUNDATION MYTHS AND EARLY HISTORY (TO c. 1100 B.C.E.)

The myths of China's founding played such an enormous role in Chinese conceptions of their history that readers would lack key connections in later writings if they didn't know them. The creation story centered on the person of Pangu, who emerged from a cosmic egg to create the universe. His head became mountains, his flesh fields, and his bones rocks. His hair became trees and vegetation, and his breath winds and clouds. His sweat was rain, and the insects, which finally found themselves on his body, were people.

It is a fascinating story, but it was a late addition to a series of much earlier "human culture" stories that were at the foundation of early Chinese mythology. Of the five legendary rulers, the first, Fuxi and Nüwa (a brother-sister pair) domesticated animals, built homesteads, taught people to fish with nets, introduced fire, channeled rivers, created writing, and focused their mythical energies on the Yellow River. The second, Shen Nong, introduced agricultural techniques and medicine through herbs and other means. The third, Huangdi, the Yellow Emperor, quelled barbarian tribes, established a calendar, and created an infrastructure for plow carts and other vehicles. Huangdi also developed the subtle agricultural techniques that would remain at the heart of Chinese life into the twentieth century. His wife, the first empress, practiced silk cultivation and began a tradition of "women's work" with silk that would last throughout imperial times. In these first three great mythical reigns, the idea of a Chinese state was created. It is the last two legendary rulers, Yao and Shun, who exemplify the core ruling myths of Chinese civilization and have appeared prominently in the rhetoric of Chinese politics for more than three millennia.

Yao was said to be born after his mother observed a dragon of the auspicious color red. He devoted himself to the people, so the stories go, and even placed "remonstrance drums" and "criticism tablets" throughout the kingdom so that people with grievances could bang or write upon them and tell him of their troubles. Yao was completely devoted to his people and to ruling in a moral and righteous fashion that would solidify the growing state. Yet when Yao became old, he looked to his own sons for the succession and was displeased. After asking his advisers to send him an upright person who could morally rule the kingdom, a commoner named Shun was brought to him. Through the force of his virtue, Shun held together what we today might call a dysfunctional family as he persistently cared for parents and siblings. Even as his stepmother sought to kill him, he remained a devoted son. He was, in reasoning that would persist for millennia, the obvious choice—for one who knew how to manage a family surely knew how to manage an empire. Family management and imperial management were, in traditional political rhetoric, two sides of the same coin.

As Shun himself grew old, he had failed in only one respect. He had not lived long enough to quell the great floods that were overtaking China in the later years of his reign. He, too, looked beyond his own sons and found, as Yao had many years before, a virtuous, hard-working young man named Yu. Yu toiled to quell the floods and passed by the crying wails of his own family, never looking in on them, so focused was he on the problems of the empire. The tension between duty to family and to empire is a part of this story, but the primary focus was on a ruler who worked for the sake of his people above all else. Yu is the first ruler that we can even remotely call "historical." He is known as the founder of the first dynasty, the Xia, for which we have only fragmented historical information. Together, Yao, Shun, and Yu are known as the "Three Rulers," and their rule has provided writers with images of strong leadership for millennia.

But Chinese history, at least as it was interpreted by three millennia of readers and listeners, is not only about the lofty good deeds of benevolent and talented leaders. We also have the stories of the "bad last rulers," such as Jie and Zhou. Indeed, the writing of Chinese history took on a definite narrative pattern: Dynasties were founded by able, hands-on, benevolent, and capable managers who would set the tone for decades, even centuries, of rule. Eventually, each dynasty would be undone by evil, lax, complacent rulers who were overthrown when they lost the Mandate of Heaven—the cosmic doctrine that anointed or dethroned rulers depending on their virtue and capabilities.

Jie, at the end of the Xia dynasty, and Zhou, at the end of the Shang dynasty, gave themselves over to excesses and luxury that shocked their subjects. Both are described as strong and even potentially heroic, but both turned their desires toward sensual and cruel pursuits. Jie had large parks built where he would have orgies in which he and his guests would float about in boats upon ponds of wine, dipping their cups, and even swimming, to complete contentment. He also ordered the construction of meat trees, from which his guests would carve off hunks of flesh. He was said to have an underground palace where even greater wickedness prevailed. He was overthrown and imprisoned until his death, and a brilliant new leader founded the Shang dynasty.

Zhou, more than six centuries later, was as flawed as Jie. He, too, is described as strong and capable yet unworthy of the kingship he inherited. In imitation of Jie, he was said to have wild orgies on ponds of wine. His excesses continued with severe punishments, including making accused people walk over greased rods above hot coals. If they fell, they were pronounced guilty. He even shot passersby with arrows, it is said, in order to examine their still-warm organs. Zhou, too, was overthrown, and his severed head exhibited on a post for all to see.

The exaggeration in these tales is clear enough, but they had a profound effect on political thought in Chinese history. The positive examples of Yao, Shun, and Yu combine with the negative examples of Jie and Zhou to provide a powerful template for later thinkers in the Chinese tradition. All a government official had to do was to mention the name of Jie or Zhou to get the attention of the sovereign. Even today, the names are almost synonymous to readers of Chinese with good government or utter depravity. An example of how lasting these foundation myths could be is found in one of China's greatest works of history, compiled by Sima Guang, a serious scholar known for his "no-nonsense" approach to government. Sima Guang quotes an official named Yang Fu, who has criticized the emperor he serves:

> [Yang] Fu again sent up a memorial, saying: "Yao's abode was of modest thatch, yet the myriad states enjoyed peace. Yu's palace was simple, yet all under heaven happily labored. Down to the time of Yin and Zhou halls measured three by nine *chi*, and no more. Jie built ornamented rooms and ivory halls; Zhou made the spacious Lu Terrace, by means of which he lost the nation. King Ling of Chu erected Zhanghua and he himself met with disaster. Qin Shihuang built Ebang—two generations and his dynasty was extinguished. Now, not measuring the myriad peoples' strength in following desires of ear and eye, there has never been one who did not perish. Your majesty should take Yao, Shun, Yu, Tang, Wen, and Wu as your standards. The examples of Jie, Zhou, Ling, and Qin Shihuang should be taken as deep warnings." (Guang 1956, 2307–2308)

Thus, two millennia after these figures were said to have lived, they were used as ways to persuade rulers to act with virtue and compassion.

THE ZHOU DYNASTY (c. 1100–221 B.C.E.)

The information we have on Chinese history before the year 1000 B.C.E. is tenuous at best. We have growing archaeological evidence that suggests a developed calendar, sophisticated agricultural techniques, and a rich Bronze Age culture. By the time we reach the Zhou dynasty in the late second millennium before the common era, we begin to get even more solid evidence of political culture as well as social and economic life.

Early historical works such as *The Book of History* give vague accounts of a battle between Shang and Zhou forces, with a great Zhou victory in 1122. Legend has it that only 50,000 Zhou troops defeated an army over ten times that size, and that many Shang troops, unhappy with their degenerate ruler—the bad ruler Zhou mentioned above—joined the winning side. King Wu, the founding ruler responsible for the great victory, died only six years later, with the territory far from completely conquered. The greatest state-building credit goes to King Wu's brother, Tan, better known as the Duke of Zhou. He is said to be the creator of the institutions that would lie at the center of the Zhou dynasty, but he was fiercely criticized at the time because he served as a regent for young King Cheng, the heir to the throne.

Officials within his government attacked him for what they took to be usurpation and rebelled. The texts tell us that the Duke of Zhou put down the rebellion, solidified the dynasty's rule, created a system of administration, organized life in the palace, and after seven years, voluntarily gave up power in favor of Cheng, who was then of age to rule. Having spent those years lecturing the young king on proper rule, he left the dynasty in capable hands.

This theme of regency is a persistent one in Chinese history. Confucius and other thinkers revered the Duke of Zhou as a leader who embodied the very ideal of regency—serving for a child, teaching the child, using his (or her, in later cases) talents to improve government, and leaving a better political situation in the hands of the heirs. The reality of regency in Chinese history was a good deal different, yet the example of the Duke of Zhou has persisted since his time.

China during the Zhou dynasty was never a wholly integrated state. The eastern half of the territory (and it is a territory far smaller than the China one will find on a map today, consisting essentially of the area surrounding the Yellow River) was held by royal family members who paid allegiance to the Zhou rulers.

The western areas, which soon became small states, were never well-integrated into the system. In the first 500 years of Zhou rule they loosely acknowledged the position of the Zhou king, but that disappeared quickly as the system weakened after 500 B.C.E. Both Chinese and Western historians have often referred to the Zhou as a "feudal" system. Although the term is a problematic one when referring to East Asian history, there was a connection between territorial lords and retainers who served them. For the territorial lords, theoretically "granted" their territories by the Zhou, there was also the expectation that they accept the Zhou king and revere the ancestral spirits of the Zhou rulers.

These somewhat tenuous ties between Zhou rule and the small territorial lords loosened in the centuries after the dynasty's founding. Beyond the border states to the north, west, and south lived tribes of unassimilated non-Chinese peoples. By the seventh century B.C.E. there was an increasing distance between these peripheral states and the heart of the Zhou order to the east. This signaled the beginning of intense warfare among states that would reduce more than a hundred small states to a handful of larger states by the third century B.C.E.

Although the Zhou kings would continue to rule, as though by default, each territorial lord was master of his own state. Interstate diplomacy became an art that limited the loss of lives from frequent warfare. Works from the period note the increasingly bloody conflicts between the so-called Warring States during the third and second centuries B.C.E. War was perpetuated because of territorial conflicts, but also for broader cultural reasons; even the earliest historical writings speak of the ideal of a unified China. The Zhou rulers did not come close to unifying their territory to any significant extent, yet the ideal remained and became a part of the philosophical debates that would help define the Warring States period.

As warfare intensified, many rulers paid increasing attention to the administration of their states. By the fourth century B.C.E. aristocratic warfare in chariots gave way to massed infantry and large-scale fighting, resulting in significant casualties. The scale of conflict required a level of organization far beyond anything previously seen in Chinese history. In addition to skilled troops and able generals, the remaining states required managers who were able to translate philosophical insight into practical administration of the realm. States vied with each other for experts in a kind of intellectual or managerial "free agency," in which thinkers would travel the land looking for the "right" leader to whom they could give political or military advice.

Although the state of Qin, protected by a prime location in west-central China, would gradually emerge as preeminent, it is necessary to understand more than the military tactics that led it to victory. During the last three centuries of Zhou rule, the great power vacuum that led to intense battles between states also led to intense philosophical disputation of a kind not often seen before or since in China. The learned arguments between schools, which would come to be known as Confucian, Daoist, and Legalist, would shape later Chinese thought in profound ways, even into the late twentieth century.

THE HUNDRED SCHOOLS OF THOUGHT (c. 500–200 B.C.E.)

Conflict on the battlefield was only part of a larger struggle in early China; the struggle over defining ideas that would shape how people ruled was inextricably linked to warfare. Even the most practical of advisers understood that winning on the battlefield had to be followed by effective rule, and that guiding concepts were necessary to make that rule effective. Though the "school" sometimes called Confucian would figure enormously in later Chinese history, it is important to see all thought in early China as fluid. It is just as important to see it as vitally connected to ruling.

Confucius taught that the breakdown of the Zhou order lay in lack of attention to the fundamentals of social life. A native of the small state of Lu, he taught groups of disciples who eventually compiled his sayings into a slender volume known as the *Analects*. He spent the better part of a decade in middle age traveling throughout north China in hopes of persuading territorial lords to put his teachings into practice. Several key concepts emerge from a careful reading of the *Analects*. One of the most significant is the importance of achieving social and political harmony through proper attention to the hierarchical roles one plays in society. As one entry puts it, "Fathers must be fathers and sons sons; rulers must be rulers and ministers ministers."

One of Confucius's great contributions was to rework core concepts that had been used for centuries, giving them new moral dimensions through his discourses. The most important of these concepts are ritual, benevolence, sincerity, trustworthiness, loyalty, filial piety, and righteousness. These English translations do not do justice to the moral subtlety of the terms as they are discussed by Confucius, but the articulation of a limited number of important terms lies at the heart of Confucius's *Analects*. Confucius cast himself as a transmitter of the old ways that had been practiced by the Duke of Zhou. His teachings were, from his perspective, merely a restatement of the core ideals practiced by the three sages—Yao, Shun, and Yu—and the early Zhou leaders. He deplored the deterioration of his society and sought to reassert the core values that would revitalize the human order.

Working in the tradition that would come to be known as *ru,* what we call Confucianism, was another great philosopher, Mencius (372–289 B.C.E.). Although Confucius's teachings were set down in the form of pithy moral maxims, often no more than a few sentences long, Mencius expanded these concepts with full historical and cultural examples that ran to many pages. He promoted the concept that people are basically good, and through paying attention to what he saw as the core ideals in human nature—not the flawed realities of what people actually did—leaders could create order in their domains and assert their dominance peacefully throughout the empire. More than any other early thinker, Mencius asserted that the heart of rule lay in promoting the welfare of the people. This can best be summarized by his statements that a ruler merely needed to exude goodness to succeed. If the good ruler did that, the people from other states would take notice and flock to him.

The texts that took shape in the late Zhou period were not written in isolation. They were products of intense intellectual conflict,

CONFUCIUS

Le plus célebre Philosophe de la Chine.

Portrait of Confucius. One Confucian concept that influenced early China is the importance of achieving social and political harmony through proper attention to the hierarchical roles one plays in society. (Historical Picture Archive/CORBIS) and the fervor with which philosophers argued their points about human nature and ruling reflected, on many levels, the contentious environment within which the territorial lords operated. Many of the texts from this period specifically attack the writings of other schools, and in virtually every passage, one can see an engagement with other texts. This is important, because states needed advisers, and all of these philosophies, even those that seem somewhat esoteric, deal with the problem of ruling—of managing a complex state and dealing with others.

The Daoist thinkers, of whom the most prominent are Laozi and Zhuangzi, argued in opposition to Confucian thinkers. Indeed, in Zhuangzi's writings, Confucius often appears as a bumbling character who is unclear about how to operate in the world around him. At the core of Daoist thinking is the concept of the Way. *Dao* literally means road or path, and this concept of the Way can be extended to human action within and beyond government. The term was also employed by thinkers of other schools, but the articulation of the concept by Daoists took on a power that persists to this day—even beyond the borders of China. The major argument Daoists had with Confucians was that the latter were trying too hard. By categorizing people by role and pushing them into molds, Confucians opposed the "way" or flow of nature. Daoists maintained that all a ruler had to do was just *be*. Numerous examples in the writings of Laozi and Zhuangzi explain that trying too hard or thinking too much destroys the flow of life.

More provocative still is the Daoist concept of *wuwei*, or non-action. This is the extreme political statement that a good ruler does nothing. By not categorizing, not making rules, and not "ordering" the people, order would be achieved. Although there is an element of in-your-face obtuseness aimed at Confucians in all of this, careful thinkers will see that there is much more than a germ of truth as well. Most everyone has seen the results of a competent manager who lets the workforce work within the flow of their jobs, the kind of leader who *seems* to do little, yet the work is accomplished, and well. Hence, the Daoist statement: "through not doing, nothing is left undone."

The Legalists formed the most practical pole in early Chinese philosophy, one that aimed unashamedly at ordering society for the sole purpose of creating a unified state that would ultimately rule the empire in a way never before achieved. Xunzi (c. 300–235) was an exponent of Confucian doctrine who inspired later Legalist thinkers as well. Arguing with Mencius's contention that human nature is inherently good, Xunzi noted that humans were intrinsically flawed; it was only through proper attention to education, memorizing the classics, and articulating the great teachings that people became good. Much has been made by later philosophers of their disagreement about human nature, and any school-aged child today can recount it. There is room for agreement, however. Both Mencius and Xunzi asserted a common thread: People stayed good or became good through attention to core values and teaching. Their differences lay in whether goodness was innate. For both, education lay at the heart of moral and practical statecraft.

Xunzi's crisp rhetorical style and careful patterns of argumentation deeply influenced thinkers for a thousand years, and it is only relatively recently that the works of Confucius and Mencius have been deemed superior, as Chinese philosophy took on new shapes in later times. At the heart of Xunzi's thought is an expansion of those two thinkers' idea that people are only as trustworthy as their actions. Xunzi focused on such actions and the practical elements of ruling, and it was just this focus that later Legalist thinkers would expand. In opposition to the other schools, Legalist thought concentrated on what the people *must* do, no questions asked. Opposing other thinkers who concentrated on the people or just "being," Legalists focused on what must be done to make the state prosper. It was an amoral philosophy that articulated the regimentation of society for the purpose of bettering the state itself.

The excesses of Qin, which we will soon discuss, and the ultimate failure of "practical" Legalism gave it a very bad reputation among traditional historians. Indeed, anyone even vaguely familiar with twentieth century world history might wince at some of the implications of Legalist language. But it is important to understand Legalist philosophy for what it was—a full-fledged articulation of the administrative needs of a strong state. What mattered to Legalists was power. Administration was for them the difficult art of manipulating people by taking advantage of their selfish interests and making it profitable for them to do what served those interests. It is not a philosophy that relied, as did Confucius's thought, on trust—not even on that of family members. The enforcement of law itself was meant to be so swift, so automatic, so dreadful that it appeared to be a part of the natural order. Above all, one sees no strains of sentimentality in Legalist writings. The people were there, and they were meant to be molded. The same was true of administrators and even the ruler himself. Indeed, if there is a weak point in the order, one might find it in the person of an all-powerful ruler who had few checks upon his own conduct. The challenge of Legalism was actually to put it into practice, to go beyond the ordering of ideas, and to manage an actual state. In the history of the Qin centralization, we see just that.

THE QIN CENTRALIZATION (221–206 B.C.E.)

The unification of China under the power of the Qin state in 221 B.C.E. initiated twenty-two centuries of centralized imperial government over eight major dynasties. Although the Zhou, even at its height, was never more than a loose alliance of powers under the nominal rule of the Zhou king, the Qin set the pattern for central rule in China. Indeed, central government under the control of a single dynasty remained a powerful, though often distant, ideal—even during periods of division. Under the unifying force of the First Emperor, Qin armies defeated each of their rivals and initiated reforms that abolished the decentralized structure of the Zhou and extended the influence of the state. The Qin reorganized the empire into thirty-six administrative divisions, which were in turn subdivided into counties, with all levels ultimately accountable to the central government—a system that persisted in its broad form throughout much of the imperial period.

The Qin also initiated a more central control through the standardization of scripts, weights, measures, and currency, and began the process of building thousands of miles of imperial highways and waterways to connect China's various regions—including work on northern fortifications that would, more than a millennium later, be part of the Great Wall. The process of standardization and centralization would play a role, both practically and symbolically, in later periods, as the Qin unification became the model of central government in Chinese history.

Enormous credit for the Qin unification belongs to King Zheng, who succeeded to the Qin throne in 247 B.C.E. and led the state to victories over each of the six other Warring States. He is known in history as Qinshi Huangdi, a flowery and imposing title meant to separate his new position from that of earlier kings. The name can be translated as "First Grand Emperor of Qin," and echoes a title previously reserved for the mythical Yellow Emperor. By calling himself the First Emperor, he assumed an endless perpetuation of the Legalist machine that he and his advisers had created.

Because his rule was extremely harsh, and because he singled out scholars of the Confucian (*ru*) school—whose descendants would

Northern fortifications built during the Qin dynasty would become part of the Great Wall of China more than 1,000 years later. (Corel)

eventually write the histories of China—he appears as a cruel tyrant in traditional histories. By almost any standard the First Emperor was a complex individual, and his reign ended in almost total failure after his death in 210 B.C.E. Yet his mark on Chinese history was indelible—his centralization of political power became the dominant pattern of later Chinese history and created a model for the state that persists to this day.

The single greatest achievement of Qin was its elimination of the decentralized nature of Zhou rule. The Qin abolished all of the old states and erected an entirely new administrative and bureaucratic structure. Centralization, however, also required standardization. The regionalism that flourished in the last centuries of the Zhou had been marked by diversity in such matters as weights and measures, coinage, scripts, and even axle widths (which were very important if a new infrastructure of dirt roads was to be created). The Qin government prescribed new universal standards in all of these areas and punished those who transgressed them.

Standardization of the vastly diverse ways of thought that marked early Chinese history was another challenge. The Qin prohibited philosophical dispute of the kind that marked the three preceding centuries, and made particular attacks on those who (like Confucius and Mencius centuries before) praised the past or criticized present policy. Although the story is perhaps apocryphal, the "burning of the books and the burying of the scholars" is important in Chinese history if only for the fact that it was spoken of as truth for two millennia. In 213 B.C.E. all previous writings were burned other than official Qin records and treatises on matters of agriculture, medicine, and technical matters. Because many scholars who developed their skills in the spirit of the "hundred schools" could not accept the new policies, the First Emperor reportedly executed almost 500 of them and buried them together as a warning to future generations.

Finally, the Qin centralization was a time of grand construction. Roads were built connecting the capital with every part of the empire. Waterways were improved, and irrigation systems (using remarkably sophisticated technology) and canals were constructed. Such massive projects were largely possible because of the extremely harsh enforcement of Qin laws, which made hundreds of thousands of convicts into forced laborers.

One of the greatest flaws in thinking about the Qin is to focus only on the practical aspects of centralization. Although the first emperor was a tough-minded ruler, he was also preoccupied with his own mortality. After surviving three assassination attempts, he became obsessed by notions of immortality and spent a great deal of effort seeking ways to lengthen his life and even discover seemingly mythical islands, such as Penglai in the eastern seas, where immortal "bird people" were said to live.

After the first emperor's death in 210 B.C.E. (while traveling in search of new elixirs), the Qin degenerated into a fight among factions of his lieutenants. It is somewhat ironic that the Qin order was largely undone by the harshness of its own laws—the very laws that had shaped Legalist philosophy but were administered, perhaps too strictly, by those who managed the Qin state. Another, perhaps apocryphal, story is enormously important because for twenty-two centuries it has explained the Qin fall: The spark that ignited the revolt was a commoner named Chen She who, put in charge of a group of laborers, was delayed by heavy rains. Under Qin law, the penalties for delay included death, with no consideration of extenuating circumstances. Chen is said to have persuaded his followers to rebel against the oppression rather than be put to death. Rebellions erupted throughout Qin, and by 206 B.C.E., the Qin order was destroyed.

THE HAN DYNASTY (206 B.C.E.–C.E. 220)

China's first imperial dynasty endured for less than two decades and had only two emperors. The Han dynasty succeeded the Qin when Liu Bang, a commoner, reunited the empire in 202 B.C.E. Building upon the strengths of Qin unification but carefully backing away from its excesses, Liu Bang and his successors oversaw 400 years of central rule. The Han dynasty cemented the institutional patterns that would define the Chinese state for the next two millennia.

Liu Bang, better known by his posthumous title of Han Gaozu ("lofty ancestor"), was the first of two commoners to fight his way to the throne in Chinese history. For that reason, and because he never completely lost his "earthy" qualities, he has always been to the popular imagination one of the most celebrated of Chinese emperors. Two further things stand out as precedents in his rule. First, he took seriously the role of advisers in the governing process and sought to heed their advice. Second, in reaction to the Legalist excesses of the Qin and in accordance with the teachings of Mencius, Gaozu and his ministers, he emphasized that government existed to aid the people.

One concession he made was to grant most of the eastern half of the empire to his followers as rewards for their efforts. In some ways it was a prudent decision that reflected the reality that Qin's level of integration was unrealistic, but it created the potential for long-term problems. The Han integration did indeed lighten the burdens on the people, but the system showed considerable weaknesses after a half-century. By then the harsh memories of Qin's rule had softened over several generations, and Emperor Wu (141–87 B.C.E.), who ruled longer than any emperor until the seventeenth century, saw the opportunity for more thoroughly solidifying central rule than his predecessors.

To begin, Wu centralized and extended imperial authority in domestic affairs, reappropriating the territories Gaozu had given his followers. He also dealt strongly with merchants who had taken advantage of Han China's relaxed economic policies to control huge fortunes, mostly untaxed, in iron, salt, liquor, and grain. Salt and iron, in particular, were made state monopolies, and Wu also created the "ever-normal" granary system in order to regulate the supply of grain through good years and bad.

Equally adept in foreign relations, Wu asserted Han strength over the northern and southern peoples who bordered the state. The greatest showdown was with the Xiongnu nomads to the north and west,

Woman in Han dynasty costume (Corel)

who would be a continual threat to Han power in subsequent decades. The Han strategy included marriage alliances, diplomacy, and warfare. Although Emperor Wu was quite successful in his dealings with northern powers, the reality of "outsiders" in the Chinese historical picture would remain for twenty-two centuries. Chinese political history needs to be read as an ongoing relationship, often not friendly, with surrounding peoples who were at times strong enough to take control of China itself.

Emperor Wu's reign was the height of Han power. Later Han rulers continued the general domestic and foreign policies instituted during Wu's reign, yet few of his successors stood out. They do, however, reflect an important problem in Chinese rule—passing power from fathers to sons created the very real possibility that successors would be coddled (growing up at court) and unable to deal well with problems of the larger world. The system benefited when a charismatic and powerful figure such as Emperor Wu emerged, but the pool for such talent was so narrow that mediocrity often became the norm.

At the beginning of the common era factional infighting marked court life, and in the countryside there was economic turmoil. Some advisers became convinced that the Han had lost the Mandate of Heaven, and prevailed upon an upright court official named Wang Mang to take over the regency for a child emperor. Wang was seen in many ways as a latter-day Duke of Zhou, whose rule was meant in every way to continue what was good about the Han. He declared his own dynasty (Xin, "new"), and undertook to reinstitute Zhou dynasty institutions and policies that, to his mind, marked a better era in Chinese history. He organized government with Zhou titles, changed the coinage system, and put into practice, as he saw it, a "genuine" form of Confucianism. In the year C.E. 9, Wang took the throne for himself.

Wang's reign was a disaster of such staggering proportion that it is difficult to see why he and his ideas might have been appealing. Wang Mang remains an odd figure in Chinese history. He was reviled by later historians as a usurper who broke Han's four centuries of rule. His was an attempt to simplify life and rule and to return to a more innocent age. Nonetheless, his reforms ultimately antagonized all classes of society, and even nature seemed (in true Chinese cosmological fashion) to vent its displeasure. Changes in weather patterns produced poor harvests. Drought ensued, and then the Yellow River flooded, eventually changing its course and killing thousands. Famine followed, and vagrants formed into bands of rebels, which included the prominent Red Eyebrows movement. In C.E. 23 rebels broke into the palace and murdered Wang Mang. By C.E. 25 the Han dynasty was restored to members of the Liu clan, and the Wang "interregnum" became a cautionary dividing line between Former Han and Later Han.

The restorers of the Han dynasty, Emperor Guangwu (r. C.E. 25–57) and his immediate successors, were strong rulers under whom the Han regained a considerable amount of the vigor and prestige it had enjoyed in Former Han. The natural disasters and agricultural devastation seen under Wang's reign gradually abated, and in the first century of the common era, the population and economy rebounded. One of the most important themes in Chinese political thought is that of restoration, and Later Han is a model for it. Following the Han precedent of domestic and international strength shown by Emperor Wu, Guangwu and his followers reasserted military strength over the Xiongnu to the north, rebuilt roads, and eased the pressures on farmers. In a general optimism of state Confucianism, Guangwu created schools and academies for the moral and practical education of children.

One can already see in the first centuries of imperial rule a pattern of unity and division that echoes the famous first lines of the epic Ming dynasty novel *Three Kingdoms:* "The empire, long divided, must unite; long united, must divide." Even within the history of a single dynasty one can perceive patterns of founding, restoration, and decline. In the second century of the common era, that decline took root, eventually ending the four centuries of Han rule. The political deterioration began with another structural flaw in the ruling system—the succession of a minor to the throne. Palace intrigue and factional infighting marked the struggles for power, and this pattern of court politics persisted into the third century. Similarly, natural disasters (another constant in Chinese history) inspired peasant rebellions by the 170s and 180s, and Daoist-inspired cults such as the Yellow Turbans and Five Pecks of Rice bands wrought havoc in the countryside. Generals were called to support the Han, and even though they restored order by 190, the pattern of regional warlordism had been set. A Han emperor would remain on the throne for thirty more years, but real power had passed to a series of generals and territorial leaders.

General Dong Zhuo seized the capital in 190, deposed the emperor, set up his chosen ruler, and murdered the empress dowager, imperial princes, and palace eunuchs. In this climate of intrigue and open warfare, Dong Zhuo was unable to maintain power, and the Han was controlled for the next thirty years by another general, Cao Cao, who styled himself as "protector" of the empire. Upon his death in 220, his son Cao Pei (r. 220–226) accepted the abdication of the Han emperor and established a new kingdom called Wei. After four centuries of rule that later ages saw as a model of imperial greatness, the Han came to a quiet end.

THE PERIOD OF DIVISION (220–589)

The late second century rebellions and warlordism signaled the start of what would be four centuries of division—the longest time the empire was to remain divided in subsequent Chinese history. Because of the rise and fall of kingdoms with little hope of anything beyond regional power, the period has traditionally been interpreted as something of a "middle ages" of Chinese history. It is vitally important to note, however, the tremendous social and cultural changes that occurred during this period—changes that would play an important role in China for centuries.

Cao Cao and his successors were never able to reunite the empire. His most significant attempt occurred at the Battle of the Red Cliffs in 208, where a combined force of his major rivals, Sun Quan and Liu Bei, defeated him. For the next sixty years the kingdom was divided, "like three legs of a tripod," between these three men and their states, Wei, Wu, and Shu Han. The time has been immortalized in the *Three Kingdoms* tales, and these generals have been known to Chinese readers and listeners for centuries through that novel as well as in popular drama and storytelling. Today, one can even find numerous comic books highlighting the period and its personalities—indeed, more than half of an English class of sixth graders in Taiwan listed the cunning *Three Kingdoms* strategist Zhuge Liang as their hero, and teachers often tell that almost all of their students score very high on history exams for this period, even as they stumble on others. These are but a few of the many ways that historical issues figure quite prominently in everyday life in China, even today.

Despite Wei's struggles with the other kingdoms, a later family usurped the throne in 265 and changed the dynastic name to Jin. For a generation, China was "united," but it was a tenuous consolidation at best, and the territory it controlled was much smaller than during Han at its height. By the beginning of the fourth century, factional infighting, assassination, and abdications marked court politics, and the regional patterns of social and economic organization that had defined the Zhou more than 500 years earlier became entrenched. By the fourth century, in fact, what we now call China was very much a

Golden Buddha, Guangzhou, China. The most significant change during the period of division was the entrenchment of Buddhism as an intellectual and political force from the upper classes to the common people. (Corel)

society dominated by large, landowning families, each with tenants and, indeed, private armies.

The Xiongnu and other northern groups took advantage of the uncertainty and moved southward, sacking the Jin capital at Luoyang in 311 and eventually killing the Jin emperor. By 316 the Jin's fragile unification was completely devastated, and for more than two centuries China was divided, north and south, into two quite different social, economic, and political groups. Widening northern and southern cultural differences are among the most important and lasting effects of this period. Although southern groups made sporadic attempts to recover lost territories, they for the most part cast themselves as the preservers of traditional civilization, even though that center had moved far southward into the marshy lands that had earlier been held by aboriginal groups. These aboriginal groups were slowly absorbed into the mainstream. But the most significant change of the period of division was the entrenchment of Buddhism as an intellectual and, indeed, political force from the upper classes to the common people.

Many Chinese saw Buddhism as a "foreign" doctrine that disrupted important aspects of family ritual and harmony (by shaving one's head and rejecting one's family, a monk or nun went against some of the most basic ideas of filial piety known in China). In the changed political climate of the northern and southern dynasties, however, Buddhism became a way for states to set themselves off from their predecessors and create a cultural and ideological identity that marked their kingdoms' rule as each vied for control of larger swaths of land. Buddhism thoroughly penetrated the north, and its popularity would eventually be a "glue" through which north and south could reconnect in the future.

Finally, although it never was to have the enormous influence of Buddhism on all levels of society, religious Daoism played an important role in the increasingly diverse intellectual climate of the time. Its focus on breathing techniques, mysterious sexual rituals, and the ingestion of materials for immortality formed a religious tradition that deeply influenced many rulers and practitioners in later China. The period of division was also a time of great vitality in the writing of poetry, the development of genres of mystery writing, and various arts from painting to ceramics.

The period of division is one of the most challenging eras one confronts in studying China. The political narrative is hardly unified, and following it is so complex, with such meager results, that it is difficult to talk about anything beyond the most general of themes. Even so, the cultural heritage is remarkably rich, for the era provided a setting in which Confucian, Daoist, and Buddhist thought would merge (although never without tension) throughout later Chinese history.

THE SUI DYNASTY (581–617)

The centuries of reestablished unity under the Sui and Tang dynasties saw a reintegration of vastly changed northern and southern territories. The Sui founder, Wendi (r. 581–604), was born into a part-nomad northern family and had the difficult task of reuniting north and south through a centralized legal code, new roads, and waterways—tasks that call to mind the Qin's short-lived centralization seven centuries earlier. Wendi's son, Sui Yangdi, the second and last emperor of the dynasty, undertook the largest centralizing efforts early in his reign, combining this work with large-scale military efforts. He attempted to gain control of the Korean peninsula, only to be defeated there and beset by internal rebellion in China. It seems that Qin and Sui, overwhelmed by the internal and external demands of reinventing central rule, were unable to reign for more than two generations.

Sui Wendi succeeded to the Northern Zhou throne as a regent and spent the next decade, after taking power for himself, integrating a southern China that was in great disarray. An able administrator, Wendi combined skillful ideological blendings of the Confucian, Daoist, and Buddhist traditions with superior military strength to subdue the southern states by the end of the 580s.

Because there had been for many decades no great wars or rebellions of the kind that marked the later Han, both northern and southern China had prospered during the sixth century, even as their cultures grew further and further apart. Wendi's greatest success was to reconnect north and south, not only through a new infrastructure but also by connecting scholars and thinkers who represented families that had become regionalized in the previous centuries of division. He rebuilt a rudimentary canal network to link his capital in Chang'an with the Yellow River, and he improved transportation and irrigation systems throughout the realm. This included the initiation of a project to link the Yellow and Yangzi Rivers by what would become known as the Grand Canal.

The Grand Canal not only represented a new political linkage between the regions but also allowed the thriving wealth of the south to be shared more readily with the north through expanded trade networks. The Grand Canal, of course, also made possible the much faster readying of troops to the south, better to maintain order in a fragile political situation.

All of this stability, however, was undone in a generation by his son, Yangdi (r. 604–618). It is a classic example in Chinese historical writing of a two-generation "good first ruler, bad last ruler" pattern, and he is remembered, along with the totalitarian excesses of the First Emperor and the debacle of Wang Mang's reign, as one of the worst rulers in Chinese history. Yangdi had many of the state-building and megalomaniacal qualities seen in the First Emperor. He built new roads and led troops on ambitious campaigns as far away as Korea and Vietnam, but he was also obsessed by building lavish new palaces and taxing the people through corvée labor and military service. He is also said, in the traditional histories, to have led a life of licentiousness that rivaled even Jie and Zhou. Domestic revolts similar to those found in the last years of Qin and Han sprang up throughout the empire.

Ordering a frontier general named Li Yuan to quell the disturbances (following the now familiar pattern of relying on outside help to regain order once the center could not hold), Yangdi fled to southern China. Li Yuan renounced his ties to the Sui, set up an heir in Chang'an, and, after Yangdi's assassination by a courtier in 618, inaugurated his own dynasty, the Tang.

THE TANG DYNASTY (618–906)

The Tang dynasty, not unlike the Han before it, gained control of China during the confusion of the last years of the short-lived Sui. The Tang founders inherited Sui's centralizing achievements, and quickly moved to solidify the state and display their military strength to the always problematic north. In both geographic expanse and cultural achievements, the Tang dynasty has traditionally been regarded among Chinese readers as the height of imperial China and a lasting model for later periods. From its capital in Chang'an, which became one of the richest and most cosmopolitan cities the world would see for many centuries, Tang slowly solidified a bureaucratic structure that would persist throughout the imperial period and began to expand its military influence in all directions, including into Vietnam, Korea, and much of Central Asia.

The Tang imperial family represented the tensions that China had seen during the centuries of disunion. On the one hand, it claimed descent from a famous Han general, linking itself symbolically to that great dynasty and its ideals. On the other hand, the family had intermarried with "alien" nobility to such an extent that it could only be considered, by Tang times, to be ethnically Han Chinese only in part. This kind of intermarriage and strategic descent claim marked northern families during the period of disunion, as well as during the Sui and Tang eras.

The Tang dynasty took its shape under the vigorous rule of Li Yuan's son, known to readers of history as Tang Taizong (r. 626–649). At the time that he and his father were fighting on behalf of the Sui, northern China swarmed with dozens of rebellious movements. Taizong solidified the north by the year 624 and eventually accepted the abdication of his father to rule in his own right. Although the beginnings of his rule appear somewhat shady, there is no doubt that Taizong was enormously successful in building upon the centralizing drive of Sui. He practiced openness toward Buddhism and Daoism while reinstituting a strong government-sponsored Confucianism. His most famous work, an edict written for his successors, notes that fostering education, welcoming advice, and choosing able subordinates were the key elements of good rule.

Solidification of Tang rule continued unabated under Taizong's son,

Gaozong (r. 649–683). He continued the military campaigns and development of key economic and legal institutions begun by his father and grandfather, but it is in his last years that one of the strangest periods of Chinese history began. Becoming infatuated with one of his late father's concubines, the Lady Wu, he recalled her from a nunnery to which she had, according to palace regulations, retired after Taizong's death. The traditional histories relate that Gaozong allowed her to intrigue (and murder) her way to the position of empress and, when Gaozong's health failed, exercise power in his place, as would a regent.

When Gaozong died in 683, Empress Wu kept her power by placing successive sons on the throne, finally taking power for herself in 690 as the only woman in Chinese history to hold the title of emperor. She proclaimed a new dynasty with the name of Zhou and ruled until 705, when she abdicated in her eighties. Traditional historians have condemned Empress Wu as a ruthless usurper. However, though it seems clear that she manipulated the institutions of government and staffed the palace with her favorites, it is hard to see a manner in which she let domestic or foreign affairs decline under her rule.

The Tang realized its height, as well as the seeds of its demise, during the reign of Emperor Xuanzong (r. 713–755). The early decades of his reign witnessed perhaps the greatest cultural displays China had ever known, as well as a capable and efficient government machinery. The capital of Chang'an became a magnet for travelers on the Silk Road and beyond. It was a place of elegance and even decadence that can best be represented by the emperor's 100 trained horses who danced, with teacups in their mouths, in vibrant yellow halters to music played by court musicians. From dancing horses and the splendid poetry of Li Bo and Du Fu, to polo matches and hawking, the Tang's eighth-century elegance masked the increasing bureaucratic and military weakness of the state.

The later years of Xuanzong's reign saw the solid framework of the first century of Tang rule undone by an emperor and bureaucracy meandering aimlessly through more than a decade of a leadership vacuum. This resulted in command of frontier armies being turned over to generals of questionable loyalty, as well as palace intrigue on a monumental scale. Although traditional historians point out the familiar villains of eunuchs, maternal relatives, and (in this case) a lovely concubine, it is clear that a combination of misrule and larger social and economic changes contributed to the mid-Tang crisis. These strains came to a head when An Lushan (d. 757), a Central Asian general, rebelled, leading his troops toward Luoyang and then Chang'an, while Xuanzong and his court fled southward into Sichuan in one of the most famous exoduses in Chinese history.

The An Lushan rebellion from 755 to 763 was extremely destructive, and though the Tang dynasty's power was eventually restored, the state was severely weakened over the next 150 years, with increasing difficulties with northern groups and ineffective central institutions. The rebellion's political significance notwithstanding, it is noteworthy to Chinese historians because of its relation to very important changes in Chinese society. Whether these changes resulted from, or coincided with, the rebellion is an enormous question, but many historians note that long-term changes—from the suppression of Buddhism to the weakening of early-Tang institutions and rapid population growth—are linked to the rich social and economic ferment of the mid-eighth century.

As the central government weakened, institutional checks on landlordism and commerce were impossible to maintain. The aristocratic "dividing line" that had set apart the great families of China since the Han dynasty was undermined by waves of massive social and economic change, and the later imperial age would see a very different social order. The long era of Tang "twilight" was finally broken by a series of rebellions that would, over a period of thirty years, destroy Tang rule. It is important to note just how long it took for a dynasty to fall in China: For both the Han and Tang it took thirty years even after power diminished, and their emperors reigned in name only.

THE FIVE DYNASTIES (907–959) AND THE KINGDOMS OF LIAO, XI XIA, AND JIN (c. 900–1234)

The fall of the Tang dynasty led to another period of division, the Five Dynasties, in which China was again divided between north and south. What are traditionally termed the Ten Kingdoms rose in succession in the south, largely unhindered by the more powerful northern states. Each state lacked the strength to consolidate the south or approach unification of the empire. Each also modeled itself on Tang-style imperial institutions, but generally enjoyed relative peace and the dimming splendor of late Tang culture.

In the north, five dynasties rose and fell, each lasting only a matter of years, as military influence passed from one set of rulers to another. These northern regimes had little time for cultural pursuits, and little inclination to support them. Far more than the dynasties in the south, they singlemindedly concentrated on maintaining what was, in fact, a very fragile military supremacy over other northern leaders and frontier groups who were building great strength on China's northern borders. Indeed, it is to these northern states that we must look for much of the flavor of later Chinese political history.

Northern peoples, often referred to by the Chinese as "barbarians," played an enormous role in later Chinese history. Throughout the Five Dynasties and the subsequent Song dynasty, non-Chinese states to the northeast and northwest would deeply influence Chinese life. The Liao kingdom to the northeast and the Xi Xia state to the northwest, with populations measuring only a fraction of that of China Proper, combined indigenous political and cultural patterns with the Chinese model for state organization during the tenth and eleventh centuries. The process of sinification, or "becoming Chinese," is extremely important in understanding foreign states that sought to influence China. On the one hand, the Qidan people adopted Chinese practices of ancestor worship, used the Chinese language in official government work, and adopted Chinese-style court regalia. On the other hand, they retained their own tribal organization and maintained their own distinctive styles of food and dress outside of court life. The Xi Xia state of the Tangut people declared its independence from Song in 1038, and its ruler declared himself an emperor on even footing with the Chinese. Its people developed an innovative writing system and adopted Buddhism as their state religion.

Although the Liao and Xi Xia states played a major role in Chinese life during the Northern Song dynasty, neither could withstand the superior power of another northern people, the Ruzhen (often written *Jurchen*), who created a Jin state that in the twelfth century would annihilate both and drive the Song southward below the Yangzi River. From their northern Manchurian roots, the Ruzhen were unified by a series of charismatic leaders who linked the ability to conquer large regions and the administrative capabilities required to rule them.

In spite of all their power, the core problem for non-Chinese states was how to rule a large land mass peopled by Chinese subjects—as many as 100 million during the eleventh century—without losing the cultural identity and nomadic hardiness that helped them to gain power in the first place. We will discuss the particular problems associated with this when we examine the Mongols, but it is important to understand from the outset that conquering large swaths of China and maintaining rule for a long period of time was difficult, indeed virtually impossible, for non-Chinese groups. The staccato patterning of northern groups conquering China and then failing to hold it would be seen, in various forms, throughout China's next ten centuries.

THE NORTHERN AND SOUTHERN SONG (960–1279)

The Song founder, Zhao Kuangyin (r. 960–976), was a capable young general in the 950s who, in a now-familiar pattern, eventually took the throne in place of a child emperor. He and his advisers felt the need for hands-on military leadership in the unstable north, and he was prevailed upon to declare a new dynasty. Creating a lasting political order from the unstable northern and southern politics of the tenth century presented several serious challenges to Zhao Kuangyin, who would later be known by his imperial name of Song Taizu, or "Lofty Ancestor of Song."

Song Taizu's first priority was to stabilize northern China. He provided his own military supporters with generous "retirement plans," and thus weakened the possibility of mutiny and rebellion. He also replaced regional governors, whose loyalties were not always dependable in times of discord, with civil officials delegated from his court. Finally, he moved the very best units from the regional armies to the palace army and put them entirely under his own command. In this way he created a military structure that consisted of a powerful, professional army that was under his direct control.

Taizu also helped to solidify his position by expanding the civil service and entrusting government administration to scholar-officials who, although immensely talented, had no power bases of their own. Like other founders who sought to create order after periods of division, he also worked to solidify the infrastructure and create a more central process of collecting taxes and administering local government. In this way, Taizu created a concentration of power in the imperial position that would influence a great deal of later Chinese history.

After solidifying the north in this manner, Taizu needed to reincorporate the southern kingdoms into his realm. In campaigns during the 960s and 970s he subjugated all but one kingdom, the aboriginal state of Southern Zhao, which retained its independence throughout the dynasty. Song Taizu died at the comparatively young age of forty-eight, with the centralization only partly completed. His younger brother Song Taizong (r. 976–997) continued the process, moving to solidify the borders (still a good deal less total territory than Tang at its height) and reunite the lands that were traditionally considered Chinese.

The Liao state offered tribute and for a short time became vassals of the Song. The Xi Xia state, in contrast, successfully held off Taizong's military campaigns. Thereafter, he concentrated on building defenses, and this defensive stance would mark the Song for the remainder of the dynasty. In fact, many readers of Chinese history are disturbed by the extent to which, during the eleventh century in particular, the Song created "peace agreements" that appear to be very much like tribute payments to what they regarded as "barbarian" states in order to hold off the possibility of warfare. These gifts started as 100,000 ounces of silver and 200,000 bolts of silk every year. These numbers were later raised in both categories by another 100,000 units, creating at least a potential strain on the economy, and limiting diplomatic possibilities.

In spite of the military tensions, the Song enjoyed internal peace and prosperity during the eleventh century, and one can see the flourishing on several levels. To begin, as part of the long-term changes spoken of above, the population reached 100 million by 1100. New agricultural methods were developed and a much more sophisticated set of commercial links marked the growing communication between north and south. Cities, some with more than a million inhabitants, were the sites of a complex urban culture. A system of examinations that led to official positions became the primary vehicle for social mobility and profoundly shaped an increasingly fluid set of class lines, with shifting fortunes representing a new norm for aristocratic families. Finally, the development of printing would have enormous consequences in later Chinese history.

Eleventh-century China was immensely prosperous, and that would continue as long as the standoff with the northern states remained. Keeping the indigenous states appeased with payments worked fairly well as long as they lacked the strength to conquer in their own right. Similarly, the northern states were not united into a single fighting force, and the division worked to the Song's advantage. This changed with the Ruzhen (Jurchen) people's proclamation of a new state, the Jin, in 1115. By 1126, Jin had marched quickly southward, laying siege to the capital. The Song emperor Huizong abdicated, and the court moved south. Diplomacy continued for two years, but on terms that were impossibly high for the Song, Finally, in 1127 the Ruzhen returned, took the capital again, and carried hundreds of members of the imperial family into captivity.

What remained of the Song dynasty was a distinctly different, and much smaller, territory with its capital based in Hangzhou. The move to a new southern capital marks the dividing line between Northern (960–1127) and Southern (1127–1279) Song. The Song ceded virtually everything north of the Yangzi River, including the Yellow River drainage area that both practically and symbolically figured so prominently in earlier Chinese history and culture. They also accepted status as essentially a vassal state of Jin and continued their high payments of silver and silk.

Throughout the almost two centuries of the Southern Song dynasty, the territory under Chinese control was but a fraction of the great dynasties of the past. Emperors of this period were entangled in powerful faction struggles and too politically weak to create unity at their own court, much less in the broader arenas required to retake the north. Although the Southern Song was a time of cultural change, with significant contributions in Chinese philosophy, painting, and poetry, the political story would be defined by reaction to the northern states, and it is to the most prominent of these that we now turn.

THE MONGOLS AND THE YUAN (1234–1368)

Few "outsiders" have had as powerful an impact upon China as the Mongols in the thirteenth and fourteenth centuries. The development of the Mongolian empire under the leadership of Genghis Khan, and the conquests of much of Europe and Asia, are a significant part of world history. The Mongols annihilated the Jin in 1234 and completed their conquest of the Southern Song in 1279. In the four decades between these dates, the Mongols controlled northern China and solidified their rule of, as the Chinese called their territory, "all under heaven."

In the early thirteenth century a young man named Temüjin defeated numerous northern tribes; in 1206 he was named paramount ruler of the Mongol peoples as Genghis, or Chinggis, Khan. His Mongol troops, led by hereditary leaders trained for lives in the saddle, could cover incredible distances as they lived on plunder in their raiding to the east and south. It has often been noted that the Mongols' psychological warfare was as effective as their legendary fighting ability. Stories of terror and devastation preceded them wherever they went, sapping the fighting strength of the mostly agricultural peoples they conquered. "Man's greatest joy," Genghis Khan was said to have declared, "is in victory—in conquering one's enemies, pursuing them, depriving them of their possessions, making their loved ones weep, riding on their horses, and embracing their wives and daughters."

The first Mongol ruler of a reunified China was Khubilai Khan,

Nineteenth-century engraving of Genghis Khan. The paramount leader of the Mongols during their rise to power in the thirteenth century, Genghis Khan was one of the world's great military organizers. Under his leadership, the Mongolian empire undertook successful conquests of much of Europe and Asia. Fifty years after his death the Mongols completed their conquest of the Southern Song. (Print and Picture Collection, Free Library of Philadelphia)

Genghis Khan's grandson (r. 1260–1294). After an early succession crisis, Khubilai Khan asserted his power over his brothers and various generals, moving his capital to Beijing and declaring a new dynasty with the name of Yuan ("beginning"). Unlike his Chinese imperial predecessors, Khubilai followed his subjugation of the southern regions with aggressive fighting overseas, proclaiming his rule as far as India and Korea, being hindered only in his attempt to take Japan.

Mongol rule in China combined strong military control with an attempt to negotiate the complex Chinese bureaucracy. Mongols occupied top posts but needed assistance from Chinese officials. Those Chinese who did serve were clearly subordinate to their Mongol leaders, and the examination system itself, long considered to be a tool of fair assessment of native ability, was altered to produce regional and ethnic quotas to reflect Mongol rule. Yet Beijing under the Mongols was a cosmopolitan center, with many foreign travelers and diplomats in the Khan's service—Central Asians, Persians, Arabs, Russians. The city under Mongol rule is celebrated in the writings attributed to the Italian merchant traveler Marco Polo, who mentioned strange long noodles, black rocks used for fuel, and money made of paper, as well as cities so large that their commercial centers themselves would dwarf those in his homeland.

The extremely centralized autocratic government of the Mongols added strength to a trend that had begun with the Song founder, Taizong, three centuries earlier—the growth of a strong imperial institution with the potential to be much more brutal and singleminded than was seen in the early empire. The ideal of remonstrance, of a government minister opposing a reflective and understanding emperor (so lauded in early writings), was an increasingly quaint memory.

As the Mongols entered the fourteenth century, the economy increasingly suffered from corruption and a government that could not effectively reach the lower levels of administration. Landlord power over tenant farmers became increasingly great, and economic life was again regionalized in numerous ways. More Chinese were reduced to tenant or even outright slave status than at any previous time in their history. The cumulative effect of this, over half a century, was loss of the countryside and, eventually, confusion in the capital. Even the Mongol neglect of agriculture, irrigation, and water control seemed to conspire against them, with a series of natural disasters in the 1340s that culminated in the Yellow River breaking its dikes and changing course. The Mongol rulers, whose terrifying fighting ability combined with the Chinese notion of the Mandate of Heaven to thoroughly occupy China a century earlier, were undone by that very same mandate. Heaven had seemingly renounced its will, causing rivers to flood and people to die. For all of their initial terror, the Mongols could not rule all of China for even a century.

THE MING DYNASTY (1368–1644)

Chinese peasants rose in a series of loosely connected rebellions throughout the 1350s, as the Mongols lost control of southern China. In that same region, a Chinese commoner named Zhu Yuanzhang gradually linked his armies with an increasingly wide collection of disgruntled groups, and having consolidated the Yangzi River drainage area, declared a new dynasty, the Ming ("bright" or "luminous") in 1368. As with all such foundings, much work remained to be done, and it was not until several years later that the last Yuan emperor was driven back into the steppe of Mongolia.

As the first commoner in 1,500 years to ascend the imperial throne, the man who would become known as the Hongwu emperor (r. 1368–1398) set out to remedy the harsh conditions in the countryside. He abolished slavery, confiscated large estates, and punished many large landowners. He raised taxes dramatically in southeastern China, where many merchants had benefited enormously from trade networks by land, sea, and river as well as from the almost nonexistent checks on trade during the confusion of the late Yuan era. He also returned to the Song model examination system and sought to raise the status of scholar-officials in his government. Although the gap between rich and poor remained great, the effect of the Hongwu emperor's policies was (like the Han Emperor Wu and other rulers who sought to even out inequities) to check the worst abuses of landlordism and monopoly that marked the mid-fourteenth century.

The Hongwu emperor also was successful in dealing with the Ming borders, and by the time his reign ended at the close of the fourteenth century, his government controlled all of what was regarded as China Proper, and dominated the northern frontier from Inner Mongolia to Manchuria. Because of his success in restoring Chinese rule and due to his commoner origins, many modern historians have made something of a folk hero out of him. The appealing qualities are clear, but there were serious problems with his reign, including a series of bloody purges that ended in the deaths of thousands of officials and their families. Indeed, as he became older, his paranoia and fear of ridicule for his humble beginnings and perceived ugliness (he is known by some as the "bean face emperor" for his pockmarked visage) led him in a direction far from his founding ideals.

The third Ming emperor, Chengzu (r. 1402–1424) came to power by overthrowing his nephew in a three-year civil conflict. From such beginnings he nonetheless proceeded to, in many ways, create a "refounding" for the Ming after the violence of the Hongwu emperor's later years and the conflict that marked his own ascent. He reconstructed the heavily silted Grand Canal, which had become all but unusable after accumulating eight hundred years of sediment, again linking north-south trade networks. He also moved the Ming capital to Beijing in 1421, where it would remain to the present. Finally, he inaugurated a series of naval missions that went far beyond anything China had seen before or for many centuries since. For a narrow slice of time, from 1405 to 1433, China was Asia's paramount naval power.

This early Ming spirit of travel was not to last, and for the most part it could be characterized as an inward-looking empire. There was little of the cosmopolitanism of Tang dynasty Chang'an, or even Yuan dynasty Beijing, with their travelers, musicians, and poets. Indeed, symbolically if not practically, the building of the Great Wall from fragments of earlier northern walls speaks to a desire to set off China from the surrounding world—a breathtaking symbol of imperial isolation, if not an effective check on northern invaders.

By the mid-Ming period, serious financial problems had beset the dynasty following decades of poor fiscal management. Eunuch management of palace expenditures, according to both traditional and more recent historiography, became a major factor in the weakening of the state. Factional politics, echoing bureaucratic divisions in the Song, also prevailed in the mid- to late Ming. On a cultural level, the Ming dynasty saw a profound growth in social, cultural, and intellectual realms, including advances in printing and the growth of the vernacular novel. The population of the north slowly recovered from the Yuan disasters, and the overall population continued on a trend that would create serious issues of resource management. In all, one sees a pattern throughout the fifteenth and sixteenth centuries of increasingly lax governmental administration accompanied by cultural richness and economic growth that led to a long period of late-imperial greatness.

The affluence of the mid- to late-Ming was not equally distributed, and the kinds of abuse that marked earlier ages came to the fore as well—especially in the form of landlordism. Exploitation of the tax system and the serflike status of tenant farmers were a further part of the problem. The later Ming emperors became increasingly remote. It is hard, perhaps, for readers accustomed to four- or eight-year administrations to imagine the kinds of problems that decades of government mismanagement or neglect might create. In brief, corrupt officials and imperial lieutenants took on enormous authority, and partisan wrangling divided the court. When the central government was most ineffective, landed families and wealthy urbanites were able to act independently, which led to further divisions.

Creating even more serious problems for the Ming was the fact that internal instability coincided with serious northern threats. A domestic rebel, Li Zicheng (d. 1645), seized Beijing in 1644, whereupon the last Ming emperor hanged himself. A frontier general invited the rulers of an increasingly powerful Manchurian state to the northeast of China to join him in putting down the rebels, and the Manchus took the opportunity to take the throne themselves. The Ming legacy is thus a mixed one. Long-term abuses in the countryside were checked, but only temporarily; and by the time the dynasty ended, the Manchu conquerors were welcomed by many Chinese as legitimate holders of power who sought to remedy the problems of greed and abuse among Chinese rulers.

THE QING DYNASTY (TO 1800)

The Manchus, who in 1644 founded China's last imperial dynasty, were related to the Ruzhen, whose Jin state had ruled northern China in the twelfth and thirteenth centuries. They adopted the name Qing ("clear" or "pure") and sought to rule China without losing touch with their northern roots. When they gained control of northern China, they cast themselves as preservers of a Chinese culture gone awry and contended that it was the Ming itself that had lost the Mandate of Heaven and, hence, the right to rule.

The Qing conquest was by no means easy, and it was far from bloodless. Indeed, the massacres that followed them from north to south were a serious point of anger for native Chinese, and stories of Manchu abuses were told for generations. Indeed, the Manchu consolidation took the better part of forty years, and it was only in the 1680s that all of southern China and Taiwan were reintegrated and various rebel groups eliminated. This "Southern Ming" resistance, as it was called, played a prominent role in later criticisms of Manchu rule and formed an ideal of resistance for many Chinese.

The Manchus organized themselves into a complex "banner" system, a social and economic institution that formed them into well-ordered fighting troops or disciplined civilians, depending on the needs of the time. Other ways that Manchus set themselves apart from the Chinese were to maintain a secret management of revenues for the imperial clan and to create a separate Manchu homeland. For at least the first century of rule, Manchu language study was compulsory, and there were restrictions on trade and intermarriage with Chinese. The most dramatic display, however, lay in forcing Chinese men to wear queues, in which the hair was braided and the front of the head shaven. Chinese resistance to this took on various forms, but the Manchus enforced it with the death penalty.

The first 150 years of Manchu rule was marked by the reigns of three extraordinary rulers who created a managerial structure that made China, in many ways, the most flourishing of the world's nations. Unchecked by foreign aggression, the Qing enjoyed more than a century of peace and stability, largely through sound, if often harsh, domestic policies, and a clear preeminence over neighboring peoples.

The Kangxi emperor (r. 1661–1722), reigned over China longer than any emperor before him. Although he was actually the second in the sequence of rulers, he had all of the classic qualities of the "good first ruler" in the Chinese political imagination. Raised in the manner of a Chinese heir apparent, he wrote poetry, painted, and enjoyed a wide range of literature. He was also deeply interested in the practical, if not religious, teachings of Jesuit missionaries. Still, he was deeply attached to the Manchurian north and quite conscious of the unique combination of personal training and insight required to remain true to his Manchu roots while being an effective Son of Heaven.

The Kangxi emperor carefully regulated the economy and worked for better water control and agriculture. This was no small feat, remembering the difficulties the Mongols had with these matters three centuries earlier. He was also a strong leader in military affairs who personally completed the consolidation of the empire during the first twenty years of his reign. He planned the campaigns to the south but also pushed the Qing borders northward to the greatest territorial extent prior to the twentieth century.

Where the Kangxi emperor failed was in controlling the succession of his heir. He was eventually succeeded by his fourth son, the Yongzheng emperor (r. 1723–1735), who gained the throne by conspiring against his brothers. He was a wary ruler who reflected the potential for autocracy in the imperial institution. His reign only seems brief in the context of his predecessor and successor, who each ruled for more than sixty years. He carried on the careful management of his father and left the empire in good order for his son, the Qianlong emperor, who would control Qing government until the end of the eighteenth century.

The Qianlong emperor (r. 1736–1796), was one of the greatest figures in the history of world imperial power. He held power for longer than any Chinese emperor, but abdicated his official role in 1796 as an act of filial devotion toward his grandfather, the Kangxi emperor. For the first forty years of his reign he was also one of the most capable rulers in all of Chinese history. Domestically, he continued his grandfather's work as a patron of the arts, and it was his inspiration that led to several monumental encyclopedic compilations that marked mid-Qing intellectual culture. Militarily, he embarked on ten campaigns that were meant to preserve and even extend Qing borders, culminating in his destruction of a pesky, resurgent Mongol presence in Central Asia. By the mid-eighteenth century, the power of the Qing military was unquestioned in East and Central Asia.

In retrospect, the Qianlong emperor's reign was damaged by two serious flaws. First is an extensive literary inquisition in the 1770s aimed at suppressing subversion in the bureaucracy. The other was the weakening of his will to rule. In the last quarter century of his reign he gradually gave power to a Manchu guardsman named Heshen (1750–1799), who controlled the government for the last twenty years of the Qianlong emperor's reign. The combination of the literary inquisition and Heshen's corruption seriously weakened Qing domestic policy and military preparedness. Indeed, in the last twenty years of the century, officers and troops on stipends were forced to subsist on low rations, and they often became petty traders or even criminals.

After more than a century of comparative peace, the deterioration of the Manchu military was clearly shown by a huge peasant rebellion that in better times could have been quickly checked. The same banner forces that had dominated Central Asia for almost two centuries took eight years to fully suppress the White Lotus Rebellion that arose in the mountainous border regions of Hubei, Sichuan, and Shanxi. Mixing religious strains with an increasingly strong anti-Manchu sentiment, the rebellion was effective both in its wide appeal to the populace and in its nonstandard, guerilla warfare tactics.

When the Qianlong emperor abdicated in 1796, the Qing's military was spoken of as unrivaled in all of Asia. By the time he died in 1799 the toll of a quarter century of neglect was increasingly obvious. As

China entered the nineteenth century, it would meet an array of challenges from within and without for which it was very poorly prepared.

THE EARLY NINETEENTH CENTURY (1800–1830)

Chinese rulers in the nineteenth century saw a series of domestic and foreign challenges virtually unrivaled in their history. Brief histories of China often make the mistake of implying that many of the deep changes in attitude and institutions that occurred during that time were the direct result of the shock of foreign presence. Without doubt, the foreign influences that would affect China during the nineteenth century were dramatic. Yet many Chinese scholar-officials themselves had begun to criticize China's ability to deal with its problems at the turn of the century.

When the Jiaqing emperor (r. 1796–1820) came to exercise full power in 1799, the Qing government saw enormous challenges—addressing the problems of military inefficiency, population growth, and a quarter-century of corruption that had marked central government at the end of the Qianlong reign. Earlier rulers had confronted each of these problems in the past, but when they occurred together, as at the end of dynasties, the problems were serious indeed. The White Lotus Rebellion was finally quelled in 1804 with a combination of latent military strength and starvation blockades. The long-term effects of the government action, however, would be serious, raising the specter of anti-Manchu resistance.

Population problems were by no means under control by the early nineteenth century. By 1800, even conservative estimates of China's population placed it in the 300 million range. By midcentury, it would increase again by half. The problems were acute: Most of the land that could be farmed was already under cultivation and had been for centuries. After stunning agricultural developments almost a millennium earlier, few new innovations in agricultural methods had occurred. These pressures were reflected at the higher levels of government in a cynicism among young men who had hopes of government service.

There were few more positions available than there had been to an official during the Song dynasty, yet the number of degree candidates had skyrocketed. This was the result of population growth, of course, but also of increased literacy. Although this could in no way be called a high level of literacy, a doubling or tripling of the relatively small numbers from earlier centuries still had profound effects. The greatest was on morale. Many scholars of great talent saw the examinations as a dead end, and increasingly as a reward for unimaginative drones who saw only the obvious in their readings. Whether or not that was indeed the case, many challenges lay ahead for Qing officials, and they were by no means organized into the tidy paradigms represented in classical teachings and examination essays.

What John King Fairbank has called "the paradox of growth without development" thus had enormous effects on China in the early nineteenth century. Government morale was low, resources were increasingly scarce, and the once-strong military structure had all but collapsed. This was the setting for two pivotal events—one external, one internal—that would shake the Qing to its very foundations by midcentury. The Opium War and its aftermath, as well as the Taiping Rebellion, would shatter the long-studied (and assumed) patterns of China's past.

WAR AND DIPLOMACY (1830–1850)

By the early nineteenth century, Chinese contact with Western countries was limited to sporadic trade and the memory of Jesuit missionary activities two centuries earlier. There were essentially no diplomatic relations in the form that one could find among European states. The series of conflicts that are often written about as the Opium War had a great deal to do with British (and other nations') desire to "open" China for a much wider trade than the Chinese wished. Just decades earlier, the Qianlong emperor had rejected British interests, reflecting a Chinese governmental world view that other nations came to pay tribute, but that the Middle Kingdom would not engage them as equals. The British envoy refused to kowtow; the Qianlong emperor stated that "we possess all things." In the late eighteenth century, it was a standoff. Fifty years later, it would be war.

Opium had been outlawed by the Qing in the early eighteenth century, but, for both internal and external reasons, its use had grown tremendously over a century. By the 1830s, members of the Qing bureaucracy were attempting to regain control of an opium trade in Canton that had gotten out of control. To begin with, it represented a serious exchange problem for the government. Connected to this was the resistance to significant foreign trade of any kind. Finally, Qing officials increasingly saw the opium problem as a moral one.

Against this backdrop, Lin Zexu (1785–1850), regarded as an incorruptible official in China but skewered in British history books for

British ships battle Chinese junks during the Opium War. (Hulton Archive)

intransigence and naiveté, was sent to Canton to put an end to the trade. Lin demanded that foreigners turn over their opium and sign a pledge to no longer trade opium, instituting the death penalty for buying and selling opium. The British superintendent of trade, Napier Elliot, ordered the opium stocks turned over. When the Chinese ultimately destroyed the opium, British merchants looked to their own government for restitution. There was a great deal of tension on both sides, and the British government felt enormous pressure to take some kind of action. In addition to this, there were a growing number of conflicts—fights, murders, general misunderstandings between foreigners and Chinese—for which there were no convenient legal mechanisms.

The war itself lasted from 1839 to 1842. The first phase ended in a tense peace in the summer of 1841, only to be broken soon thereafter. The second phase of the war saw the complete victory of the British, whose cannons were able to fire at will from ships too far away for the Chinese to resist. The defeat itself was humiliating, for it showed that the Qing military forces were backward by international standards, their administration deeply flawed, and, in a time when the rest of the world was capable of sophisticated sea travel and fighting, had nothing resembling an able navy. China had been defeated before, but not since the Mongols had it been so thoroughly and relentlessly driven into submission.

In the context of later historical events, the diplomatic results of the Opium War are perhaps more important than China's defeat. The Qing government was forced into concessions it clearly never would have made without a thorough military defeat. Hong Kong was given to the British. Five "treaty ports" were opened to foreign consuls, traders, and missionaries along China's southeast coast. The treaty also forced the Qing to pay $21 million in silver to Britain, and to give Britain special diplomatic status. Finally, foreigners were given extraterritorial rights, allowing their home governments to punish them, but preventing the Chinese government from dealing with conflicts on its own territory.

Far from the trade in opium (which remained illegal), the major results of the war lay in forcing China out of its traditional models of trade and diplomacy. The effects were great, for no amount of reading in the classics or traditional moral education could help Chinese troops defeat the superior military power of the British. What one sees in the 1840s is confusion that would last for decades, until a wide range of thinkers would attempt to resolve the apparent conflict between Western and Chinese ways.

REBELLION AND BEYOND (1850–1870)

Beyond the treaty ports, the Opium War had profound effects throughout southeastern China. The countryside, with a complex local and regional trade network that had grown for centuries, was well-connected by land and river to the major coastal cities. In the cities themselves, crime and unemployment increased, as well as a simmering resentment of the influx of foreigners. In the countryside, where there had been a long tradition of "secret societies" linked together by fictive kinship ties, religious ideals, and fighting skill, opposition to Europeans broadened to a more general opposition to China's Manchu conquerors.

In this rural context we can best see the strange case of Hong Xiuquan, the educated son of a Hakka farmer from just north of Canton. After his third examination failure at the relatively humble prefectural level, he encountered a Protestant missionary and Chinese converts. Although examination failure was a constant in later Chinese history, missionaries in the countryside were not, and this is only the first reflection of the profound changes that were taking place in rural China. Hong accepted some pamphlets and returned to his home. One year later, in 1837, he tried again for his degree. His subsequent failure set off a mental breakdown in which he lay at home, hallucinating and lashing out at "devils." One of these "devils," Hong would later relate, was the sage himself—Confucius.

Six years passed, but the pamphlets he had received eventually led him in a new direction. He crafted a "doctrine of heavenly peace" that stated, "China belonged to the Father, and yet the barbarian devils stole into Father's heavenly kingdom; this is the reason that Father decreed I should destroy them." For Hong, these "barbarian devils" were not Europeans, but rather Manchus. Once the Chinese people recovered their "original" religion (Christianity, in his teaching, was Chinese) by exterminating the Manchus, the "age of great peace" would arrive, uniting the world in universal harmony.

Western missionaries quickly realized that Hong was not a typical convert. What he said was new, and perplexing, for all of his listeners—Chinese and foreign. Hong was not merely adopting a foreign teaching; he was redefining that doctrine as inherently Chinese. He cast himself as Christ's younger brother, in a perfect Chinese model of filiality, and declared himself the articulator of world Christianity.

Hong would likely have remained an isolated, and somewhat strange, prophet in different times. It so happens that he found a ready group of listeners in a countryside discontented with massive population growth, restricted resources, official corruption down to the local level, and increased banditry and disorder. In the countryside of Canton, these listeners and their leader became the Society of God Worshippers. At least during the late 1840s, they still lacked military ambition.

In January 1851, however, Hong Xiuquan formally declared the Heavenly Kingdom of Great Peace—a radical departure from the earlier pattern of worship. He declared a new dynasty with the intent of breaking the Manchu hold on China. The resulting Taiping Rebellion represents an important blend of concepts, many of which would play out a century later in the Chinese Communist movement. Still, the official positions held to the Chinese imperial model, with Hong as the "heavenly king." It was envisioned as more than another dynasty, however. As part of the "heavenly order," it was meant to break the dynastic cycle altogether. Other prominent features included communal ideals—all followers were one family, brothers and sisters. The sexes were separated, but distinctions on the traditional Chinese family model were abolished. Finally, it was a militarized organization at all levels. Farmer-soldier groups of twenty-five replaced old alliances based on home and family with an ideological commitment to a greater cause.

For the next year they moved north, swiftly sweeping up the indigenous peasantry in the movement. Villages that resisted were often destroyed and their inhabitants massacred. Those who submitted watched all of their possessions burned to the ground before being permitted to join the movement "without ties to the past." In 1853 the Taiping forces occupied the city of Nanjing, the early capital of the Ming dynasty and a key strategic city. There, they made an enormous tactical error—they stopped moving. They settled in to stabilize and define the kingdom, but lost the momentum they had in keeping Qing forces off-balance. An even more important problem also became apparent. Once the Taiping rebels stopped moving, they, just like the government they derided, were forced to deal with the complex problems of China's countryside—poverty, overpopulation, and restricted resources.

The Taiping rebels intended to apply their teachings to society at large, and Nanjing became their foundation. From the start, however, the same kinds of structural failures that plagued China's dynastic governments were seen in Nanjing—infighting, managing generals who were inclined to self-promotion, and the problem of simply feeding their people. By 1856, the movement was in shambles, with quarreling leaders and ineffective administration. Although aided by the brilliant commander Li Xiucheng, that the Taipings remained in Nanjing until 1864 says more about Qing ineffectiveness than any residual strength of the movement.

The Qing government had a good deal more to contend with than the Taiping rebels. Coinciding with the Taiping Rebellion, several other rebellions flared throughout the country. In the end, more than 20 million people died from warfare, starvation, or natural disasters. Throughout, however, the government was also occupied by a series of escalating demands from foreign interests. By 1860, at the Convention of Beijing, eleven new treaty ports were opened, and diplomatic connections with an even wider range of governments and traders emerged. With the Xianfeng emperor (r. 1851–1861) dying and the country enveloped in foreign and domestic crises, the Qing rulers faced challenges that threatened to change the very structure of not only China's government but of its society and culture as well.

ATTEMPTS AT RESTORATION AND THE
FALL OF QING (1870–1911)

Profound changes resulted from the tumultuous period delineated by the Opium Wars and the Taiping Rebellion. The most important of these is a recurring one: local militarization. From the Warring States period 2,000 years before, to the end of the Han dynasty, the An Lushan rebellion, and the fall of the Ming dynasty, there is perhaps no more important ruling theme in Chinese history—when the central government found itself overextended, it turned to others for support. Reasserting power was rarely effective. In the wake of the Taiping upsurge and other rebellions, the Qing rule was able to survive only by enlisting the support of local militia groups. Over the last decades of the nineteenth century (and well into the twentieth) these local militia groups increasingly became independent actors. Controlling local militia was only a small part of the larger restorative process that a number of late-century thinkers espoused, however.

One of the most significant of these reformers was Prince Gong, the brother of the Xianfeng emperor. He was a talented diplomat with a vision (not unlike the leaders of the Meiji reforms in Japan at the same time) of China's role in world politics. Others who fought for Chinese "self-strengthening" during this period included Zeng Guofan, who led Hunan armies against the Taiping rebels; Zuo Zongtang, who eventually defeated the Nian rebels; and Li Hongzhang, one of the principal reform leaders throughout the later decades of the nineteenth century. All of these leaders combined a vision of a modernized society with a deep sense of military preparedness, and many, having regional power bases of their own, displayed the core contradiction of reform—the conflict between a set of national goals and protection of their regional interests.

Most of the "self-strengthening" projects espoused by Qing reformers were meant to balance *ti* and *yong,* "inner essence" and "function," in the effort to modernize. They sought to retain the inner core of teachings and moral principles that had shaped three millennia of Chinese life with the sophisticated technology and strategy shown by Westerners. Responding in their own ways to what the Chinese termed the *"tiyong* dilemma," Japanese thinkers at the same time described this dual focus as "Eastern Ethics and Western Science." Indeed, those were the categories the reformers sought to resolve, as they worked to balance what was integral, as they saw it, to their tradition, even as they realized the need to rise to a competitive scientific level with the West.

Portrait of Li Hongzhang, a principal reform leader in the later decades of the nineteenth century (Library of Congress)

This "Confucian Pragmatism" was brought to military restructuring, economics, education, and social policy. Yet the reforms, in retrospect, were flawed from the outset—no matter how well-intentioned,

The Japanese defeat the Chinese at Yalu River in 1894 during the Sino-Japanese War. (Library of Congress)

there was no systematic restructuring of education to put these blended aims into practice for future generations. Traditional-style examinations were held until the end of the dynasty, and those who argued most forcefully against the system were often self-educated on reform matters.

By the 1890s a new kind of critique was taking form. Far from the pragmatic reforms of Prince Gong and others, these came in reaction to China's humiliating defeat in the 1894–1895 Sino-Japanese War, and the subsequent Treaty of Shimonoseki, sparking deep questions about the very basis of traditional ideology. Although traditionally educated, this group, led by Liang Qichao, Kang Youwei, and others, sought not to resolve old and new ways but to abolish the traditional order entirely. They traveled, sought new ideas from the United States, Japan, and Europe, and wrote increasingly virulent attacks on Qing rule and traditional political organization.

For the failures of reform, however, one needs to look back to the end of the Taiping movement when, in the late 1860s, Qing officials proclaimed a "restoration" meant to create a new order without losing hold of power. When the Xianfeng emperor died in 1861, his son was only five years old, and Cixi, the emperor's mother, with the help of the empress and Prince Gong, seized power. The complex events resulted in the last decades of the Qing period representing a combination of Prince Gong's drive to reform and Cixi's desire to retain power at any cost.

During most of the 1870s and 1880s the court remained under the control of Cixi, the empress dowager. She dominated the young Tongzhi emperor (r. 1862–1874) and (according to legends that take on the misogynistic aura of earlier attacks on the Tang dynasty's Empress Wu) encouraged his excessive ways, leading to his early death at nineteen. To maintain her power she shocked court officials by putting her own nephew, a four-year old, on the throne. She continued to rule for the Guangxu emperor (r. 1875–1908) until he came of age in 1889. She removed Prince Gong from power in 1884, and, reformism aside, continued to build her formidable personal fortune.

Many recent historians have argued that Cixi has become too easy a target for attack in what was an extremely complex late Qing political situation. Indeed, she was not the first person to gain power and wealth through nefarious means, nor the first to concentrate on retaining power above all else. Some have even argued that *only* such a forceful personality who broke, in gender and style, the conventions of rule could control China's growing regional armies and fragile political center. With the situation so fluid, the manipulation of regional leaders was the only way to bring minimal cohesion to the Qing. Restoring central control was out of the question, for the Qing government had lackluster military resources of its own.

The dynasty's last major event would combine the nineteenth-century themes of internal rebellion and foreign influence and would shake the traditional order to its foundation. The social, spiritual, political, and intellectual tensions that had been building can all be seen in the Boxer Rebellion. Known somewhat misleadingly to Westerners in China as the Righteous and Harmonious Fists (*yihequan*), the Boxers were resentful of missionary and convert "privileges" in the treaty ports and the harsh social and economic conditions in the cities and beyond. Holding a deep belief in charms and supernatural powers, the Boxers gained official recognition in their effort to "expel the barbarians" from an unlikely source—the equally "foreign" Qing government. Changing what was at least in part an anti-Qing slogan to one that was anti-Western, the Boxers gained Qing recognition as an official military organization.

In June 1900, they entered Beijing. Eight days later, the Qing court declared war on the treaty powers. Almost 500 foreign civilians and 3,000 Chinese Christians were held under siege in the legation quarters for foreign officials. The gamble failed miserably, and their eventual defeat spelled the end of the Qing government. After miscalculating badly, the court fled the capital, and it had to pay a large

The Boxers resented missionary and convert privileges and the harsh social and economic conditions affecting China. Holding a deep belief in charms and supernatural powers, the Boxers gained recognition from the Qing court as an official military organization that supported the court against foreign influence. (National Archives)

indemnity to the foreign powers. China's international position was even more thoroughly weakened, and the loss of any realistic power center gave rise to independent action on the part of regional armies. Indeed, during the rebellion itself, several governors-general refused to follow Qing orders.

In the final decade of the Qing dynasty there were a series of efforts to prolong, if not save, the political order. The examination system was finally abolished in 1905, and a series of technical schools for Western education were established. The practice of footbinding, which had affected a large portion of women for almost a millennium, began to die out even more quickly than it had taken root in the Song dynasty. Most significant of all, however, was the fact that new groups were asserting collective voices, including students and workers. Indeed, in addition to controlling regional armies and reasserting central government, a new challenge would emerge for future leaders—harnessing the increasingly formidable power of the Chinese people.

REPUBLICAN CHINA AND THE WAR YEARS (1912–1949)

A major revolt in Wuchang on October 10, 1911, sparked a series of uprisings that led almost two-thirds of China's provinces to declare their independence from Qing rule. By December, seventeen provinces sent delegates to Nanjing, where Sun Yat-sen (1866–1925) was named provisional president of a new Republic of China. Yet only one individual at that time was able to control the growing power of regional armies and negotiate the end of Qing rule—Yuan Shikai, who had the loyalty of government troops as well as ties to both parliamentarians and the Qing court. The provisional Republican government agreed to give Yuan the presidency if the emperor abdicated. The emperor accepted, and Yuan assumed the presidency in March 1912. Yuan strove to root out his opposition, even as his government stated its desire to create a parliamentary system. In 1913 the Guomindang (Nationalist) Party, with the help of Sun Yat-sen, won a majority of seats in national parliamentary elections. Yuan Shikai then plotted the assassination of the party's leader, Song Jiaoren. Later that year, Yuan suspended parliament and amended the constitution, declaring himself president for life. The following year, he declared a restoration of imperial power and proclaimed himself emperor.

The political situation had changed dramatically, even in a few years, and provincial governors throughout China vigorously con-

Yuan Shikai assumed the presidency in March 1912. He plotted the assassination of the Nationalist Party leader when the party won a majority of seats in national parliamentary elections; suspended parliament and amended the constitution, declaring himself president for life; and then declared a restoration of imperial power and proclaimed himself emperor. (Library of Congress)

tested a reassertion of imperial power. Yuan died in June 1916 of natural causes, and these same governors filled the power void in a manner that has been seen throughout Chinese history during times of division—many combined military and political power on a local level. A dozen different warlords presided over a weak central government between 1916 and 1927, yet none was able to assert lasting power beyond his own territory. During this time it was the provinces themselves that operated with near-independence of central power.

Sun Yat-sen, who had fled to Japan during Yuan's parliamentary crackdown, returned to China in 1917 and the next year founded the military government of the Republic of China based in Guangzhou. In 1920 Sun Yat-sen was elected president of the republic, but his government remained regional and without the recognition of foreign powers.

At the outbreak of World War I in 1914, Japan had taken advantage of the Western powers' lack of focus on Asia to seize Germany's position in Shandong province. A year later, Japan issued twenty-one demands, insisting on China's recognition of its claim to Shandong, which would effectively make China a protectorate of Japan. When the fact that the warlord government had secretly acceded to most of Japan's demands became known during the Paris Peace Conference in 1919, student demonstrations ensued; the demonstrators were soon joined by laborers, merchants, and artisans. A May 4, 1919, demonstration of Chinese students against Japan in Beijing quickly spread to Shanghai and many other cities, becoming a catalyst for change— sparking a New Culture Movement that led to calls for changes from basic modernization to wholesale revolution.

Inspired by these calls for change and influenced by Communist writings, Communist groups developed throughout China. In 1921 a dozen organizers, including Mao Zedong, founded the Chinese Communist Party in Shanghai. By 1927 their membership numbered almost 60,000. At the heart of Mao's thought was a desire to harness the power of the people and the countryside. Although "the people" were referred to as an important part of traditional Chinese political philosophy, it was Mao who clearly articulated their role as a true *force* in political power, as shown by his rapid organization of a peasant and worker army.

In 1923 Sun Yat-sen became the leader of a new coalition government—the National Revolutionary government, again based in Guangzhou. Sun realized that no central power would be possible without strong military backing, and so he founded a revolutionary

Portrait of Chiang Kai-shek, leader of the Nationalist Party and president of the Republic of China (Library of Congress)

army and the Whampoa Military Academy to train officers for war against the northern warlords. Before these plans came to fruition, Sun died of cancer in 1925 and was succeeded by one of his lieutenants, Chiang Kai-shek. Chiang enjoyed rapid success, and by the end of 1926, the Nationalist Army controlled half of the country. In 1927 Chiang engineered a bloody massacre of Communist Party members and other opponents in Shanghai and several other cities. By 1928 Chiang's Northern Expedition reached Beijing, completing the unification and achieving recognition by Western powers.

Between 1928 and 1937, Chiang Kai-shek sought to eliminate the Communists and used significant resources to achieve that goal. After losing their position within major cities, the Communists sought to control the countryside, In January 1932 they established the Chinese Soviet Republic in Jiangxi province, with Mao Zedong as chairman. By 1934, however, Chiang had organized an effective blockade of Communist positions. Seeking to maintain the remnants of its forces, Mao's Red Army evacuated Jiangxi and began the "Long March" across eleven provinces and covering more than 8,000 miles, moving to a new base in Shaanxi. Though the relocation march began with tens of thousands of soldiers, only 8,000 arrived in Yan'an a year later.

While the Nationalist and Communist forces were engaged in civil conflict, Japan seized Manchuria in 1931, setting up China's "last emperor" of the Qing dynasty as the leader of its puppet government. Although this move spawned angry reactions throughout China, Chiang's focus remained on a policy of "internal pacification" to eliminate the Red Army's presence. The Japanese threat, however, sparked a backlash within the Nationalist Army, and Chiang was kidnapped by two high-ranking leaders who demanded that he turn Nationalist resources toward an alliance with the Communist party against the Japanese.

Chiang agreed and was released, and the resulting "United Front" quickly engaged in full-scale war with Japan. Attacking Chinese troops near Beijing in July 1937, Japan quickly captured the city and then moved to occupy most of China's major coastal cities. Both the Nationalist and Communist parties took a two-pronged approach to the war with Japan. Although both sought to repel the Japanese, they in turn kept wary eyes on each other and worked to build their own power bases. To this day, both sides claim that the other lacked full resolve in fighting Japan.

The acrimony boiled over after Japan's surrender to Allied forces in 1945. The Nationalists reoccupied the major cities while the

Communists controlled great portions of the countryside. Over the next four years, a complex end game of four decades of postimperial conflict took place. Although the Nationalist Army, with strong U.S. support, had a seemingly enormous advantage in terms of military resources and urban centers, the Red Army was able to take advantage of ineffective strategy and poor morale to gain the upper hand by 1949, when it captured Beijing and moved to solidify the rest of China's mainland. By the end of the year, Chiang Kai-shek's remaining Nationalist forces fled to Taiwan, where the Republic of China would continue as a government in exile.

THE PEOPLE'S REPUBLIC OF CHINA (1949–PRESENT)

On October 1, 1949, Mao Zedong proclaimed the founding of the People's Republic of China. The first years of rule were greeted by enthusiasm for an end to decades of conflict and warfare. From the outset, the Chinese Communist Party (CCP) made clear that China would be governed by a strong, central authority. All key military and government positions were occupied by party members, and Mao himself served as party chairman, president, and commander of national forces.

The challenges before the new government, however, were enormous, and the CCP acted quickly—in the manner of so many founding governments before it—to consolidate power and root out opposition. As a "people's revolution," however, the dynamics of this solidification were different from earlier eras. Although the power of landowners had always been a problem for dynastic founders in Chinese history (the Hongwu emperor in the Ming , for one, worked vigorously to check landlordism), the steps taken by the CCP to create genuine land reform were dramatic. In addition, the party launched a series of "campaigns" to transform China—the campaign to suppress counterrevolutionaries; the "three antis" campaign to root out corruption, waste, and narrow bureaucracy; the "five antis" campaign against bribery, tax fraud, cheating in contracts, public property theft, and economic crimes by businesses; and, finally, the Oppose America, Aid Korea campaign. These were more than just political calls to action. During the early 1950s these campaigns affected the lives of a large portion of China's population.

Similarly, in 1956, Mao, embracing the great tradition of political remonstrance, asked for the opinions and criticisms of a wide variety of people, including intellectuals, regarding political policy and the party. Although this Hundred Flowers campaign seemingly had an earnest origin, it was followed in 1957 by a fierce "anti-rightist" movement that led to the persecution of thousands of intellectuals who had voiced criticisms.

The first decade of the People's Republic also saw two different "five-year plans." During this time the CCP received support from the Soviet Union and modeled its industrial, banking, and commercial nationalizations on Soviet models as the first of such plans. The role of the private sector thus was effectively destroyed. In 1958 the party announced the Three Red Banner movement—consisting of the General Party Line, the Great Leap Forward, and the People's Commune—aimed at providing ideological continuity, maximization of industrial and agricultural output, and the full collectivization of the countryside.

These moves were ineffective at best, and disastrous at worst, with the death of more than 20 million people in the Great Leap Forward, as will be seen in Chapter 2. Amidst growing domestic troubles, the Chinese and Soviets broke relations after a series of increasingly bitter ideological and territorial conflicts. Mao gave up the presidency in 1959 to Liu Shaoqi, a veteran of decades of struggle who, along with Deng Xiaoping, worked to revitalize the economy through a series of measures aimed to relax state control in key industries and revitalize rural areas. Although many of these policies appeared to be effective, they raised the ire of Mao and others who saw them as leading toward capitalist actions. By 1963 Mao had reemerged to launch a Socialist Education Movement to restore teachings on class struggle and people's power.

This was just a precursor to a much larger movement that Mao launched in 1966 to solidify support among workers, students, and the army—the Cultural Revolution. The Cultural Revolution was initially a movement against traditional values and ideologies, but it quickly turned into a bitter internal war against many of Mao's political opponents, and it opened the doors for the settling of a vast number of personal scores at the local level. Many of Mao's earlier associates were demoted or dismissed. Others, including Liu Shaoqi, were killed during the conflict. Given encouragement from Mao, revolutionary committees were formed to seize power from party and government organizations, and youthful groups of Red Guards were able to act unchecked at local levels and beyond.

The intensity of the first years of the Cultural Revolution diminished by 1969, as Mao gradually extricated himself from its central

Chinese poster from the Cultural Revolution promoting the resettlement of educated urban youth in rural areas (Stefan Landsberger/Hangzhou Fine Arts Group)

leadership. From then until Mao's death in 1976, tension between a moderate group led by Premier Zhou Enlai and a "radical" group led by Mao's wife, Jiang Qing, dominated the party. The deaths in 1976 of Zhou Enlai, then China's premier; of Zhu De, the earliest military commander to support Mao; and of Mao himself threw the country into turmoil. Hua Guofeng, selected by Mao as his successor, arrested the "radical" group, later vilified as the Gang of Four, thus removing from power the strongest proponents of the Cultural Revolution. The legacy of the Cultural Revolution persisted in what has been often called a "lost generation" that was marked by enormous uncertainty, lack of organized education, and the loss of family connections and local ties.

Following Mao's death, Deng Xiaoping, who had been exiled during the Cultural Revolution, gained power in a contentious struggle. Although Deng never held the titles of president or party chairman, he exercised control until his death in 1997. Deng encouraged innovative combinations of communism and capitalism in the countryside. More

Mao Zedong, with his wife, Jiang Qing (Library of Congress)

of a pragmatist than his predecessor, he created profit incentives for businesses and encouraged a limited form of private entrepreneurship.

Deng also sought to revitalize the party through a series of purges of Cultural Revolution figures, vowing an end to the political cam-

Deng never held the titles of president or party chairman, yet he exercised enormous control until his death in 1997. Deng ordered the crackdown on demonstrating students in Tian'anmen Square in 1989 that led to hundreds of casualties. (Reuters/Richard Ellis/Hulton Archives)

paigns of the past. He abolished life tenure for senior party members and sought to check corruption at all levels. During his tenure, China established diplomatic relations with the United States and created a series of special economic zones to attract foreign investment from multinational corporations. In short, China in the late twentieth century was a growing world power that, although still defined by a central party structure, had an enormous and growing foreign economic presence and a central place in world trade.

Deng's tenure was not without controversy, however, and perhaps nothing shows that more clearly than the events at Tian'anmen Square on June 4, 1989. After weeks of student demonstrations that initially marked the death of Hu Yaobang, a popular party general secretary who had been dismissed three years earlier for a "soft" stance on student unrest, the demonstrations in Beijing quickly turned antigovernment. By the middle of May, the demonstrators had reached two million, and Deng was confronted with a serious threat to Communist party rule. After days of debating within the Politburo, Deng ordered a crackdown on the students, and in the early-morning hours of June 4, government troops and tanks expelled the demonstrators, with casualties numbering in the hundreds. The aftermath of Tian'anmen was no brighter, with mass arrests and reprisals among prodemocracy groups.

China's current leader, Jiang Zemin, came into prominence when Deng ousted his designated successor, Zhao Ziyang, for being sympathetic to the student cause. Since Deng's death in 1997, Jiang has moved cautiously to keep the economy growing while still asserting party leadership. The People's Republic of China, at its half-century mark, is in a position that its founders would not likely have imagined: While remaining in control of a centralized party power, it promises to be an enormous power in a global economy and one among the world's most powerful countries.

References

Bergère, Marie Claire. *Sun Yat-sen.* Stanford: Stanford University Press, 1998.

Blunden, Caroline. *Cultural Atlas of China.* Rev. ed. New York: Checkmark Books, 1998.

Cohen, Paul. *History in Three Keys.* New York: Columbia University Press, 1997.

Cohen, Warren I. *East Asia at the Center.* New York: Columbia University Press, 2000.

DeBary, William Theodore, and Irene Bloom. *Sources of Chinese Tradition, Vol. 1.* 2d ed. New York: Columbia University Press, 1999.

Ebrey, Patricia. *Chinese Civilization: A Sourcebook.* New York: Free Press, 1993.

Elman, Benjamin. *Classicism, Politics, and Kinship.* Berkeley: University of California Press, 1990.

Esherick, Joseph. *The Origins of the Boxer Uprising.* Berkeley: University of California Press, 1987.

Fairbank, John King. *China: A New History.* Cambridge, Mass.: Harvard University Press, 1992.

Girardot, Norman J. *Myth and Meaning in Early Taoism.* Berkeley: University of California Press, 1983.

Graham, A. C. *Disputers of the Tao.* Cambridge: Cambridge University Press, 1987.

Guang, Sima. 1956. *Zizhi tongjian.* (A Comprehensive Mirror for Aid in Ruling) Beijing: Zonghu Shuju.

Hansen, Valerie. *The Open Empire: A History of China to 1600.* New York: W. W. Norton, 2000.

Hardy, Grant. *Worlds of Bronze and Bamboo: Sima Qian's Conquest of History.* New York: Columbia University Press, 1999.

Harrell, Stevan. *Chinese Historical Microdemography.* Berkeley: University of California Press, 1995.

Hinton, William. *Fanshen: A Documentary of Revolution in a Chinese Village.* New York: Vintage Books, 1966.

Hoang, Michel. *Genghis Khan.* London: Saqi Books, 1989.

Knoblock, John. *Xunzi, Vols. 1–3.* Stanford: Stanford University Press, 1988–1992.

Kuhn, Philip. *Soulstealers: The Chinese Sorcery Scare of 1768.* Cambridge, Mass.: Harvard University Press, 1990.

Kuhn, Philip. *Origins of the Modern Chinese State.* Stanford: Stanford University Press, 2002.

Lau, D. C. *Confucius: The Analects.* Hong Kong: Chinese University Press, 1983.

———. *Mencius.* Hong Kong: Chinese University Press, 1984.

———. *Tao Te Ching.* Hong Kong: Chinese University Press, 1982.

Lewis, Mark Edward. *Writing and Authority in Early China.* Albany: State University of New York Press, 1999.

Mair, Victor. *Anthology of Traditional Chinese Literature.* New York: Columbia University Press, 1994.

———. *Wandering on the Way: Early Taoist Tales and Parables of Chuang Tzu.* New York: Bantam Books, 1994.

Mote, F. W. *Imperial China: 900–1800.* Cambridge, Mass.: Harvard University Press, 1999.

Needham, Joseph. *The Shorter Science and Civilization in China: Vol. 1.* Cambridge: Cambridge University Press, 1978.

Perkins, Dorothy. *Encyclopedia of China.* New York: Checkmark Books, 1999.

Roberts, Moss. *Three Kingdoms: A Historical Romance.* Berkeley: University of California Press, 1991.

Schaberg, David. *A Patterned Past: Form and Thought in Early Chinese Historiography.* Cambridge, Mass.: Harvard University Press, 2001.

Shaughnessy, Edward. *China: Empire of Civilization.* New York: Oxford University Press, 2000.

Smith, Richard J. *China's Cultural Heritage: The Qing Dynasty, 1644–1912.* 2d ed. Boulder: Westview Press, 1994.

Spence, Jonathan. *God's Chinese Son: The Taiping Heavenly Kingdom of Hong*

Xiuquan. New York: W. W. Norton, 1996.

———. *The Search for Modern China.* New York: W. W. Norton, 1990.

Watson, Burton. *The Tso Chuan.* New York: Columbia University Press, 1989.

Wilkinson, Endymion. *Chinese History: A Manual.* Cambridge, Mass.: Harvard University Press, 2000.

Wills, John. *Mountain of Fame: Portraits in Chinese History.* Princeton: Princeton University Press, 1995.

Wright, Arthur. *The Sui Dynasty.* New York: Alfred A. Knopf, 1978.

CHAPTER TWO
The Chinese Economy

Warren Bruce Palmer

The economic well-being of one-fifth of the world's population depends on the performance of the Chinese economy; more than 1.3 billion people are making their living in this ancient land that holds less than 7 percent of the world's cultivated acreage. Any understanding of the economic challenges and choices faced by China today must incorporate an appreciation of the magnitude of China's population.

In the eighteenth century, China's economy was the largest in the world, accounting for 25 percent of global output. China's wealth was admired and its social organization praised. Yet in a short time the industrializing world left China behind, and it tumbled into a long period of domestic crisis and relative economic stagnation exacerbated by foreign invasion. In the first half of the twentieth century China was called "the poor man of Asia." One-fourth of the world's population lived in China, but by 1949 its economy produced only 5 percent of global output, and hundreds of millions of China's citizens lived in terrible poverty.

The triumph in 1949 of the Chinese Communist Party in its civil war with the Nationalist Party produced the first effective national government in more than 100 years. The new government achieved some remarkable successes, particularly in public health, raising life expectancy from less than forty years in 1949 to near seventy years by 1978. Yet, the economic record was very mixed.

By the late 1970s China had established itself as a major industrial power by employing the Soviet development strategy, but its industry was inefficient, producing inferior products using antiquated technology. Meanwhile its market-oriented East Asian neighbors excelled at producing the newest consumer products with advanced, efficient technology.

China's industrial expansion served mainly to expand heavy industry itself, not to expand consumption or rapidly improve living standards. Even in urban China, which received preferential treatment from the government, consumer goods were low in quality, lacking in

71

Signs in Tsim Sha Tsui, Kowloon's commercial section (Library of Congress)

variety, and hard to get, even with ration coupons. In rural China, with 80 percent of the nation's population, the growth of agricultural output had barely kept pace with the growth of population, and hundreds of millions of China's rural citizens still lived in severe poverty.

However, since instituting a series of economic reforms beginning in 1979, the Chinese economy appears to be on a spectacular roll. According to official statistics, China's economic output as measured by real gross domestic product (GDP) grew 9.5 percent per year between 1978 and 2000. Because the population has been growing at a much slower rate for the past twenty-two years, economic output per person in China has grown about 8 percent per year—a doubling of average income every nine years.

These results are some of the best ever recorded by any economy. Such rapid growth has lifted more people out of severe poverty in a shorter period of time than has ever been done before. Officially 200 million people living just above the starvation level have escaped dire poverty since the start of the economic reforms. By some measures China already has the world's second largest economy, and it could become the largest by 2035 if it sustains this rapid growth in the future.

These basic statistics tell a story of China's great economic success. However, considered alone, they oversimplify the story of China's modern economic development—which is, in fact, a dramatic, complicated saga that is still unfolding and reshaping the fate of one-fifth of the world's population.

THE MODERN ECONOMY

Since 1949, the Chinese government has devoted great effort promoting modern economic development—growth in GDP per person—based on rapid industrialization. But what exactly does GDP measure? It is the market value of *final* goods and services—those goods and services not directly transformed into other goods and services—produced within a nation's territory in one year. GDP is a single number that summarizes the economic output of an entire nation. Money prices allow apples to be added to oranges, to automobiles, to restaurant meals, and to every other good and service to calculate the output of an entire economy in one number. GDP might rise because prices in general have risen without more final goods and services being produced. Economists solve this problem by adjusting their measurements of GDP for the effects of inflation, producing a measure of *real GDP* that does measure the increase in the real output of an economy.

The average citizen of a nation can become continually better off only if real GDP per person continually grows—the real GDP growth rate must be faster than the population growth rate. Modern economic growth *is* the long-term growth in average real GDP per person in a nation. In the roughly ten thousand years since the invention of agriculture, only in the past 250 years have any economies been able to sustain continual growth in real GDP per person for generation after generation. (From now on, whenever the term GDP is used, assume that it refers to real GDP—GDP corrected for inflation.)

Modern economic growth results from the systematic development of new scientific, technical knowledge and its application to the continual development and transformation of industry, commerce, transportation, and agriculture. A modern economy consists of mechanical production systems powered by inanimate energy, especially electric power, and linked together by mass transportation systems, powered by refined fossil fuels and electric power, able to rapidly move goods and information throughout the economy at low cost. These mechanical production and transportation systems greatly magnify human effort, and their continual development is caused by and results in the continual invention and refinement of new products and production processes.

The pace of modern economic growth—which has been termed a process of "creative destruction" because new products, processes, and economic relations continually replace the old—stands in sharp contrast to traditional, premodern economic growth.

CHINA'S TRADITIONAL AGRICULTURAL ECONOMY

Worldwide, the preindustrial traditional economy was a rural, agriculture-based economy powered almost entirely by animate energy—human and animal muscle power. The traditional economy did not support sustained growth of output per person over successive generations. In the traditional economy, most people lived in the countryside and worked in agriculture. The pattern of the seasons, the demands of farming, and the power of local customs ruled people's lives. Economic relationships and practices changed slowly over time, much slower than in the modern economy.

Yet even before the modern era, Chinese civilization attained high

Farmers cultivating tea in Hangzhou, China (Corel)

levels of achievement based on its traditional agricultural economy. This agricultural economy produced sufficient surplus beyond the basic needs of farming families to support large urban populations, extensive government organizations, major public works, standing armies, and active intellectual and artistic elites. For centuries China had the world's most advanced civilization, judged by its achievements in literature, art, government, science, and production technology. Yet, as Chapter 1 demonstrated, China's economic success was repeatedly disrupted by war.

CHINA'S POPULATION BEFORE 1850

In times of peace, China's population probably grew at a fairly constant rate of 1 percent per year, doubling every seventy years. However, up to 1000 C.E., China's population failed to surpass the peak of 60 million recorded in 2 C.E., because periods of war repeatedly interrupted the relatively short periods of peace (see Figure 2.1). The population then contracted as large numbers of soldiers and civilians died violently and even more succumbed to famine and pestilence caused by the wartime economic disruption. This pattern changed in the 150 years of sustained peace during the Northern Song dynasty (960–1127), when the population grew to 120 million. Two dramatic population contractions occurred thereafter during periods of invasion and civil war, but the peacetime population had grown so large that 60 million represented its lower limit. Then long periods of peace

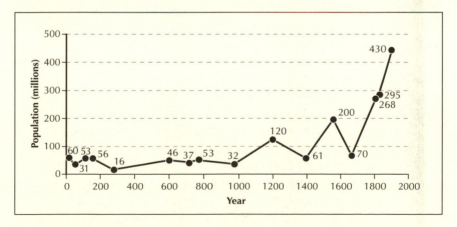

Figure 2.1: Population of China, 2 C.E.–1850

Source: Chao, Kang. *Man and Land in Chinese History*. Stanford University Press, 1986, p. 41.

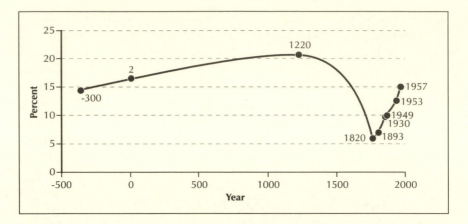

Figure 2.2: Percentage of China's Population Living in Urban Areas, 300 B.C.–1957

Source: Chao, Kang. *Man and Land in Chinese History*. Stanford: Stanford University Press, 1986, p. 60.

in the Ming (1368–1644) and Qing (1644–1911) dynasties resulted in large population growth. By 1850, China supported almost half a billion people with agricultural technology largely developed one thousand years before.

China has had a long history of advanced urban development. The total urban population, living in 36 large cities and 500 smaller cities, numbered about 4.3 million in 300 B.C.E.—more than 14 percent of the population. Chang'an, the capital during the Tang dynasty (618–907), had more than 800,000 residents. Linan (present-day Hangzhou in Zhejiang province), the capital of the southern Song dynasty (1127–1279), may have reached a population of 2.5 million in the early 1200s, including its suburbs.

These cities throughout the country were much more than simply administrative centers. Considerable productive activities were centered in the cities. Highly developed workshops existed for the production of all manners of goods used by both rural and urban residents.

As Figure 2.2 shows, the share of China's population living in cities and towns reached a peak in the 1200s and declined thereafter, falling by 1800 to a level lower than that achieved two thousand years before. The total number of urban residents probably did not increase after the early thirteenth century. The countryside absorbed the increased population. As the urban percentage of the population fell, the number of smaller towns increased, and the largest cities held fewer people than they had in the Song dynasty.

THE FAMILY: FOUNDATION OF THE TRADITIONAL ECONOMY

The ability of rural China to absorb more and more residents derived from the economic flexibility of rural families. By the 1700s China's population had grown so large that neither rampant disease, natural disaster, nor massive civil war could reverse its growth trend so long as the willingness to found and expand families continued unabated. This willingness formed the bedrock of Chinese tradition and culture, which places the highest value on family, the central economic and religious institution in China, and on the perpetuation of family through the birth of male heirs.

Family members existed to serve the living family and to worship their ancestors. Even the poorest of young men sought early marriage and the birth of sons to continue their family lineage. Early marriage was almost universal for Chinese women. The cultural family imperative resisted deteriorating economic conditions. The rural Chinese family responded by supporting a growing family on smaller and smaller farms rather than limiting the size of the family.

The average farm size in China had been generally decreasing for centuries. Even in the eleventh century the average Chinese household farmed about five acres while the typical English peasant tilled thirty acres. Yet up to the twelfth century, the Chinese were still inventing labor-saving agricultural implements. Thereafter, technological efforts were focused more on increasing output per acre than output per worker: The central economic task for the Chinese farm became how to utilize a growing population.

The rural Chinese family was a complex economic unit that uniquely tolerated overpopulation. The Chinese family system coped with the worsening land-people ratio by intensifying its agricultural efforts and diversifying its economic activities. Small-scale handicraft production for home use and for the market became an increasingly important part of the rural economy and replaced much urban production. This development increasingly drew farm families into a market economy, and in turn this further spurred the development and deepening of the market economy, including the proliferation of smaller towns mentioned above. These towns served to collect the peasant families' output and to supply them with the production and consumption goods they could not produce themselves. Paradoxically, the relative decline of large cities coincided with a greatly expanded population engaged in greatly expanded market activities in the eighteenth century.

CHINA'S ECONOMY IN THE EIGHTEENTH CENTURY

China's traditional agricultural economy reached a high point in the eighteenth century as China reached its largest geographic size and its economy accounted for approximately 25 percent of global economic output. During the Qing dynasty, an extended period of peace, the introduction of new crops, improvement in traditional crops, and expanded irrigation allowed China's population to grow and expand into formerly uncultivated lands. China's population doubled in the 1700s, reaching perhaps 310 million by the end of the century. At the same time the economy became increasingly commercialized, and GDP growth seems to have at least kept pace with population growth.

Such sustained population growth for more than 100 years might seem indicative of modern economic growth, yet China achieved this wealth without the help of an industrial revolution, such as began to transform European economies in the mid-eighteenth century. Still, China represented to Europeans the pinnacle of success. Europeans idealized and envied China's social organization and greatly coveted its fine silks, exquisite porcelain ware, tea, and other products.

China was, at best, a reluctant trading partner of European nations, even though it maintained a trade surplus during the 1700s. The influx of silver from European merchants buying Chinese goods, especially from the British buying tea, helped fuel the economic expansion and increasing commercialization of China's economy. Europeans strove to overcome China's reluctance to trade and strove to develop closer economic ties to this fabled land. Officially, China spurned its impatient European suitors. In a famous rebuff to a mission from Great Britain, the Qianlong emperor dismissed the mechanical marvels of Britain's emerging technical and industrial prowess as irrelevant to China, a tragic miscalculation.

In this, China was a victim of its own success. Because China's leaders controlled a largely inland empire that confronted threats to peace and prosperity from the interior and not from the sea, they unsurprisingly understood neither the promise nor the threat of the new inventions from the industrializing West. Instead, rulers rode a wave of great success as both the population and economy continued to grow. They were confident heirs to 2,000 years of imperial history and to a social system capable of ruling a vast nation.

Why did China not launch an industrial revolution on its own and in advance of Great Britain, Europe, North America, and Japan, either during the 1700s or under earlier dynasties, such as the Song, when China clearly led the world in inventiveness? Scholars have proposed several candidate answers: the foot binding of Chinese women that hobbled half of the population; the civil-service examination system that diverted intellectual efforts away from science, invention, and commerce and toward literary studies; the sustained population growth and the decline of farm size that eliminated the demand for labor-saving inventions; or the poorly defined property rights that undermined the initiative of entrepreneurs who experienced the arbitrary confiscation of their wealth. Probably all of these factors played some role in China's failure to develop an indigenous industrial revolution and its failure to recognize the threat posed by ambitious Westerners.

Despite the outward success of the eighteenth-century Qing government, by the late 1700s China was headed toward social crisis. The Chinese government maintained peace during most of the century but failed to respond in any meaningful way to the challenges of expanding population and commercial activity. The doubling in population saw no corresponding increase in government personnel or institutions. The government failed to support the great increase in commercial activity by developing supporting governmental institutions, such as a unified system of weights and measures, or expanded transportation systems. A costly war against internal rebellions in the late 1700s focused the government's attention inward. However, on the other side of the globe, European ambitions toward China were ripening toward aggressive expression as the industrial revolution brought technological developments at a quickening pace, transforming production, transportation, and war.

ECONOMIC CHANGE IN THE NINETEENTH CENTURY

Economically, in many ways the nineteenth century in China continued the main trends of the eighteenth century: Output continued to grow by applying traditional agricultural methods to existing resources, but now the entire economy and social system staggered under the burden of the large and growing population. The rate of population growth probably declined from 0.7–0.8 percent in the eighteenth century to 0.3–0.4 percent in the nineteenth. Still, by 1850 China had a population of more than 400 million—a remarkable achievement for a traditional agricultural economy. GDP was probably still growing, but slower than the population. From 1839 on,

Beijing in 1861 (Illustrated London News Picture Libary)

China's government slowly succumbed to internal discord and rebellion and to external political pressure and military defeat.

For much of the eighteenth century, British and other European traders had paid for Chinese goods in silver because Europe produced no product that China needed in large quantities. This balance of trade began to change when the British discovered an appetite in China for opium. The British East India Company produced opium in India and exported the product to China. The flow of silver into China reached a peak of about one million kilograms in the first decade of the nineteenth century, but the growing market for opium soon reversed the flow. By the 1830s China saw a silver outflow of almost 400,000 kilograms. This outflow contracted China's money supply, causing severe deflation and recession. As described in Chapter 1, Chinese officials' belated attempts at stopping the opium trade ended with Great Britain declaring war and then defeating China through the use of superior military technology—cannons, rifles, ships of war—made possible by the West's industrial revolution. Economically the most important result of the Opium War was not the robust growth of Britain's opium trade, which remained illegal in China, but the forced opening of China to a permanent foreign presence in five "treaty ports" and the expansion of foreign trade.

For most of China, the Opium War was of little direct consequence. Of more importance was the continual growth in population and the pressure it placed on agricultural lands. This pressure helped incite large-scale internal conflicts and rebellions, which dwarfed all foreign military incursions. The largest revolt, the Taiping Rebellion (1850–1864), almost toppled the increasingly ineffective national government. The Taiping rebels occupied Nanjing, one of China's most important cities, controlling much of the rich Yangzi River basin. Local armies loyal to the Qing government ultimately destroyed the rebellion in a series of attacks that left many of China's richest counties devastated and depopulated. Perhaps 20 million Chinese died during the Taiping Rebellion, but China's population grew with such momentum that this loss was rapidly replaced and the empty counties repopulated.

Foreign military and political pressure on China's government continued. In response to a string of military defeats, the Chinese government signed a series of treaties in the nineteenth century that progressively opened China's economy to foreigners who introduced new business practices and new technologies into the traditional economy.

The wealth and size of China beguiled foreign commercial interests who dreamed of the profits from selling to the huge China market. Foreign merchants founded modern European communities and commercial activities in the treaty ports. These cities were designated for special development and allowed Europeans special privileges. Shanghai and Hong Kong—the most prominent treaty ports—as well as lesser known treaty ports, grew rapidly in response to foreign commercial activity. By 1850 the population in China's cities began to increase faster than the overall growth in population, reversing a 600-year trend. In the treaty ports, the foreigners began building a modern industrial and commercial economy that over time became intertwined with the traditional Chinese economy. Some Chinese entrepreneurs acquired new technological skills and prospered from doing business with foreigners.

Many Chinese resented the foreign commercial activities and blamed them for damaging China's economic interests. Certainly the foreign incursions into China demoralized a people long accustomed to viewing themselves as the center of the world and exacerbated the political weakness of the government. From a modern perspective, the foreign powers perpetrated grave injustices against Chinese sovereignty and the Chinese people. Nevertheless, it is hardly credible to blame imperialism for China's economic woes in the nineteenth century. Providing for a very large and growing rural population continued to be the main long-term challenge faced by the Chinese economy.

A common charge is that mass-produced European goods destroyed China's handicraft industry. A closer analysis reveals that rural households shifted labor away from spinning, buying machine spun thread instead, and transforming the former spinners into weavers. The handicraft production of textiles actually expanded and improved in quality.

Another charge was that foreign imperialism and its economic manifestation prevented indigenous Chinese industrialization. But the Chinese economy worked with and incorporated foreign economic elements. Particularly in the latter nineteenth century, an industrial base, part foreign and part Chinese, developed in China in response to the forced opening of the Chinese economy. Chinese financial institutions began evolving to meet the challenges of new commerce, and Chinese transportation systems, particularly water transport, expanded and changed to meet the increasing demand for commercial transport. (A notable transportation failure was the slow development of rail transport, but here only government intervention could possibly solve the property rights challenges of building long-distance rail lines.)

Some regional leaders who had been instrumental in defeating the Taiping Rebellion tried to adopt foreign technology and construct modern armament and other military industries. These leaders, such as

Li Hongzhang and Zeng Guofan, strove to build up modern iron and steel works, to develop coal mines, and to develop machine tool factories. Their goal was to equip a Chinese army with modern weaponry and to create a modern navy. They were well aware that a rapidly modernizing Japan was doing the same with greater effectiveness and imperial support, and that Japan cast a covetous eye upon Chinese and Korean territory.

This budding industrial development was obstructed by the Qing dynasty, which failed to strengthen either the economy or the military by sponsoring industrial development. In one instance, Qing officials ordered the removal of the first train line installed in China. The central government also opposed early efforts at electrification. In another notorious case, the Empress Cixi, who sided with more conservative leaders opposed to adopting foreign technology, diverted funds intended to create a modern Chinese navy into rebuilding her summer palace, which was burned to the ground by the British in 1860.

The contradictory responses of China's leadership to the foreign technology of war culminated in a disastrous defeat in 1895 by the modernized Japanese army and navy. In the Treaty of Shimonoseki, the Chinese government ceded its influence over Korea and its control of Taiwan to Japan, while agreeing to pay Japan's cost of waging the war. Other nations took advantage of China's weakened state to occupy or claim expanded spheres of influence in China.

Still, at the grassroots level, the Chinese government's failures did not halt the growing connections provided by a new class of Chinese entrepreneurs between the foreign-dominated modern sector and the traditional economy. The early beginnings of Chinese industrial development were underway by the end of the century. Three sectors led the way: steam-powered transportation, manufacturing, and commercial banking. Nevertheless, most Chinese still followed the ancient patterns of traditional agriculture.

THE CHINESE ECONOMY, 1900–1949

After the demise of the Qing government in 1911, China entered an intensified period of political chaos and fragmentation that only partially ended with the establishment of a new national government by the Nationalist Party in 1929. The new government only weakly controlled many regions that were still under the control of local warlords, who often battled among themselves. In addition, the government expended great effort trying to eradicate Communist control of rural bases. Japan's seizure of Manchuria in 1931–1933 and then its complete invasion of China in 1937 extended China's political chaos and fragmentation. Japan's surrender in 1945 gave China only a brief respite from war. Soon China's extended civil war resumed as the Nationalists and Communists fought for control of China, culminating in a Communist victory in 1949.

At first glance the period of 1900–1949 appears to have been a complete political and economic disaster. Most Chinese continued to live at subsistence levels or worse after the mid-1930s. However, at the same time both the population and economic output continued to grow at about the same rate, so GDP per person did not decline. As a result, the period 1912–1936 saw some remarkable modern economic growth, considering the concurrent political disorder.

World War I produced a boom in Chinese exports and spurred modern economic development in China. Economic growth continued in the 1920s despite the highly unsettled political environment, and the worldwide depression in the 1930s had less impact in China than elsewhere. Over the whole period 1912–1936, modern industry expanded at an annual average rate of 8 percent per year. Yet, even by the late 1930s the modern industrial sector accounted for less than 5 percent of GDP while traditional handicraft production generated more than 7 percent. Traditional agriculture continued as the main source of production.

The development of the modern and traditional sectors of the economy complemented each other. Both produced outputs that the other sector used as inputs. Both produced primarily consumer goods. Most heavy machinery and other producer goods to expand industry primarily came from abroad, but the modern sector did begin to diversify its production into producer goods. The Nationalist government established state-run enterprises in heavy industry and mining. Recent research even suggests that average output per person in China may have increased between 1912 and 1936 because of industrialization. The Japanese invasion of China brought this development to a halt.

Until 1945, Japan occupied large parts of China, including the coastal areas, which had been responsible for most modern production. The war crippled production in these areas. The Nationalist government retreated into the hinterlands, carrying much industrial equipment with it. Cut off from normal transportation networks and suffering from Japanese attacks, significant industrial development in the Chinese-controlled regions was difficult. In Manchuria, however, industrial development accelerated under Japanese rule.

Japan had possessed considerable influence in Manchuria since its victory in the Russo-Japanese War in 1905. Russia surrendered all its interests in Manchuria to Japan. Under Japanese influence, Manchuria became one of China's most important industrial areas, comparable to treaty ports such as Shanghai or Hong Kong. In 1931–1932, the Japanese military seized complete control of Manchuria, which already produced 14 percent of China's manufacturing output. Thereafter, Japan further expanded industry in Manchuria, planning to make it a major source of manufacturing for Japan's imperial expansion. By 1945 Manchuria was the most industrialized region of China.

These industrial facilities would have provided a good base for Chinese industrialization after World War II. However, in August 1945, the Soviet Union declared war on Japan and invaded Manchuria. When the Soviet forces returned home after Japan's surrender, they took a large part of Manchuria's industry with them.

In addition to the Soviet confiscation of Manchuria's industry, economic revival after 1945 was also disrupted by civil war between the Communist and Nationalist parties. The Nationalist government's inept and corrupt policies undermined the urban economy, producing hyperinflation that left almost all urban residents scrambling for the most basic means of survival. For example, a large sack of rice that sold for 12 yuan in 1937 cost 6.7 million yuan in June 1948 and 63 million yuan two months later. The Nationalist government's economic failures greatly contributed to the military victory of the Chinese Communist Party.

THE MAO ERA, 1949–1978

On October 1, 1949, Mao Zedong, chairman of the Chinese Communist Party and architect of its victory over the Nationalist Party (see Chapter 1), announced the founding of the People's Republic of China, claiming that "the Chinese people have stood up."

This statement seemed more like bravado than reality. The economy was on its knees. Agricultural output in 1949 was 70 to 75 percent of its prewar peak, and industrial output was 56 percent. Inflation of 100–500 percent per month crippled the urban economy.

However, the new government backed Mao's boast with action by getting the economy back on its feet during a three-year period of reconstruction, even with China's entry into the Korean War in October 1950. Hyperinflation was halted in 1950, and prices were stable by 1952. By then production of basic foodstuffs had returned to or

Portrait of Mao Zedong (Illustrated London News Group)

exceeded prewar peak output. Food grain production was 11 percent higher than the best previous harvest, and industrial output exceeded prewar peak production by 25 percent.

Still, the new government faced great economic challenges. Traditional peasant agriculture dominated the economy. Eighty-nine percent of the population lived in the countryside, and agriculture produced 60 percent of economic output. The typical farm was tiny. Farming resembled gardening, requiring intense hand cultivation using simple tools. Even with industry restored, its output was also quite low. For example, in 1952 electricity production for the year averaged thirteen kilowatt hours per person—one kilowatt hour will light a 100-watt bulb for ten hours—and only cities had electrical service.

The new government had great ambitions. The Communists wanted to build a socialist economy that eliminated free markets and private enterprise. They also wanted to build an advanced industrial economy able to equip modern armed forces and raise people's living standards. National defense required the expansion of those heavy industries—coal, steel, electric power, petroleum, and heavy machinery—necessary for manufacturing the weapons of modern warfare. Improving living standards required expanding consumer goods industries, developing retail and wholesale commerce, and constructing new housing, hospitals, medical clinics, schools, and other infrastructure. All of this development required agricultural output to grow considerably faster than the population.

As a very poor country, China lacked the investment resources to launch rapid industrialization. What it had in abundance was unskilled workers needing jobs. China's natural advantage thus lay in labor-intensive production that required relatively little investment. China could produce consumer goods and agricultural products at very low cost for its own population and for export throughout the world, which would produce both jobs and profits. The profits then could be invested in building up other sectors of the economy, including heavy industry, that required relatively large investments and produced relatively few jobs. Japan, for example, followed such a strategy in its economic recovery in the 1950s. However, socialist goals and international events eliminated this strategy in China.

Even at its founding in 1949, China's new government had few friends and many enemies. During the civil war, the United States had strongly supported the Nationalist government. Also, the Communist Party's nationalist, anti-imperialist politics jeopardized Westerners' investments in China. Finally, China's entry into the Korean War in

October 1950 against the United States and its allies left China with only one major power for support: the Soviet Union. During the Korean War, the Soviet Union gave China financial and military support, and China also began following the Soviet Union's advice on economic planning and development.

In the 1930s under Stalin's leadership, the Soviet Union launched an all-out campaign to expand its heavy industry by placing the entire economy under central command. Other governments have taken control of vital economic sectors in times of war, but the Soviet Union under Stalin was the first nation to do so in peacetime and to extend this method to its entire economy, creating a centrally planned economy. This economy matched the antimarket inclinations of socialists, but primarily was invented on the spot to carry out the investment plans of the top leaders and to protect their political power.

In the Soviet Union, the state owned all enterprises and controlled them through a bureaucracy of industrial ministries. A central planning office created five-year plans that set the general course of the economy according to the top leaders' priorities. Central planners and the ministries then created annual plans for the actual operation of the economy. In principle, these plans told enterprise managers what outputs to make and what inputs to use. In practice the plans were quite incomplete and left enterprises scrambling to meet their plans, using semilegal, quasi-market means to obtain the inputs needed for production, maintaining high inventories of inputs, or inefficiently making the inputs themselves. The plan's failure even to balance inputs and outputs meant that little attention was focused on efficient production. Still, the planned economy achieved its main goal of building heavy industry while severely restricting the production of consumer goods. The state set wages and the prices of agricultural goods, industrial goods, and consumer goods to limit consumers' income and direct money flows into heavy industry investment.

The new Chinese government adopted a similar economic system. With the help of the Soviet Union, China launched its first five-year plan in 1953 and began centralizing the economy under state control.

China's First Five-Year Plan

China's previous government had already paved the way for national economic planning by nationalizing much of China's modern economic sectors. By 1948 the Nationalist government controlled most of the production from the metal, electric power, railroad, and petroleum industries, and 33 to 45 percent of coal, cement, and shipping. The new Communist government nationalized all foreign-owned firms by the end of 1952. However, at first the Communists moved slowly in taking over Chinese-owned enterprises, encouraging their owners to stay in business and run their companies. In 1953, privately owned firms produced 40 percent of modern industrial output. This changed during the first five-year plan. By 1957 all enterprises were under state control, as most private commercial activity was outlawed and suppressed. For the next thirty years, state-owned enterprises thoroughly dominated the Chinese economy, absorbing the bulk of investment funds.

China contracted with the Soviet Union for the design and construction of 156 key projects in heavy industry. The Soviet Union supplied entire factories in some cases and designed other projects, trained Chinese personnel, and sent engineers to supervise construction and start-up.

The structure of the Chinese economy changed with the emphasis on heavy industry. In 1952 industry only accounted for 20 percent of economic output, 64 percent of it light industry. By 1957 industry's share of economic output had risen to 28 percent, and heavy industry produced almost 50 percent.

The rapid growth of heavy industry reflects the high investment rates achieved by China's new command economy. The state channeled 24 percent of current economic output into investment, with heavy industry receiving about half of this. China paid for its industrial imports through exports and through short-term loans provided by the Soviet Union at favorable interest rates. Much of the resources had to come from agriculture, which still produced half of China's economic output. The state needed surplus agricultural output to feed the increased urban population, to provide raw materials for industry, and to pay for its loans and imports from the Soviet Union.

Land Reform and the Collectivization of Agriculture

Delivering on promises to its peasant supporters, between 1950 and 1953 the Communist government confiscated "excess" land and tools from rural landlords and gave the property to poorer peasants. Even peasant women, in principle if not always in fact, received similar rights to land as men—truly a revolutionary move in a society where women had possessed few if any rights. By 1953 land reform was essentially completed. About 10 million rural households lost some portion of their land and household property, while about 300 million peasants each received about a third of an acre.

Land reform by itself was not a step toward socialism. Land was not nationalized, socialized, or collectivized in the first land reform. In the short run, the land reform primarily strengthened the peasant market economy by expanding the number of private landowners. But the land reform movement gave the new government great prestige among the peasants and created a political organization in the countryside to eventually carry out the step-by-step collectivization of agriculture. By 1958 almost all land had been taken away from the peasants. (This collectivization would be reversed in the early 1980s.)

Land reform did not solve the basic problems of Chinese agriculture—small, fragmented fields, lack of modern inputs, labor-intensive technology, continually falling ratio of land per rural family, and intense poverty continued to hinder growth. Also, land reform complicated the government's efforts to gain enough agricultural output from the peasants for export, for feeding a growing urban population, and for use as inputs into expanding industry. Newly landed peasants had a strong incentive to increase production, since they would own the increased output, but if they consumed the increase instead of selling it, urban agricultural supplies would be threatened.

In the 1920s and 1930s about half of agricultural production was marketed, largely due to the rents peasants paid their landlords, but with the land reform's abolishment of rented land this ratio fell to less than 30 percent in 1953. In order to extract enough grain from peasants, the state enacted taxes that had to be paid in agricultural output and required peasants to sell an additional part of their output at low state-set prices. The state banned all private purchases of grain, forcing peasants to deal only with the state trading organizations. These policies increased the share of agricultural output flowing to the state, but decreased peasants' incentives to expand production. Yet, the state still needed more agricultural output.

The state could have expanded agricultural output by investing in agriculture, expanding irrigation, providing improved seed and chemical fertilizer, and mechanizing agriculture. But the state did not want to divert scarce investment resources from industrial development. Instead, its administrators hoped to increase agricultural output through the socialist transformation of agriculture.

Following land reform, party leaders first encouraged peasants to pool their resources into mutual aid teams. In keeping with party and government policy, local officials then encouraged, led, and coerced the formation of lower-order and higher-order collectives. At each stage, the number of families in the collectives increased. In the early stages of development, peasants received incomes in proportion to the land (to which they retained title), tools, and labor they contributed. In the larger higher-order collectives, income was based on labor, not on ownership of land and tools. However, peasants did retain about 5 percent of land in small plots for personal production. Peasants farmed their small plots intensively, producing by their private efforts 20 to 30 percent of China's farm income and 80 percent of its pigs in 1956. By 1957 almost 94 percent of peasant households were members of higher-order collectives, each larger than a traditional village.

China had good harvests in 1956 and 1957. Agricultural output achieved the production targets set in the first five-year plan, but industrial growth greatly exceeded its plan targets, increasing the demand for agricultural products. Unfortunately, from the point of view of the planners, the level of agricultural products extracted from the countryside scarcely changed from 1953 to 1957.

The Great Leap Forward, 1958–1960

In 1958, China embarked on the Great Leap Forward—Mao's plan to propel the economy to a new level of development by arousing the socialist enthusiasm of the people. China veered away from detailed central planning because of the low rate of agricultural growth and because Mao distrusted the growing bureaucracy of the centralized economy, fearing that it undermined socialist goals and his own power. Starting in 1957, the new strategy decentralized much economic planning and control to lower government levels and tried to replace careful planning with political fervor.

Collectivization of agriculture rapidly advanced as the countryside was organized into rural communes that combined political and economic power in a single entity. The intention was to use China's greatest resource—the agricultural labor force—to transform the rural economy through brute force. During the winter of 1957–1958 vast armies of peasants armed with shovels, baskets, and wheelbarrows constructed reservoirs and irrigation systems across China. As the Great Leap Forward moved into high gear, local leaders and political campaigns also directed peasant's energies into local industrial construction.

Still, large-scale heavy industry remained the main focus of development. Although the planning and control system was partially decentralized, the goal of rapid industrialization remained paramount. The rate of investment jumped from 25 percent of economic output to 40 percent or more, and the share going to heavy industry increased from 47 percent in the first five-year plan to more than 56 percent in 1958–1960. Many new projects were begun. Existing facilities operated more intensively, damaging some industrial equipment when they were operated at capacities beyond their design limits. The excessive growth rates and weakened coordination caused bottlenecks throughout industry. Still, according to official statistics, industrial output grew 57 percent in 1958. This growth was entirely in heavy industry, where output more than doubled; light industrial output declined during 1958–1960. These figures overstate actual growth because many factories running at breakneck speed produced low-quality or unusable products.

A messianic fervor spurred on by Mao and other top leaders gripped the country. Mao believed that the selfless, socialist enthusiasm of the people could accelerate the pace of economic development to a level higher than any economy had previously achieved. The development goals rapidly became more grandiose in 1958 and 1959. To doubt the goals became politically suspect, and even a sober statistical statement of economic outcomes was viewed as evidence of treason.

Leaders at multiple levels reported inflated production figures. Based on highly exaggerated agricultural production figures, Mao and China's other top leaders called for even faster development. More workers were shifted out of agriculture into local water control and industrialization projects. Many peasants went to work at expanding industrial facilities in the cities, increasing the urban population by one-third in three years.

The drain of farm workers prevented the harvesting of a significant part of 1958's actual bumper crop. But the extreme overestimates of agricultural yields made unharvested fields at first seem unimportant. Unfortunately, state agricultural procurements went ahead, based on the highly inflated production figures. Many communes were left with very low stockpiles for the coming winter even though peasants were working longer hours than ever before. In the winter of 1958–1959, peasants on the communes began starving.

The Great Leap Forward continued on through 1959 and 1960. Peasants continued to be diverted from agriculture and to work at a pace beyond available food rations. Bad weather hampered agriculture and aggravated the problem. China's leadership reacted slowly to the developing disaster. No unbiased statistics existed to tell the true state of agricultural production and supplies. Actually, grain output fell in 1959 and in 1960 to a level 25 percent below production in

1958, but state acquisitions of grain jumped almost 40 percent in 1959, leaving many communes without enough food to get through the winter. The one top official, Peng Dehuai, who dared in 1959 to criticize the development program lost his job. By the time the Great Leap was officially abandoned, the damage was done. Famine swept the country, and China lost 20 to 30 million people.

Recovery, 1961–1965

The setback in population growth was only temporary. In 1953, China's first modern census had counted a population of 588 million, an increase of about 200 million since 1800. By 1957 China had added 60 million new citizens. In 1962 the population was growing again and at a faster rate than in the 1950s. Because Mao rejected population control programs as reactionary, China's population would continue to grow rapidly through the 1960s.

The economic setback, although quite severe, was temporary as well. Mao relinquished control over economic policy to more pragmatic leaders such as Liu Shaoqi and Deng Xiaoping. In 1978 Deng would emerge as China's top political leader (his political and economic career would take many turns before then) and would institute economic reforms first experimented with in recovering from the Great Leap Forward.

China abandoned the Great Leap Forward strategy and recentralized economic planning. The state shut down many industrial construction projects and increased the priority of light industry. About 20 million of the new urban residents were forced to return to the countryside. The communes remained, but China abandoned the mass organization of production. The work team, a unit of production smaller than a village, became the main production unit. Liu and Deng reintroduced individual economic incentives, allowing peasants once again to farm small garden plots, raising vegetables and livestock for their own use and for sale in markets. In a foreshadowing of economic reforms in the 1980s, in some areas their policies introduced the household responsibility system, a modified form of family farming. After declining for three years, economic output rebounded, growing at double-digit rates between 1963 and 1965.

Ten Years of Disorder, 1966–1976

Mao Zedong's power and prestige had been diminished by the Great Leap Forward debacle, but his ambitions to shape economic and political policy remained strong. In 1966 Mao reasserted control by initiating the Cultural Revolution, a political movement aimed at top party leaders, who had engineered the recent economic recovery, especially Liu Shaoqi and Deng Xiaoping. Mao disapproved of their economic programs and resented their political prominence. In retaliation, he claimed these Communist leaders were leading China back to capitalism and incited rebellions across the country against the "capitalist roaders."

Over the next ten years, Mao and his allies dominated economic policy. They revived some features of the Great Leap Forward. The greatest similarity between the two periods was the extreme politicization of economic decision making. The "redness" of one's actions and words became more important than actual economic results. Again economic planning and enterprise control were partially decentralized to lower levels. In the countryside, private market activity was once more repressed, although the level of repression ebbed and flowed. Communes were urged to pursue self-reliance by creating small-scale industry and by becoming self-sufficient in grain production.

Urging communes to become self-reliant was partly to avoid the challenges of supplying the countryside with needed industrial inputs and partly to prepare for invasion. In case of invasion, each locale would be better able to resist if it was largely self-sufficient. Also, this policy of communes and local government funding their own development freed central resources for a crash program building military-industrial facilities in China's hinterland.

The Third Front Investment Program

Beginning in 1964, China secretly launched a crash industrialization program to prepare for invasion by either the United States or the Soviet Union. In case of invasion, China's leaders planned to retreat from the coast—the first front—and from the lower lands within 400 miles of the coast—the second front—into remote, mountainous regions—the third front. From there China would wage a prolonged war of resistance against any invader.

Because much of China's industry was then concentrated on the coast, the leaders endorsed a highly centralized investment plan to build new industrial facilities in these remote regions. Between 1964 and 1971 this military-industrial program absorbed the majority of China's new investment. The program moved existing factories from the coast and created complete heavy industrial systems able to produce all manner of military equipment in rugged interior locations.

The turmoil of the Cultural Revolution and the administrative decentralization of the rest of the economy did not hinder the third-front investment program. It moved ahead in great haste, starting many projects before planning was complete and scattering many new facilities in remote valleys to protect them from air attack. As a defense strategy, perhaps the program made sense, though many projects were so large that they could not be completed and placed into production for many years. However, in the absence of invasion, the investment program had a high economic cost. Many of the new industrial plants would have been cheaper and easier to build and more useful if they were located elsewhere.

Assessment, 1949–1976

By the mid 1970s, the shortcomings of China's economic development were brought into stark relief by the successes of other East Asian economies. Starting first with labor-intensive industries, Japan had quickly grown into a technological and industrial powerhouse. Other countries followed its lead: South Korea, Thailand, and Singapore. In particular, Taiwan and Hong Kong achieved great success, growing rapidly while also transforming their industrial structure.

Annual investment rates of almost 40 percent of GDP had failed to transform the lives of most people in China. The Maoist industrial system with its emphasis on politics in command, self-reliance, and administrative decentralization failed to invest the economy's savings wisely. Excess capacity existed in many industries, but investment in new capacity still continued, creating new facilities that incorporated old technologies. For example, each province had at least one truck and automobile plant, even though some produced but a few vehicles per year. State-owned enterprises dominated the economy but had no incentives to produce efficiently; their managers often lacked technical training and had to pay more attention to political concerns than efficient production. Industrial workers had guaranteed lifetime employment, while their compensation, frozen since the late 1950s, bore no relation to their economic effort. Many factories produced output that either was not needed or was of poor quality. Stockpiles of industrial output equaled almost a year's worth of production. Economic results were simply not very great for all of the effort and sacrifice that had been made.

Although China developed a high-yield rice and implemented institutional and technological transformations of its agricultural industry, Chinese agriculture barely keeps pace with the growing population. (Corel)

China was still fundamentally a poor, rural economy. The creation and development of communes and communal industries had created larger fields amenable to mechanization, greatly expanded irrigated land, and developed small-scale chemical fertilizer plants. Also China had independently developed and popularized high-yield short stalk rice. Still, the institutional and technological transformation of agriculture had failed to raise agricultural output much faster than population. Extreme poverty persisted, with most rural residents living near the absolute poverty level.

The poor performance of agriculture resulted directly from Maoist policies emphasizing self-reliance, restricting markets, and encouraging bureaucratic interference in local decision making. These policies prevented farmers from using their specialized knowledge to select products and processes best suited to their local conditions. For example, the policy requiring each commune to be self-sufficient in grain production and preventing the market transfer of grain between communes lowered cotton production as high-yielding cotton fields were replanted with wheat. Other locales, specialists in growing wheat, devoted land to local cotton production. Both wheat and cotton production suffered.

The policy of local self-reliance achieved the opposite result on the national level. By the mid-1970s China relied on imported grain to feed 40 percent of its urban population and was a major importer of other crops, such as cotton and edible vegetable oils, which it should have excelled in producing. China's production of grain per person had just kept pace with its population. The real income of rural households had barely increased since 1956.

Even in the relatively highly favored urban areas, people's economic lives were bleak on the day-to-day level. Government-run stores were poorly stocked. Consumer goods, rationed by a complex system of coupons, remained in short supply, of poor quality, and lacking in variety. Even basic foodstuffs were rationed. Money incomes were low because wages and promotions had been frozen since the late 1950s. Still, people saved money because there was so little to buy. Major consumer goods in the 1970s were bicycles (rationed), wristwatches, and sewing machines—a far cry from the goods available in Hong Kong and Taiwan, for example.

On September 9, 1976, Mao Zedong died. Within a month top Maoist leaders, "the Gang of Four," were arrested and China entered a period of uncertainty. Hua Guofeng, the new top leader picked by Mao on his deathbed, stressed self-reliance in word but not in action. The new leadership adhered to the Soviet development model and tried to revive Soviet-style central planning. At the same time, the lost economic opportunities of the past ten years made the leadership impatient for improved growth. A new great leap began in the countryside. As before, rural authorities organized armies of peasants for mass construction projects with the goal of mechanizing agriculture by 1980.

Agricultural mechanization required rapid industrial development, but this time, instead of relying on the Soviet Union, China planned to import industrial plants from the most advanced capitalist economies and to pay for the imports with income from oil exports. For a while in the 1970s China believed that its oil resources would rival those of Saudi Arabia. With the development of the Daqing oil field in the Northeast, oil production had grown rapidly. The increased production combined with the high price of crude oil in the 1970s rapidly increased China's export earnings. China would abandon its efforts at technological self-reliance and leap to the frontiers of technology by importing advanced industrial plants.

In 1977–1978 the Chinese government set off on a buying binge around the world, planning to spend more than $12 billion on imported plants for heavy industry. Actual contracts signed greatly exceeded this amount as individual ministries made deals without central coordination. The buying binge was predicated on the continual discovery of new oilfields and greatly expanded crude oil exports. However, great efforts at exploratory drilling in 1978 produced no major discoveries, jeopardizing increased oil output. China was not Saudi Arabia, and it could not expect rising oil revenues to pay for the heavy industry shopping spree. China's exports were not nearly sufficient to cover the jump in imports.

ECONOMIC REFORM, 1979–1989

In December 1978 Deng Xiaoping finally established his position as China's top leader and launched a reform program that was radical for China, but that was actually rather modest in scope. Ironically, the early steps of reform had unexpected and unintended consequences that set China's economy on the road to a market economy.

The early reforms addressed three areas: agriculture, foreign trade and investment, and state-owned industry. In agriculture the state raised the price paid for grain, permitted the revival of market-oriented household handicraft production, and granted agricultural collectives greater freedom to make economic decisions. This reform began to change the incentive systems for rural workers, directly linking individual effort to individual reward through a revival of traditional household economic activity where farm families produced consumer goods for the market using surplus labor in the household. The reforms also permitted the poorest districts to experiment with household responsibility systems. Initially a minor element in the reform, the household responsibility system permitted individual households to lease land from the commune. The household guaranteed to deliver a fixed amount of output to the commune and could keep everything else for itself.

The household responsibility system was nothing less than a return to family farming, and although its application was to be limited to only the poorest regions, the implementation of this reform slowly spread into other areas between 1978 and the first half of 1981. Then in the second half of 1981, the adoption of the household responsibility system took off like a prairie fire, racing ahead of the leaders. As word of the system spread, communes in richer regions switched to the new system, and within one year 70 percent of communes had adopted the new system without approval from higher leaders. But the leaders let it stand, as agricultural output boomed under the new system. By 1984 the commune system was dead, and farm families once again tilled China's earth.

During 1978–1984 the growth rate of grain output averaged 5 percent per year—more than twice the 1957–1978 growth rate, while the annual growth rates of other major agricultural products grew even faster. The surge in production improved Chinese diets and reduced agricultural imports. The growth in agricultural output plus the growth in handicraft production caused rural incomes to increase substantially for the first time since the mid-1950s.

The second element of the early reforms experimented with foreign trade and foreign investment in China. China set up Special Economic Zones (SEZs) in areas isolated from most of China and with close ties to the outside world. The plan was to attract foreign investment and technology, and to earn foreign currency through exports. The SEZs became grand experiments in economic reform, using their unusual freedom to introduce many market-based initiatives. Along with the SEZs came reform of China's trade system. The SEZs and the reform of China's trade system signaled an increasing opening to the world. Soon foreign tourists and foreign investors flocked to China in increasing numbers, and China, in turn, sent students around the world to study at top universities.

The third element of the early reforms expanded the autonomy of state-owned enterprises and improved their material incentives. Experimentally with a few enterprises, and then quickly across the nation, state-owned enterprises were given more control over their financial flows and partially rewarded for improving profits.

A firm responding primarily to the profit motive has a strong incentive to lower its costs through innovation and to produce products that customers actually want to buy. Both the input and output effects improve profitability and efficiency. But to get enterprise managers truly to behave according to a "prosper or perish" formula, firms must really face the possibility of failure and must really experience the rewards of success. If a poorly run firm can turn to the government for a bailout, then its incentive for efficiency will be weak.

Chinese state-owned enterprises legitimately could argue that they could not possibly show a profit, given the socialist price system that was intentionally distorting prices to help the state raise investment revenues. Consequently, profitability varied widely across sectors. Without changing prices, the reforms could not get firms to behave as if profits and efficiency really mattered.

Silk workers sorting cocoons in Wuxi. State-owned enterprises increased expenditures on employee benefits in the 1980s. (Michael S. Yamashita/ CORBIS)

Managers used their increased control of financial resources to pay bonuses to workers. China's industrial workers had long-term grievances about their wages. Under Mao's leadership, wages and promotions were frozen. Managers could not fire disgruntled workers, so a wise manager did what was necessary to keep workers happy. In the 1980s, state-owned enterprises also increased expenditures on employee benefits, especially housing.

The state also relaxed its monopoly over retailing. This reform was in response to a growing problem of urban unemployment. Thousands of urban youth sent to the countryside during the Cultural Revolution flooded back to their homes in the cities and were permitted to set up restaurants and other service enterprises. Also, the state encouraged collective enterprises spawned by state-owned enterprises in the 1960s and 1970s to expand into commercial activities. Peasants resumed selling their produce and other wares in the cities as the government relaxed the prohibition against such marketing.

The 1978–1984 reforms dramatically changed the distribution of annual economic output in China, transferring 10–15 percent of disposable income from the state to China's households. Rural households benefited most from this change. Household savings rates also increased, so all of this increase did not immediately flow back out of the households as increased consumption. Instead, the rate of household savings increased from 3 percent of household income to 15 percent or more. Still, the increased income financed increased consumption expenditures by rural and urban households on an increasing variety of consumer goods. China's consumers bought goods from newly expanded markets, and their purchases in turn encouraged further market expansion. Rural residents and state-owned enterprises also invested greatly in improved and expanded housing, further improving the quality of life.

Not all Communist Party members favored the reforms, particularly those reforms that breathed new life into the market economy, which the Maoists had done their best to kill. Despite strenuous efforts during the Cultural Revolution, extinguishing people's "propensity to truck, barter and exchange one thing for another" (in Adam Smith's phrase) proved impossible. Local officials supported reforms that increased local autonomy, and rural households embraced reforms that increased their economic independence. Reformers seldom knew for sure where a reform would lead, but proceeded ahead based on the reforms' success at spurring production and creating jobs. More conservative party leaders disliked these trends, wanting instead to stay with central planning as the main coordinating mechanism in the economy.

The struggle between the reform faction and the central planning faction created a business/political cycle as the policies of first one group and then the other attained temporary ascendancy. When expanded reforms produced enough negative side-effects such as inflation, the central planning faction tried to reexert control. But each time, their restriction of market-oriented activities caused an economic slowdown and met considerable resistance. The inability of weakened planning institutions to solve the problems of an economy rapidly growing in size and complexity then set the stage for a new round of reforms. With each complete cycle, the scope of economic reform expanded.

The pace of change initiated by the first set of reforms caused increased inflation and a corresponding backlash from the central planning coalition. Although the rural economy continued to change with the expansion of the household responsibility system, 1981 to 1983 was a period of retrenchment for reform in the urban economy.

A second round of reforms between 1984 and 1988 built on the success of the earlier reforms and tried to solve problems created or not sufficiently addressed in the earlier reforms. Some reforms increased the state-owned enterprise's participation in both input and output markets. The government froze the scope of the state plan so that firms could sell above-plan output at market prices, but they also had to buy above-plan inputs on the market as well. The lower prices for within-the-plan inputs and outputs served mainly as subsidies or taxes. Firms made decisions to increase or decrease production in response to market factors. The frozen plan meant that over time the industrial economy would "grow out of the plan" (Naughton, 1996).

In the second round of reforms, the former commune enterprises took on a new life. With the increased economic freedom, these enterprises quickly reoriented their production from producing agricultural inputs to producing consumer goods for the newly expanding markets. The increased prices for agricultural output and the increase in small-scale production increased rural incomes, which, in turn, increased the demand for consumer goods and increased the revenues of rural enterprises. Spurred by profit opportunities, local government created tens of thousands of new enterprises. These township and village enterprises produced a wide range of products for the domestic market and, in the coastal provinces, for export. The growth rate of these market-oriented township and village enterprises soon exceeded that of state-owned enterprises and became the major source of new employment for surplus rural workers.

China's participation in the world economy advanced rapidly under the second set of reforms. The government expanded the number of cities and regions open for foreign investment and greatly expanded the ability of Chinese firms to engage in foreign trade. The reforms following Mao's death brought a new openness in China and increased both imports and foreign investment.

The Tian'anmen Incident and Its Economic Aftermath

In 1988 the Chinese economy boomed and inflation accelerated to levels that caused great complaint and fear among urban residents. In an autumn Communist Party meeting, more conservative party leaders curtailed the powers of the top reformer, Premier Zhao Ziyang, and began a new retrenchment in an attempt to strengthen central control and rein in inflation. This effort gained greater momentum with the violent repression of the Tian'anmen Square protests and the ouster from power of Zhao Ziyang and other reformers. After the attack on June 4, 1989, on the protestors remaining in Tian'anmen Square, the hardline leadership restricted economic as well as political freedom. The planning faction had the freedom at last to return the economy to greater central control, increased planning, and tighter control of market activities.

Planners froze total investment in 1989 at the same level as in 1988, but because prices had been rising rapidly, this was a decrease in the real value of investment. The new policies refocused investment on state-owned firms, giving particular priority to energy industries. Planners imposed strict control on loans to nonstate firms, which hit rural industries quite hard. Planners' efforts at halting inflation exceeded their expectations and abilities. Many workers in the nonstate sector lost their jobs, and consumers became much more cautious in their expenditures. Some prices began to fall, and China entered a recession between mid-1989 and mid-1990.

Although state-owned firms were seemingly given preferential treatment under the recentralization, they did not prosper. The planners decreased the emphasis on profitability and decreased managers' autonomy. Planners increased their interference in state-owned firms' operations, requiring them to help meet social goals, such as retaining excess workers to restrain unemployment. Firms' costs rose, but sales of above-plan output suffered due to the recession. Large state firms' losses climbed and became a burden on the state budget, rather than a source of revenue.

The efforts at recentralization were short-lived. Economic conditions changed too fast for the slow central planning apparatus, and important local officials opposed policies that weakened nonstate firms. The dynamic township and village enterprises in coastal provinces had become important sources of local government revenue, and provincial officials resisted planners' efforts at restricting or rolling back their growth. Even in 1990 the planning faction began to backtrack on the efforts at reviving the centrally planned economy. This proved to be the last serious effort to return to the centrally planned economy.

In early 1992 Deng Xiaoping signaled his approval of renewed economic reforms and his disapproval of conservative economic policies by touring South China, including Shenzhen, which had most embraced market development, and by calling for renewed reform. At the Fourteenth Party Congress that October, the Communist Party officially announced the goal of establishing a socialist market economy, the first time since reforms began that creating a market economy was the expressed goal of reforms. Since then, China's leaders have announced a whole series of reform efforts, including permitting private business owners to join the Communist Party. China's movement toward a market economy is far from complete, but it is an irreversible fact.

THE CHINESE ECONOMY TODAY

To fairly and completely describe China's economy today requires more words than space allows in an introductory volume such as this one. In the final section of this chapter, however, we will highlight current economic developments.

China's Growth Record under Reform

Above all else, economic reform in China has produced rapid growth. According to the World Bank and using Chinese data, China's economic growth averaged 10 percent per year from 1980 to 2000. (India, the country most comparable in size to China, experienced economic growth of 4.8 percent per year in the same period.) These figures likely overstate the actual pace of growth, with some scholars estimating average growth closer to 8 percent. Either figure represents a considerable achievement. In the latter 1990s, however, China's growth rate slowed to 7 percent or less. In 2000 China reported a growth rate of 8 percent, but growth in 2001 was back down to 7.3 percent. Although China's growth has slowed down, output per person still is growing faster than 6 percent annually—fast enough to double output per person in just twelve years. China has achieved robust modern economic growth on a scale that matches the best record of any other nation at any other time.

The high growth rates have derived from multiple sources: growth in physical capital, in quantity and quality of labor, change in the economy's structure, and finally, growth in overall productivity. According to the World Bank, China's rapid growth relied less on increases in labor and capital inputs than did growth in other Asian economies. In China structural change and productivity growth have played a large role in sustaining high GDP growth rates. During the economic reforms, the share of workers employed in agriculture has declined from 71 percent to less than 50 percent. These redundant agricultural workers boosted output and productivity by going to work in nonstate enterprises, which had higher labor productivity than agriculture and even higher than state enterprises. According to the World Bank, this structural shift plus the growth in overall productivity accounted for 40 percent or more of China's growth. There have been many components to the economic strategy resulting in this rapid growth, but foreign trade is certainly an intriguing component, given China's long isolation from the rest of the world.

Foreign Trade

Foreign trade has played an important role in China's recent development. In 1978 China's exports plus imports totaled about $20 billion, equaling 10 percent of GDP and ranking China last among 120 nations. Economic reforms raised this ratio to 36 percent by 1990–1994, but still this level of foreign trade lagged behind that of other dynamic East Asian economies and was about equal to that of other large developing economies, such as Brazil, India, Nigeria, and Pakistan. China's role in world trade has continued to grow, and in 1999 China's exports and imports ranked ninth and tenth in the world, accounting for 3.5 percent of world exports and 2.8 percent of world imports. By 2000 China's exports plus imports had grown to $474 billion. The trajectory of economic growth and trade growth puts China on the path to become the second-largest trading nation in the world by 2020.

U.S.-China Trade

The United States runs a merchandise trade deficit with China, and this deficit has been the cause of criticism in the United States. Some industries in the United States claim that imports from China hurt their industry and decrease jobs. However, most economists consider trade deficits between two countries as unimportant, and there is good reason to be suspicious of arguments to restrict trade between the United States and China because of the trade deficit.

First, a big discrepancy exists between U.S. figures and China figures on the size of the trade deficit. In 1999 the U.S. government calculated the deficit at almost $70 billion while China computed it at $22.4 billion. There are several reasons to expect that the actual deficit is between these two numbers, and probably closer to the Chinese figure. About half of China's exports come from foreign funded enterprises, and about half of China's imports are used in making goods for

Bank of China, Hong Kong (Corel)

export. China is but one step in a complicated chain of production, with intermediate production occurring in other countries and final assembly completed in China. For example, Chinese assembly accounts for only $0.35 of a "made in China" Barbie doll with a $2.00 export price and a $10 retail price in the United States. In 1999 about 70 percent of China's exports to the United States were composed of reprocessed goods.

Second, the growth of China's export trade has done little to reduce U.S. jobs while doing much to stretch U.S. consumers' budgets. Toys, clothing, other textiles, electronics, and home appliances are cheaper than they would be without imports from China. Such imports do not cause much job loss in the United States because the United States became a net importer of such goods long before China rejoined the world economy. If China's success has come at anyone else's expense, it has been at that of other low-wage economies. Much of the production occurring in other Southeast Asian economies has shifted into China.

Finally, there are good prospects for continued growth in U.S. exports to China. Since 1990 China has been the fastest-growing market for U.S. exports, growing at an annual rate greater than 17 percent, despite U.S. government controls on exports of some high-tech products. U.S. exports to China are still relatively low, about 2 percent of total U.S. exports in 1999 and less even than U.S. exports to much smaller Asian economies, such as South Korea, Singapore, and Taiwan. U.S. exports to China should grow at a faster rate than imports as a result of China's admission to the World Trade Organization (WTO). China's WTO membership will not cause a big jump in China's exports to the United States because the United States is already relatively open to Chinese imports.

Foreign Direct Investment

In the 1990s China became the destination for a large share of foreign direct investment (FDI). From 1996 to 2000 inflows of foreign capital totaled $290 billion—about 5 percent of China's GDP. Through 1999 the United States was the source of about 9 percent of FDI in China, though the majority of foreign investment came from Asian economies with large Chinese populations, such as Hong Kong, Taiwan, and Singapore. In recent years, about two-thirds of FDI has been invested in manufacturing, particularly electronic firms. Foreign-financed firms have played key roles in China's eco-

A worker stands by an assembly line making Buick sedans at the 1.52 billion-dollar General Motors plant in Shanghai's Pudong district. (AFP/CORBIS)

nomic growth, accounting for one-third of total industrial growth in 2001.

Consumer Goods and the Growth of Private Lives

Before 1979, China had posted respectable growth rates, so growth rates by themselves fall short of telling the whole story of the economy. What matters is not simply how fast the economy grows, but what it produces and who receives the output. Unlike prereform growth, China's recent growth has expanded consumer incomes, expanded consumer choice, and thus expanded the scope of private life in China.

Prior to China's economic reforms the lives of China's urban citizens were remarkably homogenous, as were the lives of rural citizens, with a large gap separating urban and rural. For both groups, the state restrained incomes and restricted the variety, the quantity, and the quality of goods and services on which Chinese citizens could spend their income. In rural areas, the poverty of China's peasants precluded much expenditure on personal consumption, and government policies prevented peasants from exercising individual initiative to increase either their incomes or the supply of consumer goods. Rural residents had little chance of moving to cities and getting jobs; their fate was tied directly to their communes and their work teams.

Prior to China's economic reforms, the state assigned young urban residents to work units, which would be their only possible job and the source of their well-being. Urban residents depended on their work units for the basics of everyday life. The work unit provided workers' families with housing, health care, education, and access to consumer goods. Thus, the choices available to typical urbanites were controlled by their workplaces and were highly subject to political movements and personal connections. Little or no change in wages plus the deliberate restriction of consumer goods production starved Chinese appetites for goods and services readily available elsewhere in Asia.

Since the start of reforms, Chinese citizens have enjoyed greatly expanded personal incomes and greatly expanded choices in consumer goods. The Chinese responded to new market freedoms and new market choices with gusto. They abandoned the drab blue clothing and black cloth shoes of the Mao years for stylish clothing and footwear. Restaurants scarcely existed in prereform China; now Chinese have the choice of dining at Chinese restaurants, grabbing a snack from the innumerable food carts on the street, or eating at an American-style fast food restaurant. Beijing alone has eighty McDonald's restaurants, and a Kentucky Fried Chicken sits across the street from Mao's tomb.

The expansion of consumer income and consumer choice has greatly expanded individual freedom in China. This expansion of freedoms is economic, not political, but the Chinese people have greatly increased their opportunities to choose the goods they buy, the homes they occupy, and the professions they pursue. Chinese now can own houses, own cars, and own businesses.

Population and Employment

China's population growth rate has generally declined since the Chinese state began efforts to limit population growth in the 1970s and since the 1979 enactment of the "one-child program." China's annual rate of natural increase is now about 1 percent—a very low rate for a developing country. Still, China's population will continue to grow for some time because its population is relatively young and many people are just entering their child-bearing years. This has both positive and negative features for the Chinese economy. As a positive feature, China has more than ten workers for every person (children and retired workers) not in the workforce, and the ratio between workers and nonworkers will continue to grow until 2015. On the downside, the Chinese economy must generate new jobs for young workers entering the workforce just as struggling state-owned and collective enterprises are laying off redundant workers.

From 1980 to 1990 the Chinese economy absorbed 215 million new workers, by any standard a sizeable accomplishment. Until the mid-1990s state-owned enterprises, collective enterprises, and township-village enterprises were the major sources for new jobs. The push under Premier Zhu Rongji's leadership to improve the performance of the state-owned enterprises and the collective enterprises reversed their role in providing jobs, at least to formal workers. These enterprises have been laying off their formal employees in large numbers, although at the same time such firms have also been adding temporary rural workers who receive lower wages and few benefits. In 2000, state-owned and collective enterprises employed 44 million fewer workers than in 1992, reflecting the effort to improve the performance of loss-making firms. China's unemployment rate has consequently risen, although it is difficult to know how high. In 1997, for example, the official urban unemployment rate was 3.1 percent though independent researchers placed the rate at 7 percent. Laid-off workers have trouble finding new jobs, and the jobs they do find pay less and have fewer benefits than their former jobs.

Fortunately, a real labor market has developed in China to help solve the unemployment problem. Since 1994, private business has been the largest source of new jobs in China. Although privately owned firms still constitute a relatively small part of the Chinese economy, their rapid growth in the 1990s helped provide a much-needed source of new employment. Additionally, an informal market sector has taken up the slack, helping transfer in the 1990s up to 100 million surplus agricultural workers into nonagricultural jobs. These informal work arrangements escape accurate measurement, or are excluded from measurement by official policy. For example, temporary workers in urban areas who are not official city residents continue to be counted as part of the rural population and do not qualify for social services. Daily, these workers move in and out of China's cities by the millions, taking short-term, low-paying jobs that urban residents decline to perform.

Income Inequality

When economic reforms began, Deng Xiaoping argued that it was better for some "to get rich first" than for the country to continue in poverty. Indeed, early entrants into long-closed markets did reap high profits—for example, some farmers near urban centers became wealthy raising chickens and selling them in the cities. However, on the whole, the early reforms did not dramatically increase income inequality, and they initially decreased it by raising rural incomes. Through 1984, real incomes of both rural and urban residents rose with only a small increase in measures of inequality. After 1985, income inequality began to increase. In the 1985–1989 period the rich got richer and the poor got poorer. In the 1990s both rich and poor prospered, but the incomes of middle- and upper-income groups rose much faster than low-income groups, causing significant income inequality. Incomes of the richest 20 percent of the population grew faster than the overall growth rate of the economy, while the incomes of the rest of the population grew slower than the economy. Measures of income inequality in China now equal those in the United States.

The income inequality derives from continuing disparities in urban and rural incomes and from increasing regional income differences. Economic growth, especially export-driven growth, enriched coastal provinces relative to interior provinces. Even within cities, income inequality has increased, with some urban residents moving up into the middle class or even becoming quite wealthy, while other residents, transient workers from the countryside or unemployed urban residents, are truly poor.

Conclusion

Since 1979 the pace of economic and social change in China has been extremely fast. The Chinese economy is shifting from a command economy to a market economy, from a rural economy to an urban economy, and from a poor economy to a middle-income economy. Since reforms began, a new class of very wealthy individuals has emerged, as well as a growing middle class. China has been changing from a socialist society that severely restricted the scope of private lives to a consumer society with increased economic freedom for individual choice.

The Chinese economy today is a vibrant economy that delivers the goods to a population ready to enjoy the material comforts of life.

Since economic reforms began, China has changed from a society and an economy largely isolated from the world to an increasingly important player in global economic affairs. Most Chinese have greatly benefited from China's evolving economic reform package, but others have suffered from the economic reforms.

China faces great economic challenges in the next two decades. Its foremost challenge is to maintain rapid growth rates. Doing so requires continuing reform of the state-owned enterprises, many of which continue to have large losses and to be greatly overstaffed. Improving state-owned enterprises requires improving the functioning of the banking system, which suffers from too many bad loans made to too many money-losing enterprises. Rapid economic growth by itself is not enough. Layoffs from state-owned enterprises and new entrants into the job market make unemployment and job creation of top importance. China must also solve the problems of increasing income inequality, official corruption, and spreading environmental damage.

How China manages its economic transitions and challenges will determine the future well-being of the Chinese people and will have major impacts around the world.

References
Borensztein, J. Eduardo, and Jonathan D. Ostry. "Accounting for China's Growth Performance," *American Economic Review* 86, 2 (1996): 224–228.
Chao, Kang. *Man and Land in Chinese History.* Stanford: Stanford University Press, 1986.
Chen, Shaohua, and Yan Wang. "China's Growth and Poverty Reduction," World Bank Policy Research Working Paper 2651 (2001).
Chen, Yi, and Ishac Diwan. "When Bureaucrats Move Out of Business: A Cost-Benefit Assessment of Labor Retrenchment in China," World Bank Policy Research Working Paper 2354 (2001): 1. Available online at www.worldbank.org.
Dahlman, Carl J., and Jean-Eric Aubert. *China and the Knowledge Economy.* Washington, D.C.: World Bank, 2001.
Eastman, Lloyd E. *Family, Fields, and Ancestors: Constancy and Change in China's Social and Economic History, 1550–1949,* Oxford: Oxford University Press, 1988.
Fairbank, John King. *China: A New History.* Cambridge, Mass.: Harvard University Press, 1992.
Ho, Ping-ti. *Studies on the Population of China, 1368–1953.* Cambridge, Mass.: Harvard University Press, 1959.
Jefferson, Gary H. "China's State Enterprises: Public Goods, Externalities, and Coase," *AEA Papers and Proceedings* 88, 2 (May 1998).
Joint Economic Committee. *China's Economic Future.* Armonk, N.Y.: M. E. Sharpe, 1997.

Lardy, Nicholas R. *Agriculture in China's Modern Economic Development.* Cambridge: Cambridge University Press, 1983.

———. *Foreign Trade and Economic Reform in China, 1978–1990.* Cambridge: Cambridge University Press, 1992.

———. *China's Unfinished Economic Revolution.* Washington, D.C.: Brookings Institution Press, 1998.

Lin, Justin Yifu. "The Needham Puzzle: Why the Industrial Revolution Did Not Originate in China," *Economic Development and Cultural Change* 43, 2 (January 1995), pp. 269–292.

Lin, Justin Yifu, Fang Cai, and Zhou Li. "Competition, Policy Burdens, and State-Owned Enterprise Reform," *AEA Papers and Proceedings* 88, 2 (May 1998).

———. *The China Miracle Development Strategy and Economic Reform.* Hong Kong: Chinese University Press, 1996.

Myers, Ramon H. "How Did the Modern Chinese Economy Develop? A Review Article," *Journal of Asian Studies* 50, 3 (August 1991), pp. 604–628.

Morgan, Stephen L. "Richer and Taller: Stature and Living Standards in China, 1979–1995," *China Journal* 44 (July 2000).

Naughton, Barry. *Growing Out of the Plan: Chinese Economic Reform, 1978–1993.* Cambridge: Cambridge University Press, 1996.

Perkins, Dwight. "Completing China's Move to the Market," *Journal of Economic Perspectives* 8, 2 (Spring 1994), pp. 23–46.

——— (ed.). *China's Modern Economy in Historical Perspective.* Stanford: Stanford University Press, 1975.

Rawski, Thomas G. *Economic Growth in Pre-war China.* Berkeley: University of California Press, 1989.

Riskin, Carl. *China's Political Economy.* Oxford: Oxford University Press, 1988.

Spence, Jonathan D. *The Search for Modern China.* New York: W. W. Norton & Company, 1990.

Wang, Shaoguang, and Angang Hu. *The Political Economy of Uneven Development: The Case of China.* Armonk, N.Y.: M. E. Sharpe, 1999.

Wang, Yan, and Yudong Yao. "Sources of China's Economic Growth, 1952–1999," World Bank Policy Research Working Paper 2650 (July 2001).

World Bank. *At China's Table: Food Security Options.* Washington, D.C.: World Bank, 1997.

———. *China Engaged: Integration with the Global Economy.* Washington, D.C.: World Bank, 1997.

———. *China Reform and the Role of the Plan in the 1990s.* Washington, D.C.: World Bank, 1992.

———. *China 2020: Development Challenges in the New Century.* Washington, D.C.: World Bank, 1997.

———. *The Chinese Economy: Fighting Inflation, Deepening Reforms.* Washington, D.C.: World Bank, 1996.

———. *Clear Water, Blue Skies: China's Environment in the New Century.* Washington, D.C.: World Bank, 1997.

———. *Financing Health Care: Issues and Options for China.* Washington, D.C.: World Bank, 1997.

———. *Old Age Security: Pension Reform in China.* Washington, D.C.: World Bank, 1997.

————. *Sharing Rising Incomes: Disparities in China.* Washington, D.C.: World Bank, 1997.

Yabuki, Susumu. *China's New Political Economy: The Giant Awakes.* Boulder: Westview Press, 1995.

Yao, Shujie. "Economic Development and Poverty Reduction in China over 20 Years of Reform," in *Economic Development and Cultural Change* 48, 3 (April 2000): 447–474.

CHAPTER THREE

Chinese Politics and Government

John A. Rapp

FROM TRADITIONAL TO MODERN: THE TWENTIETH-CENTURY CHINESE STATE

Contemporary Chinese politics is both a continuation of traditional Chinese political culture and a reflection of modern Communist political systems. Endowed with more than three millennia of rich political and cultural history, China has only recently adopted Communism and declared itself the People's Republic of China (PRC). Communism, a Western import made Chinese through decades of political, economic, and social upheaval, guided the governance of China for much of the twentieth century. Furthermore, as discussed at the end of the

A Communist procession (Charles and Josette Lenars/CORBIS)

previous chapter, China continues to change rapidly in the economic, social, and political realms.

To understand these fast and profound changes, particularly as they relate to contemporary Chinese politics, we will look at various explanatory perspectives that might help a reader explore any era of modern Chinese politics, whether it is the dawning days of the Cultural Revolution or the most recent gestures of openness to international markets and culture. Political events and government policies in China often develop and change rapidly. For that reason, it is important to have a sense of the underlying context of Chinese government and politics so that readers may better be able to interpret future events for themselves. To help provide that context, we will examine the variations in political ideology, party-state structure, and various issues of domestic and foreign policy throughout the history of the People's Republic of China.

As we have seen in Chapter 1, the north-south divide is a long-standing theme of traditional Chinese political culture, and it continues to influence contemporary politics. Since the nineteenth century this tension has also often been reflected in the divide between China's coast and the interior. Although from one perspective Mao Zedong led a peasant-based movement aimed at genuine social revolution, from the perspective of the "coast-interior" divide in China's history, Mao's movement in some ways represented the resistance of northern, interior forces to the "corrupting" Western influence of Communists based in urban, coastal areas, who were more accepting of economic and other reforms. Thus, Mao's call during the Cultural Revolution to "drag out" those members of the party and state who were "taking the capitalist road" did not represent (as some Western and Chinese observers thought at the time) a mass democratic attempt to prevent elitism and bureaucratism. It was, instead, an attempt to enhance Mao's own power base at the expense of other party and state elites.

Mao's paranoid fear of real or imagined rivals echoes similar rebel founding emperors in earlier dynasties of China's imperial history, most notably Zhu Yuanzhang, the founding emperor of the Ming dynasty, who led his own purge of the bureaucracy in the latter years of his reign in the fourteenth century. The autocratic policies calling for "self-reliance" in the Great Leap Forward and Cultural Revolution are in keeping with the expanded autocracy of rule in China during the Yuan, Ming, and Qing dynasties. Even the attempt to build a "third line" of industries within the interior to withstand a Soviet or

U.S. nuclear attack were similar to the neo-isolationist policies of the Ming emperors, who pulled China back from sea exploration in the fifteenth century and worked to connect the various defenses that would be known as the Great Wall. Another vestige of earlier history and culture that continues to be manifest in contemporary Chinese politics is the influence of *guanxi* (connections), networks of patron-client ties that stretch from the top to the bottom of the Chinese political hierarchy. Though this concept will be examined in more detail in Chapter 4, when examining Chinese politics through the lens of such connections, the ups and downs of individual leaders and policies can be explained in terms of the relationships among the players in the Chinese political structure. In this regard, the Cultural Revolution can be viewed as a temporary triumph of Mao's *guanxi* network over those of his rivals, notably Liu Shaoqi and Deng Xiaoping. Similarly, the quick failure of Hua Guofeng to solidify his status as Mao's approved successor in 1977–1979 can be traced to Hua's relatively weak and narrow *guanxi* network within the party-state hierarchy, compared to the relatively wide and deep network of Deng Xiaoping, who quickly supplanted Hua as the paramount leader of China after Mao's death.

A last theme relevant to both contemporary Chinese politics and earlier political culture is that of the dichotomy between "Eastern ethics and Western science" discussed in Chapter 1. Nineteenth-century reformers such as Zeng Guofan argued that only by combining Chinese essence and Western technology (*ti-yong*) could China flourish. According to this view, the entire Chinese revolution, from the Opium War to the present, can be understood as attempts by a succession of Chinese leaders to maintain a Chinese "essence," shifting and varied as that essence might be, by borrowing only enough Western technology to stand up to the West while not being absorbed or "corrupted" by it. Even after the May Fourth Movement of 1919, when both the Nationalists and Communists felt the need to challenge the corrupt and decadent nature of Chinese culture, this dichotomy continued to influence Chinese politics. Similarly, Mao's attempt to adapt Marxism to the Chinese revolution, and Deng Xiaoping's efforts to pursue economic modernization without the "spiritual pollution" of "bourgeois" ideas about political reform, can be understood as continuing (and perhaps doomed) attempts to adapt to the onslaught of Western influence without changing the dominant autocratic and undemocratic strands of China's state tradition.

THEMES FROM COMMUNIST SYSTEMS

Another way to view contemporary Chinese politics is as a variant of Communist political systems. We can understand the changes in policies and in leadership in China from 1949 to the present by examining them in terms of the contradictions and tensions within Marxist-Leninist ideology. Marx had predicted that the proletarian revolution would occur in the mid-nineteenth century within advanced industrial nations. When this didn't happen, Lenin, the leader of the Russian revolution of 1917, explained that the revolution was still imminent but would occur later and in a different place scale than Marx had predicted. Imperialism, the exploitation of the poorer countries by the rich capitalist nations that developed after Marx's lifetime, had delayed the revolution, but it remained inevitable.

"Semi-backward" nations would start to revolt against the major imperialist powers, Lenin promised, when the latter were distracted by wars with each other over their colonies. Though Lenin managed to preserve the ideological credibility of Marxism, he introduced new dilemmas for Communist Party–led regimes. For Marx the only task of the "dictatorship of the proletariat" was to redistribute wealth and property among the fully socialist workers in rich countries, after which the state would famously "wither away." But for Lenin, because the revolution was expected to occur first in "semi-backward" areas, the new socialist state had no wealth to redistribute. The state would have to create wealth in the first place, redistribute the newly created wealth, and create socialist consciousness among the still not fully-educated coalition of workers and peasants.

The contradictions among these three tasks are what have led to major policy shifts within almost every Communist regime, shifts that are reflected in China's policies at different times in its struggle with communism. For example, "marketeers" or "Titoists" (after Josef Tito of Yugoslavia, who was first to break with the Stalinist model) argue for market correctives to central planning and the need to focus on creating wealth, whereas "planners" or "Stalinists" argue the need for a strong state to monopolize the ownership of property and wealth in the name of the workers. Lastly, "ideologues" or "Maoists" focus on the need to prevent the comeback of capitalism that might arise from inequalities within the socialist state. Because communism came to China through an indigenous peasant-based revolution rather than through Soviet tanks, as in much of Eastern Europe, China went much further in the Maoist or "ideological" direction, and then further in the Titoist or "marketeer" direction than most other Communist systems.

A second major theme in Communist systems relates to how the Chinese party-state apparatus works, no matter what formal flow charts might indicate about where power lies and policy is made. Under this model, three terms largely explain how policy is made and how the party controls the state in all Communist systems—nomenklatura, kontrol, and substitution.

The nomenklatura is a list controlled by the Communist Party of China (CCP, or the party) that names people loyal to the party and subject to party discipline. The list also names who the party puts in key positions in the party hierarchy, the state, the military, and other mass organizations in order to ensure its control. Nomenklatura also stands for the real inequality between the party elite and the masses based on non-wage privileges of the top elite, such as access to better housing, automobiles, food and clothing in special stores, and access to less censored information.

Kontrol stands for the fact that every person in the party-state apparatus is subject to dual and triple mechanisms of oversight and responsibility. A prominent example of this occurs in the military, where people report up not just the regular military chain of command but also up a dual network of political commissars ultimately controlled by the party. Substitution stands for the principle that even though on paper lower levels elect delegates to higher levels of the party and state, in reality it is higher bodies of the party that decide policy and personnel issues, decisions that lower bodies merely rubber stamp. Thus, following the Soviet model, in China it is typically the Political Affairs Bureau (Politburo) of the Central Committee of the CCP that hashes out key decisions. The major exception to this rule was during the Cultural Revolution, when Mao called an expanded Politburo meeting to create the Cultural Revolution Group, which for a time bypassed the Politburo and the rest of the party leaders in making key decisions.

COMBINING TRADITIONAL AND COMMUNIST SYSTEMS MODELS

Of course, in many ways contemporary Chinese politics is a combination of Chinese state traditions and modern Communist systems. Separating them helps us better analyze key issues, but there is actually a rich interplay between the themes. For example, according to a "neotraditional" view of Chinese politics, the closed and authoritarian nature of Communist systems encourages the rise of patron-client networks of authority and decision making, networks that serve to revive and intensify the traditional emphasis on *guanxi* in political decision making. Given ordinary peoples' fear of deviating from Marxist orthodoxy and telling the truth to their leaders, there is in all Communist systems a lack of "feedback" mechanisms, by which top party leaders could learn about problems and setbacks in policy. Instead, the Chinese regime relies more on informal patron-client ties in which lower-level people are able to report back honestly only to their trusted patrons without fear of retribution. Reporting to those without whom one has connections could be disastrous.

This was true in China especially after the Anti-rightist campaigns of 1957 and 1959, when Mao made clear his intentions to oppose and purge anyone within society or the regime itself who mounted open criticism of his policies. Likewise, the campaigns against "bourgeois liberalization" and "spiritual pollution" of the 1980s succeeded in firming up the *guanxi* networks of individual top leaders in China who differed over the degree of economic reform to be pursued. The imperial Chinese state, however, had a similarly closed structure, and it was only through the ideal (sometimes carried out in practice, but usually only by someone who felt he had a strong *guanxi* network at the center) of remonstrance that those on the lower levels of the hierarchy could advise, even correct, their superiors. The problem of getting advice "from below" is a part of the structure of both ruling models.

We will draw upon all the above themes in examining the shifts and variations from Mao to Deng and beyond in Chinese Marxist ideology, party-state structure, and selected foreign and domestic policy issues.

IDEOLOGY

The government of the People's Republic of China claims to be a socialist state under the leadership of the Chinese Communist Party (CCP). As such, it follows orthodox Marxist-Leninist doctrine, which dictates that Communist parties in semi-backward (and even "fully backward") nations on the one hand help their citizens finish the job of capitalism—that is, build up wealth and abundance—while at the same time work to restrict the inequalities and inequities of capitalism. Besides making this claim of bringing wealth and equality to its citizens, the CCP also took advantage of Marxist-Leninism's fusion of socialism and nationalism. Beginning in its guerrilla days in Yan'an in the 1930s and 1940s, when Communist forces rebuilt their strengths in the relative safety of the interior, the CCP claimed to be the truly nationalist party, in contrast to the Nationalist Party (Guomindang, sometimes written as "KMT" in histories and political texts because of an earlier system of transliterating Chinese). It has carefully protected this mantle of nationalism throughout the radical shifts and changes in official ideology up to the present. In addition, the party claims that it maintains democracy within the one-party state by carefully listening to and taking into account the views of all the various classes among the people. This is remarkably similar to the remonstrance ideal of earlier times, in which "listening" was idealized but dissent was not tolerated.

This claim that the party follows a "mass line" harkens back to the days when the CCP, under the leadership of Mao, forged its basic ruling ideology during the second Sino-Japanese War. Under the "Yan'an Line" the CCP claimed to be developing Marxism with Chinese characteristics, free from Soviet domination, most importantly by including several classes among "the people." Chinese communism embraced not just the urban workers but also the rural farmers (whom Marx had referred to as a reactionary, petty capitalist class) and even small, medium, and large capitalists, as long as they joined first the anti-Japanese coalition and later the coalition against the Guomindang during the civil war.

In the party's Yan'an headquarters, Mao first posited that the CCP was leading China through the "New Democratic Revolution" and would only much later move on to the socialist revolution, where private property would be collectivized and nationalized. According to Mao, each epoch was shaped by a "principle antagonistic contradiction" between the enemy and the people, which had to be overcome by violent revolution. "Nonantagonistic" contradictions between the various progressive classes, however, could supposedly be settled by peaceful means. The CCP leaders also took pains to demonstrate that their party was close to the masses, as seen in campaigns to rectify party members' outlook by sending them down (*xiafang*) to live and work among the peasants. The CCP also organized criticism and self-criticism sessions for new party members at Yan'an not only in order to push the New Democratic Revolution but also to enforce party discipline. Scholars now point out, however, that for all its populist rhetoric and democratic claims, the party's rectification campaign in Yan'an served to purge dissent and independent thinking within the party and served as the impetus for its harsh ideological campaigns

Residents of Shanghai celebrated the founding of the People's Republic of China with unprecedented zeal. Here students carry portraits of Mao Zedong, Chairman of the People's Government of the People's Republic of China, and Zhu De, leader of the People's Liberation Army. (Bettmann/CORBIS)

and purges after 1949. Most important, who would be named "enemy of the people" and who would be named "of the people" was decided by the CCP. Later, during the Great Leap Forward and Cultural Revolution, just Mao and his personal followers were the arbiters of such judgments, thus inevitably undermining the basic principles of true mass democracy.

In 1949 China renamed itself the People's Republic of China (PRC), and its leaders began to refer to this period as "after liberation." At first Mao and the CCP claimed that the New Democratic Revolution would continue for many years. This could be seen most famously in the Land Reform campaign of 1949–1950, in which peasants were given their own plots of land to till and landlords were eliminated as a class. Though the Land Reform campaign was violent and also served to legitimate the party dictatorship, it was, ironically, an essentially capitalist land reform. Along with allowing small private businesses and joint state-private businesses in urban areas, the campaign incorporated protomarketeer or Titoist policies that would later play an even more important role in CCP ideology.

After a series of campaigns against bureaucratism and bourgeois corruption, the party emphasized its anti-imperialist, nationalist credentials in the Oppose America, Aid Korea campaign in response to the Korean War. In 1952 Mao and the CCP shifted back toward a Stalinist version of Marxist ideology, which brought China diplomatically closer to its Western neighbor. Recognizing that China needed help in constructing socialism, the CCP suddenly shifted to a line of "leaning to one side," that is, accepting aid and advice from the Soviet Union. The party declared that the New Democratic Revolution was over and that the CCP was now leading China into the socialist phase of the revolution.

As such, throughout most of the early and mid-1950s, China copied the command economy from the Soviet Union, nationalizing all industry and taking on Soviet advisers. In agriculture, land was gradually collectivized, also according to the Stalinist model. Fortunately, the early collectivization of Chinese agriculture took place without as much violence and peasant resistance as occurred in the Soviet Union in the 1930s, which took millions of lives.

As collectivization progressed, however, Mao and members of the CCP more personally beholden to their personal *guanxi* networks became emboldened by the seemingly easy successes of building rural cooperatives. First in 1955, and then after a brief interregnum in the Great Leap Forward of 1958–1960, the party, echoing its Yan'an roots, claimed that socialism could be constructed at the same time as building up the economy. Mao announced that China's peasants were poor and untouched, and that they had not yet been corrupted by capitalism, so that China might "leap ahead" of the USSR to an advanced stage of communism, the full flowering of social and economic equality, in the very near future.

The goals of the Great Leap Forward, as noted in Chapter 1, aimed to make town and countryside equal and end the gap between rural farming and urban industry. Production would be increased, the party proposed, not by the coercive methods of the Stalinist five-year plans or by the private plots and material incentives of the Titoists, but by moral or "ideological" persuasion. Under this policy, the practice of criticism and self-criticism sessions and study of Marxist-Leninism–Mao Zedong thought was expanded beyond party members to the masses. Class struggle, rather than efforts to build up the forces of production, was Mao's key emphasis. Mao claimed that the class enemies were not outsiders but the forces within the party taking the capitalist road—in other words, anyone who favored market-based economic reforms.

In contrast to the Maoist ideological demand for unanimity, 1956 allowed for a brief moment of sanctioned dissent within the party. This temporary openness came shortly after Nikita Khrushchev's "secret speech" to the Soviet Communist Party Central Committee denouncing (some of) the crimes of Stalin. At the same time, other leaders of the CCP managed to have "collective leadership" put into official party ideology and stressed the idea that class struggle would have to take a back seat to building up the forces of production—that is, building up wealth and abundance. That year, intellectuals and others briefly were encouraged to speak up to criticize shortcomings of the regime; this was known as the Hundred Flowers movement. The events of 1956 had the effect of expanding reform beyond the economy to include the political arena, though only for a short time. Mao turned on his critics the next year, labeling them "poisonous weeds."

Whether Mao was overconfident and expected minimal criticism or was trying to "lure the snakes out of the grass" (to smoke out his opponents), in 1957 he led in effect a coalition of Stalinists and Maoists in an "Anti-rightist" campaign against all criticism of the party, a wide-scale purge of all opposition led and supported by Deng Xiaoping, though later Deng admitted that the campaign went too far. Most observers now view this campaign as the precursor to the Great Leap Forward. It eliminated all potential ideological opposition to Mao outside the party and scared off would-be opponents within the party, clearing the way for the radical Maoism of the late 1950s and the Cultural Revolution of the late 1960s. Similarly, the second Anti-rightist campaign of 1959 against Marshall Peng Dehuai further scared off any potential rivals or critics from challenging Mao's policies directly. Peng Dehuai's crime was that he had dared to give internal criticism of Mao's Great Leap policies at the Lushan plenum of the party.

The Maoist ideological stress on self-reliance during the Great Leap Forward and Cultural Revolution also produced an ideological break with the Soviet Union as China declared itself the purest socialist state. Though China continued to denounce U.S. imperialism, the CCP now also denounced the Soviet leaders as "social imperialists" and "revisionists" who were taking the USSR back down the road to capitalism. According to the CCP, China represented the most progressive forces in world socialism. Thus the CCP under Mao could claim that

China had not only "stood up" to imperialism by declaring a new regime in 1949 but continued to defend a strong national state that would become a leader in the world.

As noted in Chapters 1 and 2, the extreme Maoism of the Great Leap Forward ended in economic disaster, and Mao was forced to retire to the "second rank" to allow other leaders to try to restore the economy in the early 1960s. In 1961–1963, a coalition of CCP leaders developed a combination of Stalinist central planning, modest market reforms, and other material incentives to help the country get back on its feet. Unlike the Hundred Flowers reform experiment of 1956, these reforms did not include any accommodation for political or intellectual openness. Mao, reluctantly perhaps, went along with this change in ideology, while biding his time for a comeback.

But Mao wasn't interested in lying low for long. He was determined to refocus politics on the ideology of class struggle. Mao launched an ideological counterattack, first using the People's Liberation Army (PLA) during the early 1960s under the leadership of Lin Biao, and later in the country at large during the Great Proletarian Cultural Revolution of 1966–1976. Mao built up his own cult of personality and once again stressed the need for continuing class struggle even after the revolution. This doctrine of "Continuing the Revolution" was trumpeted during the Cultural Revolution as Mao's main contribution to Marxist-Leninism. Probably in order to gain the acquiescence of key leaders such as the prime minister, Zhou Enlai, Mao largely exempted the countryside from the class struggle of the Cultural Revolution, though in the end the struggle became especially fierce throughout China.

From 1976 to 1978 under the leadership of Hua Guofeng, the CCP tried to maintain the Maoist focus on class struggle and ideological campaigns while it also built productive enterprises, favoring especially large-scale, Stalinist-style, state-owned industries such as the Baoshan steel complex and the Daqing oil fields. Given Hua's weak *guanxi* network among the administrative leaders, as well as the shortages, bottlenecks, and disincentives that Stalinism brought to the economy, Hua ultimately failed to institutionalize his authority and develop sufficient support for his policies.

Beginning in late 1978, Deng Xiaoping emerged as the paramount leader of the PRC and returned to the ideological approach that emphasized the development of productive forces within the economy. Claiming to return to orthodox Mao Zedong thought, Deng and his supporters announced that once again, the struggle to build up the productive forces was a political and economic imperative. According to Deng, Mao's doctrine of the "Continuing Revolution" was only a deviation of his later years, when he became divorced from the masses. Deng declared that "practice was the sole criterion of truth" and that the party was not departing from Maoism but in fact continuing the lessons Mao and others had taught in Yan'an. Deng justified the shift by claiming that the early Communist leaders of China would endorse a departure from Marxist-Leninist orthodoxy in economic matters when Chinese conditions demanded experiment and change.

As the shift toward production unfolded, the party also expanded attempts to allow positive economic incentives first in the countryside and later in urban areas (as discussed in Chapter 2). Deng's supporters justified the market reform experiments as particularly suitable to the Chinese definition of socialism. Other significant changes followed. First, intellectuals were relabeled as "workers of the mind," as opposed to the pejorative "stinking ninth label" (that is, added to the traditional eight "bad" class elements of landlords, rightists, etc.), as Maoists referred to them during the Great Leap Forward and Cultural Revolution. Next, as the market reforms progressed, some Chinese prospered and others did not. To justify the inevitable inequalities produced by the market, the party officially declared the country in an early stage of socialism. Interestingly, the PRC now contradicted Mao's earlier doctrine that worked to restrict inequalities as much as possible during the later stages of the Cultural Revolution. Deng's followers denounced radical Maoist egalitarianism as "eating out of one big pot" that at best led the country to equality of poverty.

At worst, Deng and his followers charged that this radical Maoism only led to hypocrisy. Deng's coalition tried to expose the excesses of top Maoist leaders and put Mao's widow, Jiang Qing, and other Cultural Revolution leaders on trial in 1980. While denouncing the "deviations" of Mao and his personal followers from Mao Zedong thought, Deng and his group claimed they were the true inheritors of the May Fourth tradition (of those patriotic students in 1919 who first called for opposition to Japanese and Western imperialism) because they stood up for a strong Chinese nation. They claimed that for all the talk of self-reliance, Maoist policies in fact nearly bankrupted China and that it was Deng's reform policies that would bring prosperity and strength to the Chinese nation.

Deng's new coalition of Stalinist central planners and economic reformers was not without its own contradictions and tensions, however, as was revealed in new ideological campaigns of the 1980s. First in the Democracy Wall movement of 1978–1980 outside the party, and later in inner party movements of the 1980s, members of Deng's coalition at the middle and lower echelons tried to test the limits of his pro-market line and push the connection between economic and political reform. At first with some support from Deng himself, political reform was put on the agenda, including separation of party and state, rehabilitation of past critics of the regime, and steps toward "socialist legality" and legal reform.

These steps were perhaps necessary to guarantee the permanence of economic reforms to both an internal and external audience. Internally, limited political reforms were needed to reassure people who justifiably feared being labeled "bourgeois elements" in some future Maoist backlash if they expanded their private plots or small businesses or made too much money in the rural or urban "responsibility systems." Limited political reform was also necessary externally in order to reassure foreign nations and businesses investing capital in new projects in China that their properties would not soon be renationalized. Though political reform in China still had its limits, and criticism of China's Communist tradition was still suspect, in 1984 an official editorial in the CCP national newspaper *People's Daily* declared that the works of Marx and Lenin could not solve the problems of the present. A few days later it was partially retracted to say that Marxism could not solve "all" the current problems.

To take advantage of this possible political opening, certain intellectuals, writers, and artists throughout the 1980s called for wider and deeper political reforms that might include democratization, improvements in human rights, and an end to restrictions on criticism of the regime. Deng, however, remained committed to the hardliner ideological campaigns of the 1980s and against "bourgeois liberal" elements.

Most illustrative in this regard was the 1983 campaign against "spiritual pollution" in which Wang Ruoshui, a deputy editor of *People's Daily* and a Central Committee–level CCP member, was purged from his post for arguing that "alienation" continued to exist within socialist China. Drawing upon Marx's early writings as well as the ideas of the Eastern European Marxist democrats of the 1960s and 1970s, Wang argued that the problem of the Cultural Revolution was its failure to focus on humanism. Humanist goals should have been the main socialist project in China, as Marx's early writings indicated, but instead people turned on each other in bitter class strife and internecine warfare.

Wang and other critics stressed that the roots of the Cultural Revolution remained. During the Cultural Revolution, the personality cult of Mao turned him into a god to be worshiped, while the people turned themselves into passive and obedient subjects. Critics outside the party, such as Wang Xizhe of the Democracy Wall movement, went further; he labeled Mao a "feudal fascist emperor." Wang Xizhe claimed Maoism was not a socialist doctrine but merely the ideology of a rural peasant rebellion that had once opposed tyrannical regimes and in the end merely served Mao's personal autocracy and that of his personal followers.

This attempt of some intellectuals to push the limits of the Deng-era ideological line met with fierce opposition, and Deng, again either willingly or out of necessity, allowed periodic campaigns against such critics, culminating in the 1989 suppression of the student demonstrators at Tian'anmen Square. Just as the political reformers pushed the limits of reform, so too ideological hardliners would try to exploit the crackdowns to push ideology in a Stalinist or even neo-Maoist direction. The fears of backlash materialized. Led by people such as Hu Qiaomu and Deng Liqun, these crackdowns, especially in 1983, 1987, and 1989, turned not just against those who called for democracy and human rights but, increasingly, against those with Western dress or attitudes, or even those making too much money. Whenever such campaigns went too far, Deng, whether out of his own beliefs or in order not to lose the support of economic reformers, stepped in to limit and end the campaigns, restoring economic reform to a high point.

The ideological justifications for increases in economic reform and simultaneous limits in political reform varied over the years and were not always made explicit. Some continuing themes, however, were repeated. First, beginning in 1979 and repeated in the antibourgeois liberalization campaigns of the 1980s, Deng Xiaoping emphasized the "four cardinal principles" that were forbidden to be criticized: Marxist-Leninism–Mao Zedong thought, socialism, the People's Democratic Dictatorship, and most important, leadership of the Communist Party. Second, following the line of his protégé, the premier and later CCP general secretary Zhao Ziyang, in the late 1980s Deng indicated that he favored a view of the PRC as a "neo-authoritarian" regime. Almost openly comparing itself to Singapore, South Korea, and Taiwan (the latter two before their liberalization and democratization in the late 1980s and early 1990s), the PRC claimed it had to limit democracy. The party alleged it needed to limit democracy not to preserve the interest of old elites and stall economic reform, as under

Mao, but to carry out economic reforms, which in the short run could lead to inflation, unemployment, and other hardships before their pay-offs became clear. Especially after the fall of Communist regimes in the USSR and Eastern Europe, the PRC even more openly pointed to the "disasters" of political reform within those ex-Communist systems as justification for continued repression of dissent in China.

Nationalism played an important role on all sides of the ideological disputes in the Deng era. This can especially be seen in the 1989 Tian'anmen demonstrations and their aftermath, in which the students tried to project themselves as patriotic youth who through self-sacrificing hunger strikes and criticism of official corruption were the true heirs of the May Fourth Movement of 1919. At the same time, the students implied that the regime was the heir of the weak Qing dynasty of the late nineteenth century and the warlord governments of the early twentieth century (see Chapter 1). The CCP countered this by denouncing the students as corrupt lackeys and dupes of Western imperialism, implying that it was the PRC leadership that stood up to the West.

Throughout the twentieth century, but especially in the later part of the century, China struggled to balance its openness with a measured caution toward Western influence and interaction with the West. Not only in the aftermath of the Tian'anmen demonstrations, but continuing after events such as the bombing of the PRC embassy in Belgrade during the NATO war against Serbia, the missile crises over Taiwan of the mid 1990s, and, most recently, the downing of a U.S. spy plane in 2001, the CCP's ideology at times briefly slips into harsh neo-Maoist rhetoric. The party has accused the United States of pushing "peaceful coexistence," in effect trying to roll back communism. However, given the continuing need for foreign investment and China's new links to the global economy, both Deng and Jiang Zemin have had to rein in strong language that might jeopardize economic relations with the West.

Even before Deng's death in 1997, but of course more openly since that time, the current leader of the PRC, President and CCP General Secretary Jiang Zemin, has been trying to gain approval as the chief representative of the "third generation of leadership" of the PRC. In official ideology this has included, first, a continuation of the view that China remains in an early stage of socialism that requires economic reforms to further free up markets, as well as continued privatization of state-owned firms. Second, and more recently, Jiang has tried to credit himself as a great ideological innovator by getting the CCP to admit members to its ranks of representatives of nonproletarian classes, including even large-scale "patriotic" capitalists. In this regard Jiang is continuing Deng Xiaoping's return to the ideal of New Democracy of Yan'an while also deepening the Mao-Deng approach to developing a particularly Chinese form of socialism.

Whether Jiang and his successors can maintain the uneasy ideological balance between political hardliners and economic reformers, or whether Chinese capitalist interests and global economic pressures in the party will eventually splinter the Deng-Jiang ideological line, is still not yet clear. It is perhaps too soon to tell whether such internal and external pressures will lead China to return to harsh nationalist rhetoric along the lines of Serbia under Milosevic or other politicians of the far right in Europe, or whether Marxist-Leninist ideology in China will gradually open up to include political liberalization and democratic reform. Even though Jiang Zemin has officially retired as general secretary of the CCP and as president of the PRC, he is likely to retain his influence, officially as chairman of the party's Central Military Commission, and informally through the numerous protegees he has managed to put onto the CCP politburo and its standing committee.

PARTY-STATE STRUCTURE

The PRC is, on the one hand, a typical Communist regime in which the party controls the formal and informal levers of power through the nomenklatura, kontrol, and substitution principles noted earlier in this chapter. On the other hand, the PRC contains many neotraditional formal and informal structures inherited from the modern state tradition. Despite major changes in party-state structure from 1949 to the present, there has been a basic organizational continuity since 1954, when the core organs of state power were set up. Party, state, military, and mass organizational structures all include four levels: national or center, provincial (*sheng*), counties (*xian*), and municipalities (*shi*). But similar to the Ming *lijia* and Qing *baojia* mutual surveillance systems, the Chinese Communist Party-State has tried to penetrate society beneath the county and municipal level in formal and informal ways, as we will see below.

Party

The basic level of the CCP is the Primary Party Organization (PPO), a carryover from the revolutionary cells of the 1930s and 1940s. Under the PPO system, party members in every work unit (*danwei*) officially elect delegates to higher levels of authority. As in all levels, upper levels of the party enforce discipline upon PPO members and limit their real choices. The PPO elects delegates to a Primary Party Congress, which in turn elects members of a local party committee, led by a local party secretary.

Officially, the Primary Party Congress sends delegates to the County Congress. This in turn sends delegates to the Provincial Party Congress, which sends delegates to the National Party Congress. Each of these congresses, under the Leninist principle of "democratic centralism," officially elects a Central Committee, headed by a party secretary and a standing committee of other secretaries. In practice, of course, under the substitution principle discussed earlier in the chapter, upper levels make key decisions that the lower levels largely rubber stamp, and party committees and party secretaries act in the name of party congresses at every level.

In the reform era from 1978 to the present there has been some experimentation with allowing nominations of more than one person for party elections at the primary and local levels. Also, during the Maoist periods of the Great Leap Forward and especially the Cultural Revolution, an emphasis was put on decentralization to local and provincial party levels, which in practice often meant not democratization but control by party elites loyal to Mao, or "little Maos" at the local level.

In the early years of the Cultural Revolution, party and state organs were temporarily eclipsed by "Paris Commune" type mass organizations on the model of the abortive 1871 uprising in Paris, which claimed to be organizations of direct, mass democracy, but which Mao quickly ordered abandoned in favor of "revolutionary committees" in which "three-in-one" combinations of representatives of the military, mass organizations, and returned cadres or officials would supposedly rule together.

When the party-state apparatus was restored in the early reform era, Deng Xiaoping introduced some structural reforms of the party organization, especially at the national level. Today, the National People's Congress meets more regularly than the once-every-five-years dictated by the party constitution (in fact during the rule of Mao there was no party congress from 1956 to 1977) and officially elects not only a Central Committee of typically two hundred to several hundred members that meets once or twice a year, but also a Central Discipline Inspection Committee (CDIC), in charge of investigating party members at all levels for corruption and deviation from party discipline. This organization represents a typical kontrol function, in which party members report up to dual and triple lines of authority in order to ensure the party's control of the state.

This mechanism can be seen most clearly in the military, in which decisions have to be approved not just by the military commander in each unit but by the political commissar as well. The CDIC also represents a carryover from the tradition of the censorate in imperial China, which was an administrative unit separate from the rest of the central bureaucracy whose function was to maintain loyalty to the center and prevent the rise of "mountain-top kingdoms," or decentralized feudal bastions. Likewise in the PRC the CDIC was one institutional attempt to maintain loyalty to the national government in an era of much economic decentralization.

Another committee officially elected by the National Party Congress was the Central Advisory Committee (CAC), which Deng Xiaoping introduced in order to induce the retirement of key members of the party elite who might resist his reforms. After most of the potential opponents of his reforms were shunted to this committee and then retired or died, the CAC was abolished.

As in most Communist systems, the Central Committee also officially elects a Central Military Commission, which sits at the top of the political hierarchy within the People's Liberation Army and is the main method by which the party maintains control over the military, or, as Mao would say, the way the "party controls the gun."

In addition, the Central Committee officially chooses the general secretary of the party and the various other heads of the party secretariat, which includes departments of the Central Committee that mirror the ministries and bureaus of the state. The post of general secretary was held by none other than Deng Xiaoping up to the Cultural Revolution, when the post was abolished. When Deng gained control over the party in the late 1970s and early 1980s, he restored the post and gave it to his protégés, first Hu Yaobang and then Zhao Ziyang, and finally, after the successive purge of both men for being too weak against "bourgeois liberalization," Deng named Jiang Zemin.

Finally and most important, the Central Committee elects a Political Affairs Bureau, or Politburo, of fourteen to twenty-four members who meet on a regular basis and formally make key decisions on policy and personnel, which are ratified by lower levels. Departing from the Soviet model, in the PRC another body, the Standing Committee of the Politburo, made up of from four to seven members who meet weekly (as far as is known, since it meets in secret) is truly the most powerful body of the party and contains the key leaders of the PRC, who may also hold dual posts in the state and military apparatus. In the Mao era, there were also the posts of chairman and vice-chairman of the party, who headed the Politburo and Secretariat. As part of his reforms officially separating the party from day-to day control of the state, Deng abolished the posts of chairman and vice-chairman in 1982 and restored the general secretary to the official leading role.

As revealed by Zhao Ziyang before his sacking in 1989, however, by agreement of the Politburo, Deng Xiaoping himself remained the paramount leader of the CCP even after he retired, while other retired cadres also maintained influence over the leading bodies of the CCP through their ability to have their protégés appointed to the key top posts. This phenomenon was very similar to that of the *genro* who ruled behind the scenes in Meiji Japan, but it also resulted from the Deng-era reforms requiring people to retire from their posts after a set number of terms and/or at a certain age. In fact Jiang Zemin himself and other key leaders retired from their party posts in 2002 at the party congress and from their government positions in 2003 at the NPC Congress, and may hope themselves to maintain influence from behind the scenes by putting and keeping their own protégés in office. There was speculation that Jiang had been reluctant to retire from all of his official posts, a reluctance that may have been behind the delay in the originally scheduled September 2002 opening of the CCP Party Congress. Even though in the end he did hand over his post of general secretary to Hu Jintao, the fact that Jiang was powerful enough to delay the party congress and at least consider retaining his posts—even against Deng Xiaoping's structural reforms that would seem to have required Jiang to do so—yet at the same time not powerful enough to gain immediate approval for staying in office, shows the remaining importance of informal *guanxi* networks and the need for top leaders to have deep and wide bases of power among Chinese political elites.

State

The structure of the state mirrors that of the party. Of course, despite officially being elected by and responsible to lower levels, in fact all top state leaders are subject to party control and supervision. In 1954, the state constitution officially set up a national body in charge of enacting legislation, ratifying treaties, and electing higher officers—the National People's Congress (NPC). The NPC contains up to three thousand or so delegates officially elected by provincial people's congresses, and is chosen every four years and supposed to meet at least once a year in plenary session. The NPC has at least nine commissions that meet more regularly, plus a standing committee of 150 or so members that meets on a monthly basis, and a chair of that committee. That post was known in the Maoist era as chairman of the state (a post held by Mao himself until he relinquished it to Liu Shaoqi in the early 1960s and in turn abolished the post after Liu's purge during the Cultural Revolution, though always retaining for himself the post of chairman of the party). The chairman of the NPC is now treated more as a speaker of the legislature, since in the reform era Deng Xiaoping introduced the new posts of president and vice-president of China, which theoretically sit on top of the NPC hierarchy. The NPC also elects a Central Military Commission, which mirrors the Military Affairs Commission of the party and in fact may be identical to it in its membership and meetings.

Finally, the NPC chooses a state council, including the premier, vice-premier, state councilors, and heads of other ministries and commissions. The state council also has a standing committee, or an inner cabinet, that works on a daily basis, but of course is responsible to the Politburo and its standing committee. Though the NPC is mostly a rubber stamp, as with the formal legislatures in all Communist systems, in the Deng era more dissent was allowed, including abstentions and even negative votes against both unpopular ministers (including the premier, Li Peng, after Tian'anmen) and controversial policies (including Li Peng's pet project of the Three Gorges Dam on the Yangzi River, which has environmental and reform critics). Some observers, both in and outside of China, speculate that the NPC may be the arena within which real rule by law may develop in the future, but only if the CCP relaxes its nomenklatura and other mechanisms that currently ensure its dominance over governmental institutions.

The central state structure is mirrored at provincial or municipal, city or county, township, and village or basic levels, in which congresses elect their own standing committees and government leaders. During the reform era, the CCP has allowed some real nominations and elections at village level posts, monitored by international observers, but so far it has refused to extend this to the township, county, and provincial levels.

Four large cities, Beijing, Shanghai, Tianjin, and most recently

Chongqing, have the status of provinces, while some provinces, especially those with non-Han ethnic majorities, have the official status of "autonomous regions." There may also be autonomous counties and lower levels within the provinces, but due to party control of the state, in practice there is very little actual autonomy in these structures. A new status, Special Administrative Region (SAR), was granted to Hong Kong upon its return to the PRC in 1997 and to Macao in 1999 (see below), a status that the PRC proposes to grant to Taiwan upon reunification. SAR status does include a great degree of real autonomy, though the governor of Hong Kong is in effect picked by a committee of the National People's Congress of the PRC and is subject to control by the CCP.

Military

As with other organizations, the military is subject to party discipline and control through the party's Military Affairs Commission and General Political Department, which has representatives at all levels of the army, navy, and air force down to the basic unit. The Minister of Defense of the State Council is the administrative head of the People's Liberation Army (PLA), which includes the service arms of the army, navy, air force, and People's Armed Police. Some key Maoist leaders attempted during the late Cultural Revolution to expand the People's Militia, especially in urban areas, as a counterweight to the PLA, but today it has been largely relegated to rural areas and put firmly under the control of the People's Armed Police. Besides being organized into service arms, the PLA is organized into military regions and districts. Historically these four to seven regions replicated the main armies of the civil war period and spread across regular administrative boundaries of the state. The *guanxi* networks of top leaders, at least up to the Jiang Zemin era, often have their roots in various field armies and military regions. Top CCP leaders thus periodically shift the commands of these regions, and in the case of Deng Xiaoping change their number and boundaries, in order to solidify their own control and prevent the possibility of a military coup.

Mass Organizations

As with most Communist regimes, the PRC officially allows many mass organizations to form—for women, artists, peasants, journalists, and so on—but all of these organizations are firmly under the control of the CCP through its nomenklatura function, naming the key heads of those organizations. The peak group of these organizations, the Chinese People's Political Consultative Congress (CPPCC), in fact served as China's legislature from 1949 until the creation of the NPC in 1954 and continued to meet after that time as part of the CCP's line that it represented all progressive classes in society. In fact, the CPPCC constituent organizations include non-CCP political parties (even a rump Guomindang, consisting of members who never fled to Taiwan), all of which, however, are subject to control of the CCP. The CPPCC was eclipsed and repressed during the Cultural Revolution but has functioned again in the reform era as a rubber stamp advisory body for party congress decisions, though as with the NPC, allowing some limited dissent as long as it does not change party policy.

Penetration of Society

In addition to the formal structure of the Chinese party-state, one must talk about other informal or semiformal institutions that help extend the state-reach beneath the county or municipal level. In the Cultural Revolution, the "People's Communes" at the township level formally extended state control for the first time in Chinese history beneath the county or *xian* level, officially in an attempt to build support for socialism from among poor peasants. In reality, some observers contend, Mao's real goal was to militarize the peasants and use them as a counterweight to central officials in order to augment his autocratic power, similar to the *lijia* and *baojia* systems of mutual surveillance networks in the Ming and Qing dynasties. In the reform era, the official line is that commune- and township-level organizations must be officially separated, just as party and state organs should be separated at higher levels. Nevertheless, other informal or semiformal mechanisms of social control remain, if also weakened by market-oriented reform policies.

Criticism Groups (Xiaozu)

Criticism and self-criticism in workplace and neighborhood small groups (*xiaozu*) were hallmarks of Maoist organization. Essentially extending Communist Party discipline beyond the party and into the workplace, the *xiaozu* were a mechanism of mass mobilization to ensure that CCP policies were obeyed and carried out by ordinary people. In the reform era, though not eliminated, the *xiaozu* have been de-emphasized as a forum for criticism and self-criticism sessions and as a vehicle for mass mobilization, and are instead used mostly just to announce party policy.

Danwei

In the 1950s the PRC copied the Soviet model of control through work units, or *danwei*. Especially in Stalinist periods, when central planning and rationing of key goods was emphasized, the *danwei* were an effective method of social control. Workers in state-owned factories gained access to subsidized housing, ration coupons for basic essentials, welfare, and retirement benefits, as well as permission to travel, marry, and have children all through the *danwei*. With the large-scale privatization and foreign investment of the reform era, the *danwei* are also declining in utility and importance, though they will remain of at least some importance as a method of social control for the foreseeable future.

Hukou

After 1949, the regime attempted to control movement into the cities so as to prevent the rise of shantytowns and urban blight associated with many Third World countries, but also to maintain social control generally. As a result, Chinese citizens in urban areas were assigned *hukou,* or urban residence permits, that designated what size and type of urban area they were allowed to live in. In the reform era and the decline of the requirement for a *danwei,* the number of laborers in the cities without the proper *hukou* permit increased drastically; many Chinese were working in the cities on temporary contracts and thus did not have formal legal access to public education, housing, and other benefits. The possibility for unrest, in addition to the threat from peasants in the countryside suffering from overtaxation and extra fees imposed by township- and village-level officials, may come from this relatively unprotected urban sector. As a result, the regime announced moves to officially relax the *hukou* requirement in the 1990s, in effect ratifying what has already occurred as many people without the proper *hukou* take advantage of nonstate sector jobs and informal support networks, including nonofficial schools in order to survive, however precariously. The regime continues to control migration to the largest cities, however, where recent urban migrants remain at a severe disadvantage in terms of housing, jobs, public education, and the like, a situation that may yet lead to social unrest in the future.

DOMESTIC POLICY: HUMAN RIGHTS AND DISSENT

According to human rights monitors such as Amnesty International, Human Rights Watch Asia, and even the U.S. State Department, despite the relative openness of the reform era, the PRC continues to engage in a number of serious abuses of human rights. This would include arrest and imprisonment, either through the formal legal system or through sentencing to the *laogai* (labor camps), to which people can still be sent for terms of three years by local officials without a formal trial. Whether in the formal systems of courts and prisons or in the *laogai,* prisoners in the reform era may be required to work in prison factories at low or even no wages, some perhaps producing goods for export.

There are several categories of prisoners, first among them the human rights and democracy campaigners from the Democracy Wall and Tian'anmen movements, including some who tried to form a new democratic political party. Another category is of religious dissenters, including Catholics loyal to the Pope instead of the party-controlled patriotic Catholic Church, as well as nonregistered Protestants and devotees of Falun Gong and other "evil cults" based on traditional Buddhist and Taoist health and spiritual practices. An overlapping category of repressed people includes members of ethnic minorities from Tibet and other strategic provinces along China's central and inner Asian frontiers charged with being ethnic separatists. Human rights criticisms also include condemnations of the PRC's use of the death penalty not just for crimes of murder and kidnapping but for more ordinary and economic crimes. The charge has also been made that the regime fails to stop, or even condones, the selling of organs from condemned prisoners for transplant operations.

FOREIGN POLICY: CHINA AND GLOBAL POLITICS

Due to political and economic pressures from the international system, Chinese foreign policy has not always varied along the three lines of Communist systems (Stalinist central control, Titoist markets, and Maoist ideological campaigns) and developed in harmony with domestic policy. Nevertheless, there has been change and variation over time in PRC foreign policy along ideological lines.

In 1945, just before the civil war heated up, and again in 1949, the PRC sent out feelers to the United States about easing their relations. But due to the Cold War and Republican accusations that the Truman administration "lost China" to Communism, U.S. relations with China were frozen, and the United States continued to recognize the Guomindang regime on Taiwan, known as the Republic of China, as the official Chinese government. The Republic of China also retained China's permanent seat on the UN security council. The PRC's interest in pursuing relations with the United States cooled with the outbreak of the Korean War (1950–1953), especially after U.S. forces under General Douglas MacArthur advanced to the Yalu River separating North Korea from China. In response, Chinese "volunteers" were sent into Korea to fight the Americans to a costly standstill, and the PRC's rhetoric quickly shifted to an anti-U.S., anti-imperialist line.

China's pro-Soviet stance of "leaning to one side" in the early 1950s led the country to sign a thirty-year Treaty of Peace, Friendship, and Mutual Assistance with the Soviet Union. The United States in turn sent the Seventh Fleet to patrol the Taiwan straits, thus preventing the PRC from taking over the island (while also preventing Chiang Kai-shek from launching any attempt to retake the mainland). Throughout the early and mid-1950s, China was heavily dependent on the Soviet Union for protection and support. After a crisis in 1954 when the PRC shelled two offshore islands controlled by Taiwan, the United States signed a mutual defense treaty with Taiwan, which only increased China's dependence on the Soviets.

Beginning in 1953, with the death of Stalin and the July truce agreement that halted the Korean War, the "lean to one side" policy was moderated. Especially with rapid decolonization in the mid-1950s, China under Premier Zhou Enlai shifted its foreign policy to support newly liberated colonies in the Third World, even if they did not themselves lean toward the Soviet Union. Most notably at the Bandung Conference in Indonesia in April 1955, Zhou Enlai announced conciliatory policies toward Third World states in Asia and Africa, and later Latin America. These policies even included a very modest foreign aid program and a stated willingness to start discussion with the United States. China continued to refer to the "Bandung spirit" in later years as the basis for claim to leadership of the Third World. Though never translated clearly into concrete institutions or actual leadership, China did receive much international sympathy and increased formal recognition at the expense of Taiwan due to its efforts during this period.

In the late 1950s, China shifted its foreign policy even further away from the Soviet Union, culminating in the official Sino-Soviet split of 1960. The reasons for this major split were many and complicated, but at its root, the PRC was based upon an indigenous rural revolution that succeeded without much Soviet aid and support, and indeed, at times China succeeded when it went against Soviet advice. After the Soviet Union refused to give the PRC nuclear weapons in its dispute with Taiwan and the United States over the offshore islands, after Khrushchev denounced some of the crimes of Stalin in his 1956 speech and announced polices of "peaceful coexistence" with the capitalist world, and after the Soviets denounced Mao's Great Leap Forward and pulled out their advisers, the stage was set to extend Maoist policies of self-reliance to the area of foreign policy.

This new policy included support for wars of national liberation in the Third World, including perhaps support for the attempted coup d'état by the Communists in Indonesia and support for opposition parties and movements in Africa and Latin America. China also fought a war with India in 1962 over a border dispute, and, although China won militarily, its involvement in the war prompted other nations to take notice. When China began testing its own independently developed nuclear weapons in 1964, it aroused fears and undermined China's support in the Third World. By 1965, the Afro-Asian conference was postponed indefinitely after China failed to have the Soviet Union excluded.

During the early years of the Cultural Revolution China's foreign policy left it extremely isolated, with Albania as its only official ally. China's Red Guards criticized the official foreign policy establishment for being too influenced by bourgeois tendencies. To express dissent the Red Guards attacked the foreign ministry itself and launched a brief seizure of the British embassy and other violent incidents in a number of foreign embassies, including Hong Kong. Chinese foreign policy was paralyzed for a time, and all ambassadors save the one to Egypt were recalled. The Soviet Union was denounced at this time as a "revisionist" and "social imperialist" country that was led by "capitalist roaders" (an ironic accusation in retrospect, since any real prospect of market-based reforms that might have occurred in the Soviet Union were quashed by Leonid Brezhnev after his purge of Khrushchev in 1964). Tension with the Soviets increased to the point that border skirmishes in the Northeast occurred in 1968–1969, including a serious one in the Ussuri River in March 1969, when Chinese border guards fired on their Soviet counterparts, who responded in kind. This incident led to further border clashes in Central Asian provinces bordering the USSR. For a time, rumors were rife throughout the world of a possible Soviet preemptive strike against China's nuclear facilities in Xinjiang province, and China was increasingly isolated from the world community.

Mao and other CCP leaders began to see the Soviet Union as the main enemy and came to favor reengagement with the rest of the world in the late 1960s, including the return of most ambassadors to their posts, and apologies and even some restitution for the attacks on foreign embassies during the height of the Cultural Revolution. Most famously, China initiated a new policy of rapprochement with the United States in the early 1970s, beginning with the "ping pong diplomacy" of April 1971, when an American table tennis team was allowed to visit China. The United States acquiesced to the PRC taking over the Chinese seat in the UN and acquiring a permanent seat in the Security Council in October 1971. In 1972, U.S. president Richard Nixon visited the PRC, and China shifted its policy away from isolation and toward rapprochement with the United States This all occurred even as the United States was involved in the war in Vietnam and as the Cultural Revolution was officially continuing. The real chief impediment to full normalization of relations between the United States and the PRC, however, was the Taiwan issue. In the famous "Shanghai Communiqué" issued jointly at the end of President Nixon's 1972 visit, the United States and the PRC declared "all Chinese on either side of the Taiwan Strait maintain that there is but one China and that Taiwan is part of China. The United States government does not challenge this position." This public statement did not incite a public outcry in Taiwan at the time because of the Guomindang's tight control and repression of any pro-Taiwan independence sentiment percolating within its borders. Today a democratized Taiwan is home to many outspoken proponents of an independent Taiwan, which may lead to greater tensions and possibly even war in the Taiwan straits.

In the early 1970s, however, President Nixon agreed to reduce U.S. military support for Taiwan and began a process of normalizing relations with China. This began with the establishment of a liaison mission headed by George H. Bush and culminated in the establishment of full diplomatic relations on January 1, 1979, during the Carter administration. America pulled out its military advisers from Taiwan,

President Richard Nixon attends an official banquet during his historic trip to China in 1972. (National Archives)

abrogated the U.S.-ROC Mutual Security Treaty, and increased markedly its trade, cultural, and other contacts with China. In response, the U.S. Congress passed the Taiwan Relations Act in April 1979, which some analysts conclude gives Taiwan more promises of aid than the previous security treaty, but in any case codified into law previous executive branch pledges to sell defensive weapons to Taiwan to prevent its being attacked by the PRC.

This full normalization of relations with the United States occurred at the start of Deng Xiaoping's reform era in China. In 1974 Mao's view divided the world into three camps: the United States and the Soviet Union; Japan, Europe, and Canada; and China along with the whole of Africa, the rest of Asia, and Latin America. Though according to this view China acted against the hegemony of both First World powers, Deng reformed China's policies to move closer to the United States. Trade and investment from the United States and Europe greatly expanded in the Deng years as China joined the World Bank and the International Monetary Fund and began long negotiations that culminated in its joining the World Trade Organization in 2002. This tilt toward the United States and the West started in 1979, after China fought a war with its communist neighbor, Vietnam, and after that country invaded Cambodia and expelled the Pol Pot regime allied to the PRC.

China proceeded to further distance itself from the Soviet Union. After the Soviet Union subsequently allied itself even more closely to Vietnam and obtained military bases in Cam Ranh Bay, the PRC abrogated its 1950 treaty with the USSR, and after the Soviet invasion of Afghanistan, China suspended talks aimed at negotiating a new treaty. In the 1980s, however, Chinese frustrations with the United States increased as American arms sales and military transfers to Taiwan continued and as the United States continued to put restrictions on imports of Chinese textiles. As a result of these frustrations, China moved to a more equidistant policy between the United States and the Soviet Union, a policy that culminated in Mikhail Gorbachev's visit to Beijing in May 1989. A new Sino-Soviet treaty was signed, the two countries' longstanding border disputes were settled, and a mutual demilitarization of the Sino-Soviet and Mongolian-Soviet borders was declared. Deng Xiaoping perhaps intended this treaty to be his final crowning achievement in foreign policy, but of course Gorbachev's visit was completely overshadowed by the Tian'anmen demonstrations of April–June 1989. After June 4, 1989, when the demonstrations were brutally repressed, China's image and relations with the rest of the world were temporarily damaged. In 1992 the world's interest in relations with China resurfaced when Deng Xiaoping toured the south of China and ordered a speed-up of market reforms, which included further openings to Western investment.

Despite the end of China's isolation from the rest of the world and the opening up of its economy to foreign trade and investment, some observers fear that China may become again an enemy of the West and a threat to world peace in the new century. Evidence for this supposed new threat includes increased Chinese missile sales and nuclear-related exports to Algeria, Pakistan, Syria, Iraq, and Iran. China has also raised international concerns in its aggressive territorial claims of islands in the South and East China seas, which could lead to military tensions with Japan and the nations of Southeast Asia, and its close ties and support of the repressive military regime in Myanmar (formerly Burma). Tensions with the United States spiked upwards in recent years, first with the U.S. bombing of the Chinese embassy in Belgrade during the NATO war against Yugoslavia in 1999 and later with the shooting down of a U.S. spy plane over the Taiwan Strait in 2001. Others argue that China is only assuming its rightful place in Asian and world leadership and that its need to continue to improve its peoples' living standards by participating in the global economy will prevent it from becoming a military threat.

In the past decade or so, Chinese foreign policy has perhaps been most greatly affected by the Taiwan issue. As Taiwan liberalized and democratized its own political system from the late 1980s on, and as it shifted to a more "flexible diplomacy" in which Taiwan increasingly accepted contacts and relations with countries who recognized the PRC, ironically the threat of Chinese military action against Taiwan increased. First with the selection of the first native Taiwanese, Lee Tenghui, as president of the Republic of China (ROC) and the Chinese fear that he held a secret independence agenda despite his leadership at the time of the Guomindang, China began a series of missile tests and war games in the Taiwan Strait in 1995–1996 that led the Clinton administration to send U.S. aircraft carriers into the Taiwan Strait.

Especially with the later rise to power of President Chen Shui-bian of the opposition Democratic Progressive Party (DPP), at least half of whose members favor eventual Taiwanese independence, there were periodic revivals of tensions in the Taiwan Strait in the early years of the new millennium. Continuing international tensions and domestic politics on all three sides (China, Taiwan, and the United States), in which politicians often have to play to their hardliners and prove their nationalist (or, in the case of the United States, anti-Communist) credentials, guarantee that this issue will be a contentious one well into the future. Most recently, the announced policy of U.S. president George W. Bush of an end to "strategic ambiguity" (as to whether the United States would always come to the aid of Taiwan in case of an attack) and his reference, mistaken or not, to the "Republic of Taiwan," may yet serve to increase tensions.

Upon his election as president of the ROC on Taiwan, Chen Shui-bian had announced that he would not declare Taiwan independence or even call for a referendum on the issue in the future, and he has recently opened up Taiwan to direct trade and contact with the mainland, policies that helped to allay the fears of the United States and increased Taiwan's support in Washington. Recently, however, Chen Shui-bian has declared that Taiwan is already de facto an independent country and that it may have to consider calling a referendum on independence in the future if the PRC threatens reunification by force. As a result, talks between Taiwan and the PRC have stalled, though as yet tensions have not heated up to the point of the late 1990s, perhaps due to the PRC's need to maintain relations with the

United States and the Western world in order to continue to improve its economy.

Nevertheless, after the repression of the Tian'anmen demonstrations and continuing with the crackdowns against Falun Gong and regional autonomy or separatist advocates in the 1990s, CCP leaders are even more dependent on nationalism as a strong component of the regime's legitimacy. If Chinese economic growth and development stall in the near future, the temptation of the PRC regime may be to play the nationalist card over Taiwan in order to maintain its legitimacy. Again the question is whether China's need for global trade and investment will outweigh that need of its leaders to prove their nationalist credentials and lead instead to a more demilitarized foreign policy.

"GREATER CHINA" ISSUES

A major component of the reforms begun by Deng Xiaoping was his change of official PRC policies toward Hong Kong and Taiwan (as well as the former Portuguese colony of Macao, now mostly a gambling haven), the only parts of China officially colonized by Western powers in the nineteenth century.

Hong Kong

Though Hong Kong island and the adjacent Kowloon peninsula were ceded to Great Britain in perpetuity in the Opium Wars of 1839–1842 and 1860, the "new Territories" that Britain leased for 99 years from China in 1898 were due to go back to China in 1997. People on all sides realized that Hong Kong as a whole was not a viable colony without those territories and that China could bring Hong Kong to a standstill merely by turning off the water. As a result of pressure from businesspeople and others concerned about long-term leases and other business deals, in the early 1980s Great Britain began negotiations with China over Hong Kong's return to the PRC, culminating in the Basic Agreement of 1984, in which Britain agreed to hand over Hong Kong to Chinese sovereignty in 1997 and China agreed to a policy of "one country two systems" under which Hong Kong would be declared a Special Administrative Region (SAR) of the PRC and allowed to keep its capitalist economy and autonomous political system for at least fifty years after accession. The PRC openly announced that this policy was meant as an example to Taiwan, which it offered a similar deal under even more generous terms, by which Taiwan's SAR could maintain Guomindang control and even its own military as long as it agreed to officially declare itself a province of the PRC. In Hong Kong, by contrast, People's Liberation Army troops replaced the British as the main police force when the colony became a SAR. Hong Kong and Taiwan, however, have key differences that so far have led to different results of the "one country two systems" offer.

In the first place, Hong Kong was a British colony that never had pretensions of being an independent state, and second, it was never a democracy. The British-appointed governor ruled Hong Kong, advised by an appointed executive council and an appointed and mostly indirectly elected sixty-member Legislative Council (LegCo). When the last British governor of Hong Kong, Christopher Patten, increased the number of directly elected seats, China strongly protested this action as an abrogation of the Basic Agreement. When China promulgated the Basic Law (Hong Kong's mini constitution) it returned the number of directly elected seats to eighteen and declared China's National People's Congress as the final site of appeal for Hong Kong's courts. Since Hong Kong's return to the PRC in 1997, though the feared mass exodus of its citizens has to date not materialized, recent NPC decisions overturning lower Hong Kong court decisions on issues such as rights of

A Chinese tour boat in Hong Kong Harbor (Corel)

abode in Hong Kong for certain immigrants, as well as recent resignations of civil servants and journalists, proposed new laws limiting the rights of free assembly, and denial of visas for Falun Gong members and others indicate to many that Hong Kong's real autonomy may be eroding. Hong Kong also has yet to fully recover from the Asian financial crisis of the late 1990s, and also may be threatened by the revival of Shanghai as a site of international investment and banking now that China has joined the World Trade Organization.

Taiwan

Taiwan was a colony of Japan from the end of the first Sino-Japanese War in 1895 to the end of World War II in 1945. After a brief period of rule by a corrupt Guomindang governor from 1945 to 1949, which included a massacre of Taiwanese after a riot in 1947, Taiwan became the site of the national Guomindang government under Chiang Kai-shek after it lost the civil war on the mainland in 1949. With the rise of the Cold War in Asia, the United States committed itself to the defense of Chiang's regime and sent its Seventh Fleet into the Taiwan Strait to prevent a PRC takeover (and, less widely known, to prevent Chiang from attacking the mainland, as noted above). Far from being the bastion of "Free China" that its advocates in the so-called China lobby in the United States proclaimed, from 1949 until its liberalization in the mid-1980s, Taiwan was a one-party military dictatorship, in which martial law was declared and all independent political activity outside the Guomindang was banned, with Taiwan independence advocates especially subject to arrest, imprisonment, and torture.

The Guomindang did carry out a series of economic reforms, beginning with land reform, that, aided by Japan, created industrial infrastructure, heavy amounts of U.S. aid in the key early years, and a free trade environment for its exports into the 1960s, resulted in an economic miracle and huge development on the island. Under Chiang Kai-shek's son and eventual successor as president and head of the Guomindang, Chiang Ching-kuo, Taiwan gradually started to liberalize its political system in the mid-1980s, also due to heavy pressure from *dangwai,* or independent nonparty forces. Eventually this led to democratization in the 1990s under Chiang's Guomindang successor, the native Taiwanese Lee Teng-hui, who eventually legalized non-Guomindang parties, including the Democratic Progressive Party, at least half of whose members favored Taiwanese independence. As noted above, this democratization process culminated in the election of the

Chiang Kai-shek memorial in Taipei (Corel)

DPP's Chen Shui-bian as president in 2000, followed by the loss of the Guomindang's majority in the legislature for the first time in 2001.

As Lee Teng-hui changed Taiwan's policy from the "three no's" (no contact, no negotiations, and no compromise) with the PRC to one of "flexible" or "substantive diplomacy," as the PRC's image suffered after Tian'anmen, and as democratization on Taiwan increased, international sympathy and support for Taiwan increased and global public perceptions of Taiwan as intransigent and the PRC as conciliatory reversed. Nevertheless, the rise of the DPP and the end of the rule of the CCP's old enemy, the Guomindang, ironically increased tensions between the two sides since the ruling party on Taiwan no longer has any stake in claiming to be the sole legitimate government of all China and represents mostly native Taiwanese (descendants of immigrants from southern China from the seventeenth to nineteenth centuries) who have no identification with either the CCP or Guomindang.

Nevertheless, Taiwanese investment in the mainland greatly increased in the reform era, just as the Taiwanese economy improved to the point where it lost its advantage of cheap labor and needed to move investments offshore. Although China is much less dependent on Taiwanese investment given its much larger size, any action against Taiwan—such as a missile blockade if not an outright invasion—could severely hurt investment and trade from other countries. It is in this light that global public opinion and sympathy for Taiwan as it democratized plays such a large role. Nowhere is the relation between economic liberalization and political reform more apparent and obvious. Whether Taiwan will prove an example of how China itself will democratize in the future or whether tensions between the PRC and Taiwan will lead to military hostility and war is the main question for Chinese politics and foreign policy in the years ahead.

References

Amnesty International. *Annual Report 2001: China.* Reprinted at http://web. amnesty.org.

Andrew, Anita M., and John A. Rapp. *Autocracy and China's Rebel Founding Emperors: Comparing Chairman Mao and Ming Taizu.* Lanham, Md.: Rowman & Littlefield, 2000.

Bernstein, Richard, and Ross Munro. *The Coming Conflict with China.* New York: Alfred A. Knopf, 1997.

Dittmer, Lowell. "Bases of Power in Chinese Politics." *World Politics* 31, 1 (October 1978), pp. 26–61.

Dreyer, June Teufel. *China's Political System: Modernization and Tradition.* 3d ed. New York: Addison Wesley Longman, Inc., 1995.

Friedman, Edward. *National Identity and Democratic Prospects in Socialist China.* Armonk, N.Y.: M. E. Sharpe, 1995.

Gurley, John G. *Challenges to Communism.* San Francisco: Freeman and Co., 1983.

Hammer, Darrell P. *The USSR: The Politics of Oligarchy.* 3d ed. Boulder: Westview Press, 1990.

Human Rights Watch Asia. *World Report 2002:* China and Tibet. Reprinted at http://hrw.org.

Kelly, David. "The Emergence of Humanism: Wang Ruoshui and the Critique of Socialist Alienation," in Merle Goldman, Timothy Cheek, and Carol Lee Hamrin (eds.), *China's Intellectuals and the State: In Search of a New Relationship.* Cambridge, Mass.: Harvard University Press, 1987: 159–182.

Lieberthal, Kenneth. *Governing China: From Revolution through Reform.* New York: W. W. Norton, 1995.

McCormick, Barrett L. *Political Reform in Post-Mao China : Democracy and Bureaucracy in a Leninist State.* Berkeley: University of California Press, 1990.

People's Republic of China and United States. "Joint Communique." February 27, 1972. Reprinted in *Peking Review,* March 3, 1972, p. 5.

Schurmann, Franz. *Ideology and Organization in Communist China.* 2d ed. Berkeley: University of California Press, 1968.

Solinger, Dorothy (ed.). *Three Visions of Chinese Socialism.* Boulder: Westview Press, 1984.

Walder, Andrew G. *Communist Neo-Traditionalism: Work and Authority in Chinese Industry.* Berkeley: University of California Press, 1986.

Wang, James C. F. *Contemporary Chinese Politics: An Introduction.* 6th ed. Upper

Saddle River, N.J.: Prentice Hall, 1999.

Wang Xizhe. "Mao Zedong and the Cultural Revolution," in Anita Chan, Stanley Rosen, and Jonathan Unger (eds.), *On Socialist Democracy and the Chinese Legal System: The Li Yizhe Debates*. White Plains, N.Y.: M. E. Sharpe, 1985, pp. 177–260.

CHAPTER FOUR
Chinese Society and Culture

Tamara Hamlish

Most Americans have encountered some piece of Chinese culture without ever traveling to China. In nearly every town across the country we find the familiar aromas of Chinese foods in Chinese restaurants. We recognize the highly stylized architecture of Chinese arches and pagodas from the Chinatown districts of major U.S. cities. We can puzzle over the subtleties of Chinese painting from the scrolls that are housed in American museums. And while these small slices of Chinese culture may be familiar to us, they also remind us of tremendous differences between our cultures. Encountered as isolated pieces against the backdrop of daily life in the United States, Chinese culture often seems even more distant, more exotic, and more mysterious. In this chapter, we'll create a portrait of Chinese culture that puts

Stilt walkers at a New Year's celebration, Hohhot, China (Corel)

those isolated fragments of culture into the context of the larger whole of contemporary Chinese society.

We'll look more closely at who the people of China really are, and challenge some of our assumptions about what it means to be Chinese. We'll explore the importance of language in Chinese culture, and how language shapes the cultural and political environment. Following this, we'll focus on social relationships—family, friends, colleagues—and how important a network of relationships is in Chinese society. This naturally leads to some questions about how families are organized, especially in terms of generational and gender differences. Finally, we turn to a discussion of daily life in contemporary China. Before we begin, however, it is helpful to think about some tools that we can use to make sense of the myriad new ideas we'll encounter in China.

The image of "Chinese boxes" nested inside one another, each one opening to reveal not just one more box but another perfectly matched set, is an image that works well when considering the complexities of Chinese culture. Although human society is never so perfectly matched and organized, the image is useful because it reminds us that cultural differences are relative. Each box may be useful, or interesting, or beautiful in its own right, but it is also appraised in relation to the size and the shape of neighboring boxes. Similarly, cultural differences between, for example, China's north and south only make sense in relation to the "bigger box" of China as a whole and to the "smaller boxes" of local and regional cultural practices.

History and geography also offer useful categories for thinking about the unity and the diversity of Chinese culture. Chinese express tremendous pride in the length and richness of Chinese historical records, which date back thousands of years. This includes not only historical documents but also things such as ritual objects, books of poetry, clothing, art objects, and a wide range of other artifacts used in daily life, all of which give insights into the beliefs and practices of life in China over the course of several millennia. Chinese people today often trace contemporary beliefs and practices to the beliefs and practices of Chinese people who lived thousands of years ago. Quite often, the historical record is broken or is not as clear as it could be, but its importance is not so much to trace backwards as to bring the past into the present. These artifacts and documents give the Chinese people a sense of belonging to a long and rich tradition, rather than documenting the actual provenance of a particular idea or behavior (a task that is better left to professional historians).

Similarly, Chinese frequently note the geographical reaches of Chinese culture. They can readily identify numerous shared customs and beliefs that provide a sense of familiarity and comfort, despite the vast distances that separate individual Chinese communities. For example, even something as seemingly mundane as using chopsticks is a powerful cultural practice—in part because of the simple fact that it allows people from different regions and local cultures to sit down at the table together without thinking about how they will get their food from their plates to their mouths. (Anyone who has watched someone use either chopsticks or knife and fork for the first time can readily understand the importance of these cultural practices, especially because your ability to use these critical tools is generally just assumed.) Celebrations of Chinese holidays like the Spring Festival, the Lantern Festival, or the Mid-autumn Festival mark the rhythms of the seasons with holiday foods and customs that are the same in Chinese communities throughout the world. Although history and geography are often used to trace where something began, we will use these concepts here as ways to think about cultural connections—of pulling the past into the present and building bridges across the vast distances.

Nested boxes and a historical and geographical continuum are also important in understanding Chinese culture and society as more than a list of customs or dates or places, but rather as the shared experiences of real people, embodied in their daily lives. Chinese culture and society are constantly changing even as they shape the lives of future generations.

PEOPLE

The population of China is largely composed of Han Chinese, an ethnic group that traces its origins to the original inhabitants of the Yellow River valley. By far the dominant ethnic group in contemporary China—today comprising nearly 92 percent of the population—the Han live in the most densely populated regions of China, along the eastern coast and through the river valleys. The remaining 8 percent of China's population consists of approximately fifty-nine government-designated minority groups. Differences between Han and these non-Han minority groups are often readily apparent in the way people dress, the languages they speak, the food they eat, the architecture of their homes and other buildings, the images and materials used in art, and in the organization of family life. Government-designated ethnic minorities often live separate from their Han neighbors, either in small communities within larger Han communities or in one of the

A Han Chinese mother and son (Corel)

five more remote autonomous regions. Despite significant diversity among Chinese ethnic minorities—from the hill tribes in the mountains of the southwest to the horsemen of the northern steppes—the richness of particular cultures is often obscured through the simple opposition between the Han majority and non-Han minorities.

Yet even within the Han majority we find tremendous cultural variation. One of the most prevalent oppositions is the classic rivalry between north and south China. Northerners see themselves as honest, hardworking, loyal, and trustworthy, whereas southerners tend to regard northerners as slow, stupid, rude, and arrogant. Conversely, southerners see themselves as smart, sophisticated, educated, and cosmopolitan whereas northerners are quick to describe them as sneaky, and prone to lying and cheating. Southerners have a reputation for being talented at business, and northerners are said to dominate the political landscape. Beyond these kinds of rivalries, there exist more practical differences between north and south in people's daily lives. For example, despite common stereotypes of rice as a staple at every Chinese table, inhabitants of the northern plains generally rely on wheat-based staples like noodles or steamed breads. The labor-intensive industries of the south (rice cultivation, silk production) often require the cooperation of large extended families that operate as corporate groups, as opposed to the smaller, more loosely organized family groups in the north.

Although it remains one of the most powerful oppositions in Chinese culture, the north-south rivalry is occasionally overlooked by highly educated, urban sophisticates who see themselves as part of a cultural elite, rather than as part of regional communities. This is not to say that the north-south rivalry disappears—but rather that it takes a backseat to the more important distinction between elite and popular culture. Although this difference is often talked about in terms of geographical differences—between city dwellers and village peasants—geography has become far less important in contemporary society. As China becomes increasingly industrialized, and sophisticated systems of transportation and communication make it easier to move around the country with greater ease and speed, the difference between elite and popular culture has become less a question of the difference between urban and rural ways of life and more about people's attitudes and the habits of their daily life. Local, folk culture—including things such as "home-style" cooking, decorative arts like papercuts and woodblock prints, and extended families living under a single roof—not only reflects the social and economic position of China's lower classes but gives us a window into their attitudes and beliefs about family, society, and the workings of the universe. Members of the urban elite are familiar with these aspects of rural life, but they often dismiss it as crude, old fashioned, or seeped in superstition.

Not surprisingly, Americans are most familiar with the elite culture of what is often described as "traditional" China—the habits and customs of China's scholars and government officials. The members of this group produced and perpetuated a rich legacy of fine art, including literature, calligraphy, painting, porcelain, and poetry. They were charged with developing and maintaining social order through elaborate educational and political structures. The elites were known for their sense of refinement and their dedication to leisure through activities such as the appreciation of fine teas and culinary delicacies, or the construction of elaborate homes, gardens, and temples. In contemporary China, these continue to be important qualities of elite culture. One of the most striking differences, however, is the impact of globalization and the subsequent struggle to make sense of China's "high culture" not only in contrast to "high culture" from other parts of the world but also in the context of the popular culture of Hollywood movies, fast food, and mass production and commodification of consumer goods. One of the greatest challenges for members of today's Chinese elite is to find a place for the rich legacy of China's past in the globalized world of the present—and the future. The tensions between these cultural spheres brings with it a vibrant cultural synthesis, seen for example in contemporary Chinese film, cuisine, fashion, and architecture, as well as in the daily habits of people who shift between several worlds of shared customs and beliefs—without leaving their homes and offices in Beijing or Shanghai.

The impact of globalization is not limited, however, to the elite. Successive waves of emigration have created strong ties between Chinese who have settled in other countries and their family and friends who remain in China. Within these overseas communities, people form informal associations with others from the same place, in part because they speak the same local dialect, enjoy the same kinds of food, and, most important, have an immediate bond of trust based on shared networks of family and friends back in China. Overseas workers often send money home to help support aging parents or spouses and children who remained in the village. Families use these funds to symbolize the success of their overseas relations, building new houses or cars, or funding public works projects such as local clinics or schools, or, most recently, providing the necessary capital to start a small business. Those who return home bring with them not only material goods such as microwave ovens, digital cameras, and DVD players, they also bring with them their experiences of another world and certain changes in the habits and expectations of their daily life, including things such as the convenience of owning a car or having hot running water. Finally, they support future waves of emigration when they help family and friends navigate the intricacies of immigration, apply to foreign colleges and universities, or find a job. One hundred years ago, Chinese peasants who wanted to move up the ladder of success had few options beyond the traditional civil service examination system. Today, with the influx of cash from overseas, and the opportunity to follow others who have emigrated, the simple distinction between "popular" and "elite" is becoming far less rigid.

All of these differences, however, point to a more broadly encompassing sense of "the Chinese people," since these differences are not irreconcilable but are instead clustered around similarities. Similarities, in turn, often reveal subtle but important differences. It is the ability to understand when and how people call upon these similarities and differences—how they use them to express where they stand in relation to someone else—that symbolizes most clearly the complexities of Chinese culture.

LANGUAGE

Language provides us with tremendous insights into culture and society, in part because it defines the boundaries of communities of people who are able to communicate effectively with one another. It also has a profound effect on how we live, what we recognize as important, and how we relate to the people around us. This is certainly true of the central role of language in Chinese society and culture. It is easy to attribute exotic, mysterious qualities to Chinese language because it is, in many, many ways, so different from American English. And while these comparisons may be entertaining and easy to understand, they are also often superficial and provide little insight into the intersection of language and culture in Chinese.

Opening the "nested boxes" of language reveals a distinction between written language and spoken language. For people who use an alphabetic writing system, this distinction is often difficult to grasp, yet it is crucial to understanding the significance of language in Chinese culture. Chinese traveling throughout the country can read a street sign, a menu, or a local newspaper as if they were in their native county. Spoken language, in contrast, varies dramatically, sometimes even across extremely short distances. Regional differences in spoken languages—often defined as dialects—can range from slight differences that require little translation to differences so extreme that no one outside the local community could possibly decipher what is being said. Although the written language permits communication despite differences, spoken languages emphasize those differences and clearly define the boundaries of local communities.

There are seven major dialect groups: Mandarin, Wu, Xiang, Gan, Kejia, Cantonese, and Min. Most of the local languages spoken throughout northern China are some form of Mandarin, so that roughly 70 percent of the population is considered to be Mandarin-speakers. Yet even within these groups—and especially among the southern dialects—local differences can be so marked that local languages that are classified as the same dialect are nonetheless mutually unintelligible. As soon as they begin to talk, outsiders are readily recognized—and treated accordingly. In the early part of the twentieth century, following the fall of the imperial government, Chinese scholars recognized the challenges various dialects would pose for a budding democracy. The government proposed a standardized system of pronunciation based on the northern Beijing dialect. Mandarin is now the official language throughout both the People's Republic of China and Taiwan. Because it is the language used to teach in schools, most children are now comfortable using it. Nonetheless, people continue to use local dialects in many other aspects of their daily lives.

Beyond the practical functions of communication, and the symbolism of cultural identity, there is yet one more dimension to the richness of Chinese language, seen most clearly, perhaps, in the "sister arts" of calligraphy and poetry. It is in poetry and calligraphy that we can truly begin to understand the implications of some of the distinctive characteristics of Chinese language—characteristics that give both beauty and depth to these uniquely Chinese art forms. In both calligraphy and poetry, every character is carefully chosen so that the sound, the meaning, *and the visual form* are in harmony.

What makes this even more unusual is the fact that both poetry and calligraphy are generally "improvised," that is, created spontaneously in response to a particularly emotional event. Once an artist has either composed a poem of his own or called to mind a well-known poem that conveys the sentiments of that particular moment, he picks up his brush to capture it all on paper. Calligraphy involves the use of delicate brushes loaded with ink and applied to highly absorbent paper—a technique that leaves no room for error. The piece must be completed in one continuous movement, without pauses or hesitations, in order to portray the immediacy and urgency of the moment, captured at the intersection between the spoken language and the written language.

It should be clear by now that what we commonly call "the Chinese language" is, in fact, a complex system for creating cultural communities through both writing and speech. Yet despite this seeming complexity, the various dimensions of Chinese language are part of the everyday activity of communicating with others in every Chinese community. People draw upon the resources of the language to express themselves—to bargain at the market, chat with a friend, close a business deal, or create a work of art. This can be seen in most social interactions where even a brief conversation is generally accompanied by hand gestures that depict the corresponding characters in order to add emphasis or to make something clearer. It is not unusual to see people using their index finger to "write" on the palm of the opposite hand or trace a character in mid-air. You might even be able to

Calligrapher writing on a scroll. Calligraphy involves the use of delicate brushes that are loaded with ink and applied to highly absorbent paper. (Owen Franken/CORBIS)

judge the seriousness of a conversation by the moment at which pen and paper are pulled out and verbal exchanges are accompanied by the writing of entire phrases (as opposed to single characters casually "scribbled" in the air). Meaning in Chinese language is not just about the meaning of words but also about whether words are spoken or written, whether they are the local dialect or standard pronunciation, whether they are formed in the air or carefully inscribed with a brush. It is not just about the meanings of words but about which words are chosen and through what medium they are conveyed.

SOCIAL RELATIONSHIPS

Guanxi

If language is at the center of Chinese culture, then social relationships are at the core of Chinese society. It is in the area of social relationships that the metaphor of nested boxes may be most useful because it can help in visualizing the system of social relations that extend outward from each individual, shifting in size and complexity over the course of one's life. Nearly all social interactions in Chinese societies can be understood in terms of *guanxi*. It would be difficult to overstate the significance of these networks, since they apply to a broad range of relationships, from the family to international affairs. In fact, some scholars suggest that *guanxi* even extends to the supernatural world of gods, ghosts, and ancestors.

Social relations in China are not simply about getting along well with others but about building a network of people upon whom you can count (and who will count on you) to help make things happen, from finding housing or a job to reserving a seat on a plane or a train during a busy holiday season, getting access to good medical care, or being admitted to a top school. Through the continual exchange of both tangible and intangible goods, people develop a sense of mutual obligation that cements their network of social relationships and insures that they are able to get what they need and want.

This attitude toward social relationships is unfamiliar to many Westerners, who clearly distinguish between relationships based on rational, economic needs (that is, your relationship with the clerk at the local grocery store) and relationships based on emotional needs and desires (that is, a spouse, children, close friends). The Chinese system of *guanxi* may seem like a cold and calculating approach to personal relationships based on what you can get out of it. But the calculations are not as utilitarian as they may appear, and relationships are always mutual, with a clear expectation that both parties will give *and* receive. In fact, the fundamental principles of Chinese social relations are abstract qualities that have more to do with a person's character and integrity than with material resources.

Concepts such as *ren* and *xin,* refer to qualities such as trustworthiness, credibility, endurance, tolerance, and respect. The concept of *mian* ("face") is perhaps familiar to many Americans though not always fully understood: One has the ability to enhance the reputation of others (to "give face" to others) as well as the desire to preserve one's own reputation (to "save face"). In other words, relationships are not entered into casually, nor are they considered short-term. *Guanxi* requires a deep commitment and a long-term investment of time and energy, and like all social relationships, offers the potential to reap considerable returns.

One of the most important principles that defines Chinese relationships, however, is *xiaoxun,* generally translated as "filial piety." This one concept encompasses all of the concepts described above— trustworthiness, tolerance, and reputation—but refers to one's parents. The overarching quality of *xiaoxun* points to the importance of the family as the model for all social relationships, both in the abstract and in more practical assessments of someone's integrity and character. In one of his landmark studies of Chinese culture and society, anthropologist Fei Xiaotong notes that social responsibility in China begins and ends at the gate to the family home. Family loyalties take priority over all other relationships, and family background is a key factor in determining an individual's place in society. Family resources are pooled, with all family members expected to devote at least a portion of their labor or other resources to the family, with the expectation that individuals will use these resources in ways that will enhance the well-being and the reputation of the family as a whole. It is therefore easy to see why people's behavior inside the family is taken as a good indicator of how they will behave outside of the family.

Family

The words that are used to identify kin are extraordinarily complex, in part because they are an expression of the nature of family obligations. Relationships are clearly and precisely defined on the basis of gender, age (birth order), and generation. Hierarchical values are attached to each category, with senior generation, first-born males ranking highest. Unlike English, where the term "cousin" includes all the children of all of the siblings of both parents, Chinese kinship terms identify each individual through a specific term that traces the relationship through distinctions between mother and father, the sex and birth order of the (parent's) siblings, and the sex and birth order of the children of the siblings. Thus when someone talks about a "cousin" in Chinese, it is immediately clear who the actual person is, even without mentioning a name.

This complex system of kinship terms speaks to the importance of "knowing one's place" within the wider family—and the wider social world. Families are organized hierarchically, and older men are treated with the most respect—even if their actual power has been usurped by their sons or their spouse. Although changes in Chinese laws over the past forty-five years have given women more rights, family property, wealth, and other family resources are often transferred to sons before daughters. In rural areas, where agriculture is still the primary livelihood, this is often justified by the fact that young couples generally move in with the groom's parents after they are married, and it is in that household that both husband and wife make their greatest investment of time and energy. Although this scenario has changed dramatically among urban families in China today, many families continue to privilege sons over daughters.

In the past, marriages were arranged and were seen as alliances between family groups. Today, despite the disappearance of formally arranged marriages, many people still rely on "introductions" from family or friends in their search for a spouse. Unlike marriage and family in European and American society, which focuses on the sexual relationship between husband and wife, the primary bonds in Chinese families are intergenerational, between parents and children. Resources, including children, are regarded as belonging to the family, with not much emphasis on individual ownership. In urban areas, families often live in nuclear units (parents and children) with aging parents close by, in part because of space and privacy, and in part because (as wage earners) they may seek to establish some independence. Still, families in China are far less independent than nuclear families in the United States. Extended family (grandparents, aunts, and uncles) often participate in decisions about disciplining children, making major purchases, choosing a school, or changing jobs—in other words, anything that will affect either the resources or the reputation of the family as a whole. In rural areas, families may live with several generations together under a single roof, or children may live with their grandparents while their parents go to the city or overseas in search of better economic opportunities. Although it is certainly easier to control resources when people live together—or at least in close proximity—the cultural value of *xiaoxun* brings with it a strong sense of obligation that is not diminished by long distances or infrequent visits.

BEYOND HOME: SCHOOL, WORK, AND THE LOCAL COMMUNITY

The principles that govern relationships within the family can also be seen in social relationships that extend beyond the family, in social networks that emerge at school, at work, and in the local community. In many of these contexts kin terms are used to express respect, admiration, or the desire to sustain the relationship into the future—classmates are referred to as brothers and sisters, or neighbors may be addressed as "auntie" or "grandpa." This does not, however, imply that these relationships are meant as substitutes, or even extensions, of actual kin relations. What these relationships do suggest are the kinds of parallels among these different networks—in terms of age, gender, or generation, for example—and the principles that define the responsibilities and obligations of the people involved.

The social networks that connect classmates provides a good example of both the parallels between kin and other kinds of social relations, and of the "nested box" quality of social relations in general. Although elementary school is obligatory for all children, the kind of school a child attends depends in large part on his or her family background and academic abilities. Children who attend local village schools often know their classmates from other contexts as well, and the school relationship simply adds another dimension to an existing relationship. Children in urban areas who are sent to specific schools in order to build a foundation for future academic endeavors begin to establish a different kind of social network. As their education progresses, however, children are channeled into schools that are seen to match their abilities and talents.

There they encounter others who share similar talents and interests, and who they will likely eventually encounter in a professional context. As students move into higher education, they become part of a highly select group, drawn together from various places and family backgrounds to prepare for their future as educated professionals. The networks of relationships that are formed in this context produce extremely strong lifelong ties and loyalties. Unlike the alumni associations of U.S. universities, which are formal networks built on a sense of loyalty to an alma mater, relationships among Chinese students form an informal network that grows out of shared interests, experiences, and expectations.

For those who do not attend college, important networks are built in the workplace or work unit, especially when people have recently migrated from a rural to an urban area. Residence in a workers' dormitory or other kinds of shared housing, the rhythms of daily life and work schedules, the shared experience of the work that they are doing, all contribute to establishing relationships of mutual dependence and obligation. Much like college students, young factory workers or shop clerks may use kin terms such as "brother" or "sister" to define and express the nature of their relationship. But these networks often do not endure in the same way as the networks established by college students, in part because they grow out of the activities of daily life rather than shared academic experiences or intellectual interests.

In recent decades, the Chinese government instituted a "one-child policy" in order to curb the vary rapid growth of the population. Families were limited to one child, a rule that was enforced by requiring parents to pay for medical care, schooling, and other needs for additional children. This policy, however, has also had an effect on social networks. In a culture where family is always first priority, and extended family provides a ready-made extended social network, the one-child policy has reshaped the nature of social networks in China in ways that are not yet wholly apparent. Some studies have suggested that only children become spoiled after being the center of attention for six adults—mother, father, and two sets of grandparents. Other studies suggest that these children are smarter, more focused, and more well-rounded because families have sufficient resources for a better education and a more sophisticated lifestyle. Although the first generation to be born under this policy is just now coming of age, it is difficult to assess the long-term impact of a society full of sibling-less children. Yet it is clear that extended social networks, whether through school, work, or local communities, will become increasingly important. Certainly the extensive use of terms like brother, sister, or auntie will shift as the kin relations become more limited. That is why the principles that define relationships, rather than the relationships themselves, are so important for understanding social networks in China.

A Chinese couple with an infant daughter stands in front of a sign advocating family planning.(Owen Franken/CORBIS)

WOMEN IN CHINESE SOCIETY

There is one more aspect of social life in Chinese society where the importance of social networks is revealed, this time by its relative absence. This is in the situation of women in China. In many respects, Chinese women enjoy opportunities that are missing for women in other parts of the world. In the first decades of the twentieth century, during the early years of the new Chinese nation, women's rights were an important priority. Women were encouraged to get an education and to pursue their professional ambitions. They became doctors and research scientists. Marriage laws were enacted to protect women from being forced into arranged marriages, to leave marriages where they were being abused, and to protect their rights in property and give them some control over their own resources.

Although these reforms brought about significant changes in the status of women in China, they had little effect on women's cultural value, their importance to the perpetuation of Chinese culture and society. As Carma Hinton points out in her documentary film *Small Happiness,* female children are welcomed into the family as a "small happiness" while boys are received as a "great happiness." The ratio of men to women in China is different from the global averages, a difference that is often attributed to abortion, the abandonment of female children or unconfirmed accounts of female infanticide. Despite the social reforms that now make it possible for women to work outside the home—especially before they are married—and to contribute more money into the household, they are still largely seen as a drain on family resources. It is expected that daughters eventually will marry and that their education, their talent, and their labor will then benefit their husband's family. In addition, women often earn less money and have fewer opportunities to advance in their careers, which further encourages a preference for sons who will likely earn more and advance further in their professions.

Historically, women who were articulate, talented, and well educated often did not marry but instead became the highly valued and much-adored concubines of wealthy and powerful men. Those who did marry pursued their interests within the confines of the household. Today, successful or ambitious women similarly may have difficulty finding a spouse who understands and supports their professional goals. And like women the world over, those who do marry often have difficulty balancing their domestic and professional responsibilities. All of the efforts that have been made to afford women equal opportunity in the workplace have generally not been matched with efforts to demand equal work from men in the home. Chinese women continue to be held responsible for shopping, cooking, cleaning, and caring for both children and elderly parents, at the same time that they are expected to take advantage of the opportunities to contribute to the household economy through wage work outside the home.

Although social reforms have introduced significant changes for women's lives in contemporary China, they have not resulted in deep and lasting changes in society. Most important, they have not changed the ways that women participate in the vast networks of social relationships that are the foundation of Chinese society. We see this quite literally in the term *neiren,* a word for wife that, translated directly, means "insider." When a woman marries, she moves from being a stranger or "outsider" to standing at the very core of the household. She takes on the obligations of wife, mother, and daughter-in-law in exchange for the benefits of becoming a family insider, who is represented to the rest of society through her husband and eventually her sons.

Social activists and scholars debate the reasons for women's limited social networks. Some point out that women's household and family responsibilities leave them little time to cultivate social relationships with people outside of the family. Others protest the idea that women are fundamentally different from men and do not possess the same qualities of trustworthiness, endurance, or respectability. Finally, some maintain that women have simply not been given sufficient opportunities and that social reforms in education, marriage laws, and professional advancement will naturally lead to expanding their network of social relations. Although women may maintain a small, local network of friends and colleagues, they are largely dependent on the social network of their husbands to fulfill their own needs and desires, as well as the networks of their own families.

DAILY LIFE IN CHINESE SOCIETIES

The rhythms of daily life in Chinese societies reflect China's social structures and networks of social relations. For example, while people in China draw distinctions between home and office, or between friends and colleagues, as different networks of social relations, these two spheres do not differ dramatically in the kinds of activities that take place. In other words, there is no sense of job-related "work" as a distinct kind of activity, nor is there a sense of "leisure." Working or "taking care of business" (*gongzuo, zuoshi*) is contrasted with "resting" (*xiuxi*). Resting refers not only to brief breaks during the day but also vacation days, closing time, and going to bed. In agricultural communities, it can also refer to seasonal changes in activity. In other words, the cycle of daily activity is defined not so much by where is it done, or who you are with, but by the activity itself. The contrast between work and rest is found throughout Chinese society, among office workers and small businessmen, and among laborers in factories or in agriculture.

In urban areas, where people work in offices or run small businesses, the Chinese work week often extends through midday Saturday and there is little time for leisure activity as we know it in the United States. Yet for many Chinese, the workday is far less stressful than for their American counterparts because it is punctuated by frequent breaks. Midday naps are common—it is not unusual to walk into a post office, a bank, or a department store in the middle of the day and find people with their heads down on their desks "resting," with no intention of interrupting their nap to "work." Meals are also a "resting" time. Even if people eat out of a container at their desk, they rarely work at the same time. Job-related events that take place in the evening and might be characterized as social activities—for example, a birthday celebration for a colleague—are instead seen as an extension of work. In most cases, spouses and families do not participate, and, even when coworkers truly enjoy each other's company, they keep these two spheres of social relationships distinct.

This alternating cycle of "work" and "rest" extends beyond the workplace. Without many of the conveniences available in the United States—such as a large refrigerator to store a week's worth of food, or a private car to run a quick errand, or an automatic washer and dryer to wash clothes, to name just a few—much of any day is engaged in "taking care of business." Job-related work is seen as just another kind of work that must be done over the course of the day.

Factory workers may face a more tightly regulated work schedule, dictated by the demands of a long assembly line and supervisors who are far-removed from the factory floor. Breaks are determined by the pace of the entire factory, and the length of the work day depends on the demand for the goods being produced. Because many of these workers are young and unmarried, they often live in dormitories on the factory "campus." They eat their meals together in a common mess hall and spend the greater part of every day standing together on the line running machinery. The beginning and end of the workday are marked by announcements and music played over a loud-speaker that can be heard throughout the factory grounds. Many factories, especially state-run enterprises, resemble small villages, with schools, clinics, movie theaters, and athletic facilities all on the factory grounds. In this highly structured, all-encompassing environment, workers often form close ties with one another as they move through the cycle of daily life in unison.

For those engaged in agricultural work, the cycle of daily life is embedded in a larger cycle of seasonal changes. Much like peasants and farmers throughout the world, periods of work and rest follow the seasons. During periods of intense activity, the day begins before the sun comes up and ends after the sun has set. Much of the agricultural work in China is still done by people rather than machine and therefore requires that each member of the household contribute to the process. Activities must be carefully coordinated among members of the household so that each step is accomplished on time and things move smoothly into the next stage. Labor-intensive activities, such as harvesting or threshing, may require cooperation among several households, and an entire community may pull together for an intense cycle of work. People are heavily dependent on each other, and a strong network of social relations—either extended family or neighbors or both—that can be called upon whenever they are needed is critical for survival in Chinese agricultural households.

In contrast to this continuum between work and rest, Chinese clearly distinguish between public and private spaces in daily life. Great care is given to activities and relationships that occur inside the family or among colleagues or coworkers. Within these places, there is much attention to keeping order and observing the responsibilities and privileges that go with rank and status. Once outside these environments, however, order and civility are replaced by determined self-interest and a strong sense of anonymity—whether jostling for a place on the bus, negotiating the line at the market, or disposing of scrap paper in the garbage. Similar to what we've already seen in the contrast between the cycle of work and rest, daily life in China is also punctuated by a constant cycle of public and private behavior, between roles clearly defined by family or work unit and the anonymity of the world at large. As we shall see below, these distinctions set the boundaries of daily life, as well as the possibilities for activities and events that are set apart.

Inside the "nested boxes" of the perpetual cycle of work and rest that comprises daily life can be found the smaller box set aside for

A small family picnic in a park, Chengdu, China. Chinese typically spend their free time with family. When the weather is nice, families generally head outside to a park or other public space for an outing and a leisurely meal. (Julia Waterlow; Eye Ubiquitous/CORBIS)

free time. For most Chinese, daily life leaves little time for leisure activities. Typically free time is spent with family, including married siblings, children, and parents. When the weather is nice, families generally head outside to a park or other public space for an outing and a leisurely meal. On Sunday afternoons in most Chinese cities, towns, and villages, public spaces are crowded with multiple generations of families simply spending time together. In China's big cities, large shopping malls provide a diversion for all ages, while small town public squares give families a place to sit and relax. At home, families spend time watching television or playing cards or games like mahjong.

Celebrating family events such as a wedding, the birth of a child, or the birthday of an aging parent involves a larger circle of family, friends, and colleagues. At these times, the boundaries between home and work are blurred, and invitations are extended to all who are part of the daily life of the host. Most families try not to flout the ideals of a Communist society while finding a way to mark important life-cycle events. They try to keep a careful balance between celebrations that are too small and simple and those that are too elaborate and ostentatious. In all cases, detailed records are kept to insure that proper social relationships are maintained, and that gifts and invitations to future family events are adequately reciprocated. Finally, distinctive, and symbolic, food and drink, dress, and activities mark these times as different from the work-rest cycle of daily life.

In addition to celebrating family events, Chinese families often prepare elaborate holiday celebrations. The Chinese calendar includes both national holidays and ancient lunar holidays (based on the cycles of the moon). National holidays include National Day, marking the founding of the nation (October 10 for the Republic of China and October 1 for the People's Republic of China), Teacher's Day (September 28, the birthday of Confucius), and International Labor Day (May 1). These dates are fixed on the solar calendar. Lunar holidays such as the Dragon Boat Festival, the Mid-autumn Festival, and the Lantern Festival are observed through ritual foods and activities, such as dragon boat races or lantern parades. But the most elaborate holiday observance is the Spring Festival, commonly known as the Lunar New Year, which generally falls in January or February. Businesses close for an extended holiday—often up to two weeks—and nearly everyone travels home to be with family. Starting the new year with the family together symbolizes wholeness and bodes well for the new year, so most families make a concerted effort to have everyone at the table for the elaborate ritual meal that is supposed to begin late in the evening and continue well past midnight. Mothers serve their families symbolic foods such as fish (*yu*, a homonym for "plenty"), noodles (symbolizing long life), and eggs (symbolizing family unity). Some of the most extravagant fireworks displays take place at midnight of the Lunar New Year. In addition, gifts are given, often in the form of money bundled in red envelopes, from parents to their young children and from adult children to their parents. It is customary for a married woman to spend New Year's eve and the first day of the New Year with her husband's family, and then travel on the second day to see her own family. Similarly, after the first day, people head out to visit friends or invite extended family and friends into their own homes. Days are spent eating, playing cards or mahjong, watching television extravaganzas and variety shows, napping, strolling through the neighborhood, and chatting with visitors. Shops and offices are closed, and virtually no business occurs during this time—although growing participation in a global economic community has resulted in greater pressure to get back to business sooner rather than later.

Daily life in China is thus regulated by the contrasts between work and rest, and between one's public persona and one's personal, private identity. Routine is punctuated by holidays and life cycle events that offer a notable contrast between the mundane and the exceptional. This contrast is further accentuated by the "traditional" beliefs and symbolism that are found throughout holiday and family celebrations, despite the fact that these beliefs and symbols have often disappeared from daily life, particularly among those who are living and working in large urban areas.

SELECTED THEMES IN CHINESE CULTURE
Robert André LaFleur

In the rest of this chapter, we will look at contemporary Chinese culture from a number of perspectives. Any reader who has come this far will have seen many examples of the continuity and change that is so much a part of contemporary China. Cultural themes are no different. In education, religion, literature, and popular culture, one can see abrupt breaks with the past as well as a flowing continuity. That these can often be seen *at the same time* within complex sets of events and practices is one of the things that makes the study of Chinese culture so interesting.

Education

The language of education in China (and this is also true in Taiwan and of much Chinese instruction in Southeast Asia) is Mandarin. That, in itself, is an important step toward creating an integrated educational experience. As we've seen, China is made up of a number of distinctive regions, each with its own geographical, historical, linguistic, and cultural peculiarities. To paraphrase an old saying in China, when one travels ten miles, speech becomes fuzzy; when one travels fifty, speech is incomprehensible. The fact that the northern dialect of Mandarin (*guoyu,* "national language") is used in all instruction is significant. It doesn't mean, however, that speech has become standardized; regional variations still persist, with many people speaking the regional dialects at home and using Mandarin for more public communication. The curriculum, though, is standardized, and the books that students will read throughout their academic careers are determined by the Ministry of Education and are the same throughout China. This is also true for entrance exams through middle school and high school, and all the way to college.

There are, as one might guess, significant continuities and contrasts with earlier forms of education in China. The idea of a standard six-, nine-, or twelve-year educational program for all members of society was rather late in arriving. It was not quite as elitist, however, as some general textbooks imply. As early as the Song dynasty (960–1279) private academies and clan-based charitable organizations were developed that often held the ideals of educating all young men in their family grouping. Still, even with these charitable institutions, there were significant gaps in access to education. Women, in particular, had far fewer opportunities than men, and it was not unusual for families to teach women the domestic arts but not reading and writing. The ideal for many households of means was for women to spend their lives in the "inner quarters," not venturing out into the broader world except for very special events.

The exceptions do prove the rule, though. During the Han dynasty, Ban Zhao was one of the foremost minds of her time. Educated at home alongside her talented brothers, she wrote poetry, essays, and, with great skill, finished the monumental historical work begun by her father and continued by her brothers, the *Han Shu* (*History of the Han*). Yet she is as widely known for her statement that a woman should devote her life to three men—her father, her husband, and, ultimately, her son. Given her educational achievements, such a statement is surprising, but it remains the case that it was the rare woman in imperial China who exerted intellectual influence beyond her family unit.

Li Qingzhao, a Song dynasty poet, is another great example of exceptional talent in the literary arts. Her poetry has long been anthologized, and her pieces read with a grace that is hard to underestimate. She was raised in a literary family and had an unusually close relationship to her husband, whose literary interests she shared until his death in 1129. Only about seventy of her poems survive, but they show a depth of learning and emotion that few poets attained. There are many more examples of such talent, but what unites them is the exceptional nature of their education. They had access to the greatest works and the finest instruction because they had fathers who were willing to educate daughters and who were affluent enough to do so. By the Ming and Qing dynasties, highly educated women were not unusual. Still, it was not until the twentieth century that women attained equal access to education.

In a similar fashion, access to education was not easy in the past (and often in the present) for working families. In fact, so rare was the ascent from working in the fields to the higher reaches of the examinations in imperial China that it became something of a distant ideal, not unlike that of "from a log cabin to the White House" in earlier American history. Yet even though the reality was often quite different, examples of perseverance work their way through many of the books that Chinese children studied in their early years.

The *Three Character Classic* was one of the first books that a child would memorize at the age of six or seven. Although arranged in a sing-song fashion with an emphasis on brevity (each line is three characters long), it is filled with educational ideals espoused during the later imperial period. The opening lines address the famous philosophical debate about whether people are born good or become good through learning. It then goes on to address education, which starts in the home and continues with strict teaching and diligent study:

> To raise children without instruction
> This is the father's error
> To teach children without strictness
> This is the teacher's indolence.
>
> If children fail to study
> This is inappropriate
> If they don't learn in youth
> What will happen when they are old?
>
> If jade is not carved
> Its potential is incomplete
> If people do not study
> Righteousness cannot be known.

The text goes on for hundreds of characters to describe key points in Chinese history and philosophy, before closing with the following lines that again exhort students to remain diligent and to study for the sake of their families and the good of society. It particularly addresses the concerns of those who don't have the means to obtain a good education. Whether it is making their own books for composition practice, keeping awake after a hard day of work, or reading by "natural light," the *Three Character Classic* gives examples of dedication:

> One youth cracked open cattails to make scrolls,
> Another scraped bamboo to make tablets.
> They possessed no books,
> Yet both knew to exert themselves.

> One youth, to stay awake, suspended his head from a ceiling beam.
> Another pierced his thigh with an awl.
> They had no instruction,
> Yet they toiled of their own accord.
>
> One youth made a lamp of a bag of fireflies,
> Another read by glare of snow.
> Although their households were impoverished
> They studied without cease.

Learning, we are told, is what separates us from the rest of the natural world. It is what makes us human. Just as the culture heroes described in Chapter 1 transformed the world around them into a place of order and continuity, so, too, must the diligent child learn while young and serve the sovereign and the people with superior knowledge:

> Silkworms emit silken thread
> Bees produce honey
> If people do not study
> They are not equal to the animals.
>
> Learn in youth
> Put it into practice when grown.
> Above, influence the ruler;
> Below, aid the people.

And finally, another exhortation to the student:

> Perseverance leads to success
> Idleness has no benefits
> Be ever vigilant
> And exert your strength!

The entire text can be found on the Beloit Asian Studies Web site listed in the References at the end of this volume.

Until the last imperial examination was given in 1905, a traditional education consisted of memorizing basic "beginner" texts such as the one above and moving quickly on to the "Four Books": Confucius's *Analects,* Mencius's philosophical works, and two small sections of the *Book of Ritual*—the *Doctrine of the Mean* and the *Great Learning.* From there, students would read philosophy, history, poetry, and the like, with an aim toward passing the many levels of examinations that began at the local level and ended in the imperial examinations, given once every three years in the capital. Those who passed were the "superstars" of Chinese society, and both they and their families spent years preparing for the day they would start their official careers.

One might ask what possible connection there can be between a traditional education and today's educational system. To be sure, China has made enormous strides in educating its people, and the literacy rate grew tremendously in the twentieth century. The current Chinese education provides six years of primary school and six years of secondary school (which takes a student through the equivalent, in years, of an American high school education). There is also a state-organized university system, with key campuses (and fierce competition for admission) at Beijing University and Qinghua University in Beijing, Fudan University in Shanghai, Nankai University in Tianjin, and Zhongshan University in Guangdong. In addition to these major centers of higher education, each province has its flagship campus (not unlike land-grant colleges in the United States). There are also hundreds of institutions, large and small, of higher education specializing in technical training throughout China.

The curriculum has changed a great deal from earlier times, although a Chinese student still receives thorough instruction in history, philosophy, and literature through middle school. Science and math are also a very important part of the curriculum, and the Ministry of Education has put a good deal of emphasis on building technical expertise—the very kind that nineteenth-century reformers wanted as part of a new set of skills with which to challenge the West. One thing that has stayed consistent, though, is competition. Admission to the university system takes place in a nationwide competition, and the jockeying for position, dreams, and stresses (on students and a wide variety of family members) remains great. There is also a significant urban-rural divide in educational access. Rural schools have far less flexibility in attracting quality teachers, and even funding remains, for the most part, a local concern beyond urban centers.

Although the strides toward national educational integration and equal access are great, there remains a number of significant challenges. The most obvious is that, since the end of the imperial examination system less than one hundred years ago, China has gone through turbulent changes in economic and political fortunes. One can look at the twentieth century and say that it is only in the 1980s and 1990s that we have seen the kind of consistent policy and institution building that takes many decades, and several generations of

Students at Beijing University, a key campus of China's state-organized university system. Students face fierce competition for college admission in China. (Dean Conger/CORBIS)

students, to build. Even a cursory reading of the last sections of Chapter 1 will show that the fall of the Qing dynasty, the ensuing period of warlordism, the war of resistance against Japan, and the civil war with the Nationalists have not been conducive to building continuity in education. The history of the People's Republic has been equally eventful, with major breaks in the system through the Great Leap Forward and the Cultural Revolution. In fact, many survivors of those eras refer to themselves as "Lost Generations," and it is education to which they most often refer in that loss.

Today, China has almost 350 million students, a number larger than the total population of the United States. Nine years of education are compulsory, and that is followed by competitive placements in senior secondary and university educations. The 2000 census figures show a literacy rate in China of just over 85 percent, which is based on a knowledge of 1,500 Chinese characters in rural locations and 2,000 in urban ones. Because of the sheer size of China's population, this still means that 150 million Chinese fall below these fairly minimal literacy rates. Women lag slightly behind men, although the gap is narrowing. Fairly optimistic Chinese government projections show

China climbing to a 94 percent rate in 2005, a 97 percent rate in 2010, and a 99 percent rate in 2015.

The challenge for the Chinese government will be to continue to make strides in integrating urban and rural, male and female, rich and poor into a system that provides a stable educational base for a large percentage of students and the facilities to provide for high-level training as well. As we have seen in previous chapters, the theme remains similar for all institutional goals in contemporary China. In order to build institutions, continuity is needed. The apocryphal Chinese curse, so often quoted by Westerners—"May you live in interesting times"—has been remarkably pertinent to China in much of the twentieth century and has resulted in a formidable challenge for educators of all kinds.

Religion

The English word *religion* does not convey the same range of attitudes and ideas in China that we often find in the West. Aside from Christianity, Judaism, and Islam (none of which enjoys full freedom of observance in China today), religious practices tend not to be concentrated in one place (such as a local church, temple, or mosque). In Taiwan, and for overseas Chinese in southeast Asia, North America, and Europe, many family homes have shrines with connections to what are often called "Confucian" family rituals. There is often a complex mix of Buddhist and Daoist themes as well. Traveling in Taiwan for the first time more than fifteen years ago, I came upon a temple in the southern Taiwan county of Ping-tung (Pingdong). Two things immediately caught my eye. The first was the hurried movement of many of those passing into (and quickly out of) the temple. The second was an oil filter resting on the nose of one of the lions carved into the stonework near the entrance. Thinking from the perspective of my own experience in the Norwegian-Lutheran Red River Valley in North Dakota, I thought it just short of blasphemous. Adding to my confusion, I asked someone near the entrance, "What kind of temple is this?" With a look that seemed to answer "Well, a busy one," he asked what I meant. "Buddhist, Daoist, or Confucian?" I asked in my best pronunciation. His wordless answer might best be translated as "All of 'em."

And none of them, I would later learn, at least in a purist's terms. The key word in this is *syncretism*—the blending of three traditions into a lived whole. During Chinese history, there certainly were strug-

Worshippers burn candles and joss sticks at the Shi Jing Temple in a rural area near Chengdu. (Bohemian Nomad Picturemakers/CORBIS)

gles for ascendancy among doctrines, and, as we read in the Tang dynasty section, the suppression of Buddhism in the eighth and ninth centuries was quite severe. By the later imperial age of the Ming and Qing dynasties, however, a saying had taken root that is quite telling, even to the present, in a China where religious practice is not officially recognized: *Sanjiao heyi*—the three teachings (*Ru,* or "Confucian" thought, Daoism, and Buddhism) merge into one.

This was often described in memorable ways, to represent a day in a life, or a life itself: In the morning, it is said, we are bustling, frenzied Confucians, striving for order in our lives and hoping to accomplish a great deal. By afternoon, however, as we begin to tire, we take on the thoughts of a Daoist, wondering what the rush and hurry is all about, and perhaps trying to find a way to perpetuate the relaxed feelings of the afternoon. Finally, by evening, we tire and will soon be asleep. The Buddhist focus on the transience of life overtakes us as we drift off to sleep.

Whether described in terms of a day or a life, the intertwined doctrines of China have withstood the test of time. Many people still tend to think of their lives as "blends" of traditions, not a single overarching one. Not even the new ideas that took root in China in the late 1940s, and beyond, with the rule of the Communist Party have shaken the power of syncretism in daily religious life.

A fellowship adviser at my college once counseled me against studying Chinese religious practices, telling me that they were destroyed in the Cultural Revolution. That is quite untrue, even though it would be equally foolish to say that traditional religious practices (indigenous and Western) are thriving in China today. Roman Catholic churches are open in Shanghai and other cities, but some followers have been harassed by officials. Popular Daoist cults remain in practice on the southeast China coast. As we will see in the section on popular culture, many traditional practices are so ingrained that it is hard to trace their roots to Buddhism or Daoism. Governmental persecution is real, but religious practices remain alive. These kinds of statements have perplexed many readers, and I hope at least to give a sense of what they mean in a broad, cultural sense.

Those who argue that Communist ideology has terminated what we call religious beliefs in China misunderstand on at least two fundamental levels. First, it is an extremely short-sighted perspective. All of the major religious practices—Buddhism and Daoism in particular—have endured fierce persecutions, only to emerge later with renewed strength. Although it was challenging, the second half of the twentieth century was arguably not the harshest period such religions have endured. Second, to assert the end of religion in China is a profound misunderstanding of the way that religious beliefs are intertwined with life as it has been lived in China for centuries, even millennia. Family rituals that make up a great amount of what we might call Confucian religious belief are so much a part of living as a father or a son (or a part of any other family relationship) that it is difficult to imagine them dropping from sight. To be sure, the one-child policy and economic changes will have an impact, but this is not the first period in Chinese history in which traditional practices have been challenged.

Another example is the examinations that were discussed in the previous section. Five hundred years ago, in the middle of the Ming dynasty, parents and loved ones would go to temples to pray for the success of an aspiring candidate. Today, one sees similar practices aimed at ensuring that a son or daughter (or grandson or granddaughter) will emerge from the college entrance examinations, or get into a prestigious university such as Qinghua in Beijing or Fudan in Shanghai. What I have called elsewhere "a rhetoric of fate and future" is alive in these practices, and they are far from needing churches or other edifices to work. They are built into the practice of daily life.

A final category worth noting is the "religious" groups about which the Chinese government is most worried. Falun Gong is one that has gotten a good deal of press, and the outside observer might well wonder what all the fuss is about. A martial arts cult with supernatural overtones is something that many Westerners might think of as an exotic, idiosyncratic side issue when it comes to matters of political power. Such groups have often worried Chinese governments in the past, however, and several have directly contributed to the overthrow of dynasties. Secret societies tied to various martial arts and supernatural powers were significant parts of the Red Eyebrows movement in the first century, the Yellow Turban uprising in the second century, and countless others throughout China's imperial history. In just the past two hundred years, in fact, there have been significant threats from the White Lotus Rebellion (late eighteenth century), the Taiping Rebellion (mid-eighteenth century), and the Boxer Rebellion (early twentieth century). Even if overthrowing the current order was not the goal (as in the latter case), they have often had a highly destabilizing effect.

The point here is not to condone the Chinese government's actions but rather to place them in an historical perspective that gives them context. It is sometimes difficult for Westerners to see why *organized* religious movements (whether or not they are institutionalized in a broader sense, as is the Catholic Church) send warning signals, and have for centuries, to those in power, while the individual practices Westerners would also call "religious" are mostly seen as a normal part of daily life. The classical Chinese phrase *shehui,* "gathering at the grain shrine," has become the modern Chinese phrase for "society." Groups are perceived as powerful and, potentially, as threats. By gathering, whether for the purpose of sharing political opinions or common worship, individuals become greater than the sum of their parts, and the Chinese government has always taken notice. There is a kind of cruel consistency to the reactions of autocratic governments throughout Chinese history in this, and it opens new ways of interpreting religious life.

Literature

The Chinese literary tradition is one that has for millennia mixed our themes of continuity and change. The earliest writing in China can be found on oracle bones, (mentioned in Chapter 1) where early scribes created short divination texts to gauge heaven's will in matters of importance to the state or the ruling family. The development of the Chinese script and a compressed literary style continued apace and, by the time we reach the fifth century B.C.E., we can see the development of a literature in which ideas were read, quoted, refined, even turned upside down. The lively philosophical disputes of the late Spring and Autumn and Warring States periods (c. 550–250 B.C.E.) was important in the growth of Chinese literature as well as philosophy and ruling. To use a basic example mentioned in Chapter 1, both Mencius and Zhuangzi expanded upon the brief texts of earlier writers to create extended arguments that carried many strands of complexity. Both are also read today as fine examples of classical prose style.

The Chinese poetic tradition is closely tied to the writing of prose, and just one reason among many is that educated individuals saw poetry as a natural part of their intellectual lives. Most wrote in a series of prose forms that ranged from highly personal reflections to very formal public documents, and then they would compose poems during their travels or in moments of leisure. The other key literary distinction lies within prose. Classical, or literary, Chinese (*wenyan*) was the language of the highly educated and was employed in all official correspondence and the examinations themselves. Writing in the vernacular (in the manner in which one spoke) was not acceptable in most official settings. Vernacular prose did begin to take root during the Southern Song dynasty (1127–1279) and eventually formed an important dimension of later imperial literature, but classical expression remained the key to literary success.

It is important to point out, however, that there is not an absolute divide between "classical" and "vernacular" writing. One thing that students find most perplexing in their reading of Chinese is the many classical phrases and allusions that appear in contemporary writing. These range from the use of grammatical particles that have their roots in classical usage all the way to themes from important literary works dating back to the early myths, histories, and philosophical works discussed earlier. (Such references are challenging in any language, of course. Many Western readers are puzzled by contemporary references to scenes in the *Iliad,* or from Plato's *Republic* or *Symposium.* Indeed, references to passages from the works of Shakespeare or the King James Bible can be difficult for many, even though they formed a common literary background for readers of

English only a few generations ago. Language from the epic poem *Beowulf* and Geoffrey Chaucer's *Canterbury Tales* can be positively forbidding.)

Chinese readers have a relationship to their literary past that few Westerners possess, and this goes far beyond the stereotypical observation that the Chinese care more about their history than do other civilizations. The first is that the tradition is continuous, and it is seen by many as a single "river" of literary culture. Far more important, however, is the fact that the Chinese characters themselves have masked the enormous changes in the language over many centuries. Readers of English will note challenges in texts only a few centuries old. The Chinese writing system gives the *appearance* of being consistent for more than two *millennia*.

I can sit down to read the *Shiji* (Historical Records) of the great historian and prose stylist Sima Qian, who wrote in the second and early first century B.C.E.. As long as I have a solid grasp of the grammatical constructions used in literary Chinese, it will appear to be a similar language to what I might read in an eighteenth-century text. The fact that characters don't match changes in speech patterns creates the illusion that the literary tradition is timeless and accessible. A fellow graduate student from China once told me in rather abrupt fashion that "I can read everything from the oracle bones down to today's newspapers with equal ease." If the language were an alphabetic representation of the spoken language, that would be impossible. In short, the Chinese have both an incredible advantage and a powerful illusion in this "masking," for it makes even those with high-school educations closer to the rich tradition of China's literary past than most Westerners can ever be with theirs.

For that reason, even the language of contemporary China is overlain with references to classical events, scenes, and phrases. Up until the twentieth century, every well-educated Chinese reader had not merely worked through a wide variety of challenging texts, he hadn't even just studied them very carefully; he had *memorized* them. Those readers who have memorized texts in the past will know their power. Memorized phrases are always at the ready and in two ways that are extremely significant for the understanding of Chinese literature. First, they create what one of my professors liked to call an "*aha!* effect." Reading along in a narrative, one catches sight of a passage memorized years ago, and the instant recognition solidifies a bond between reader, text, and tradition. Second, for writers, the use of memorized phrases can give what would otherwise be a personal "take" on a subject a weight of authority and precedent.

This is not always for the better. One of the greatest criticisms of traditional "examination style" education in China was that it was so heavily-laden with classical allusion and historical precedent that it detracted from positive, present-minded solutions to problems. The important thing to remember, though, is that direct prose writing was possible (and not uncommon) in the Chinese past, and snatches of memorized material remain a part of literary life today—even in reading a daily newspaper. Perhaps the most common is the use of *chengyu* (sometimes translated as "idioms," but meaning much more than the English term). These little phrases are usually four characters long and pack whole stories, situations, and classical allusions into them. They are so common, and so important, that one of my students, whose Chinese ability was already at a very high level, said that if he had more time in China he would devote himself solely to studying *chengyu*. Without a good grasp of them, he felt that his ability to function in contemporary China was limited.

A brief example will have to suffice here. Throughout Chinese history there are examples of two strong figures vying for power. The story line of the opera in the film *Farewell My Concubine* has two leaders at the beginning of the Han dynasty fighting for control of China. As readers may recall from Chapter 1, Liu Bang won and became the founder of the Han Dynasty; Xiang Yu, the king of Chu, lost. *Lianghu xiangdou*—"two tigers mutually contending" or "two tigers fighting"—goes the phrase, and everyone listening or reading would immediately grasp the situation, the precedents, and the power of a short phrase in a language that has continuity and precision. Even more interesting is the almost-always unstated phrase that follows: (When two tigers fight) *one is sure to lose.* In just the week before writing this passage, I have used or heard that single phrase four times in conversations ranging from Chinese history to American politics. I have been teaching *chengyu* in my classes for years, and they are one of the best windows available to understanding the themes of continuity and change in Chinese culture. Hundred are used almost daily, and thousands are listed in comprehensive *chengyu* dictionaries that remain quite popular in Chinese bookstores.

Chinese literary history has another dimension that separates it from other traditions. Whether it is a fair characterization or not, each dynastic period has come to be associated with the development of a specific literary genre. There are problems with such schemes, of course, but there is much we can learn from this traditional representation. To begin, we have the myths and legends discussed in Chapter 1. To this day, virtually everyone in China understands these references. Following that, we have the development of the Five Classics, which deal with poetry, ritual, government documents, and even a narrative of the tiny state of Lu during the Zhou period, said to be authored by Confucius himself.

The Han dynasty is known for the development of a sophisticated historical prose championed by Sima Qian and Ban Gu, who in their two voluminous works (separated by about a century in composition) brought the narrative of Chinese history up to the present— two millennia ago. For Western readers accustomed to thinking of "history" as a dry recitation of names and dates, it is important to realize that history was first among the genres of writing in China. It was the medium many felt best suited to a flowing and memorable prose style. One must think of the writing of history in China as the very finest example of *literature.* In fact, when critics praised books from the much later Ming dynasty, they often did so by noting how much like the narrative of Sima Qian's *Historical Records* the novels were.

The development of poetry followed similar lines but far more profoundly mixed the experience of life in the fields with that of life at court. From the *Classic of Poetry* to southern verse called *Chuci* ("Lyrics of Chu"), the sorrows of individuals and their experiences of life predominate. In the Han dynasty, the government bureau of music collected *fu,* a combination of rhyme and prose on small details of life—precisely the kind of theme that was often lost when writers sought to address "weightier" topics. All of these created a precedent in poetic writing that would not be nearly as powerful a part of prose writing: a playful quality that could be an outlet for even the most serious of writers. To be sure, much Chinese poetry deals with refined literary themes, but the potential for spontaneity was always there.

This can best be seen in the contrast between Li Bo (Li Po) and Du Fu (Tu Fu) in the Tang dynasty. Chinese students read these writers in school, and everyone who has learned to read will know stories about them. Living at about the same time during what began as a flourishing period of the Tang, and then enduring the An Lushan Rebellion and its aftermath, both writers showed their quite varied personalities through times of joy as well as trouble. Li Bo (701–762) is known to many as exuberant, and one of his most famous poems,

"Drinking Alone beneath the Moon," describes his companionship with the moon when it comes out at night as he drinks. His shadow gives him a drinking companion.

> Among the flowers, a jug of wine
>
> Drinking alone, no companions accompany me.
>
> Raising my cup, I beckon the luminous moon.
>
> My shadow makes us three.
>
> Yet the moon, in the end, was unable to drink.

Du Fu (712–770) is a good deal more sullen, and the beauty of his poems certainly carries a sadness as well. One of my Chinese students recently told me that Du Fu is "just too sad." Sad, but beautiful. In fact, my cousin's husband (he was born in Shanghai) told me that he reads Du Fu's poetry to his young daughter. I was both happy and concerned. On the one hand, she will have an appreciation of a magnificent poet. On the other, the tone is so wistful, so mournful, that one wonders about her state of mind! This poem, too, deals with the moon, but in a melancholy manner. Affected by the great rebellion, Du Fu's moon in "Evening Moonlight" is not the companion found by Li Bo.

> This evening, under the Fuzhou moon
>
> My wife gazes alone from her chamber.
>
> Distant sorrow I feel for my little sons and daughters.
>
> They do not remember me, in Chang'an.
>
> The fragrant mist wets her cloudlike hair
>
> Under the clear moonlight, her jadelike arms chill.
>
> When again shall we lean together by the empty curtain
>
> Gazing at the moon, our tears drying on our cheeks?

A flowing lyric style emerged in the late Tang dynasty and the early Song. In the thriving entertainment quarters in cities such as Hangzhou, which numbered over a million residents by the twelfth century, courtesans and scholars would meet to drink and talk. The subject matter and tone of the lyrics they wrote dealt with matters far removed from official life. They were composed by writers who set down lyrics as singing girls in the entertainment quarters sang and played instruments. Even as they were often filled with emotion, they were not taken as seriously by scholars as their other writing, but the lyrics have lasted (and have an impact on the twenty-first century literary world) in a way that most of their other writings have not. The light-hearted touch, imagery, and emotional themes have made them a lasting presence in Chinese literature.

Above all, Song lyrics (the pun works beautifully in English, if not in Chinese) were words linked to popular tunes. They were meant to be sung, and the titles often begin with the phrase "To the Tune of . . .." The rhymes and the rhythms of the lyrics were intimately connected to popular music, and though we no longer have the tunes on which they were based, the musical connection is evident in the cadences and the titles—even the imagery in many places.

New words were written—and these at the brush of highly literate, deeply read individuals—to fit the original melodies. The best contemporary example I could give would be lyrics written in a teeming environment of literary intelligence and musical knowledge to the tunes of "Yesterday," "American Pie," and "Stairway to Heaven." One can often find images of scholar, singer, and tune embedded within these rhythmical little narratives, as in these lyrics written by Yan Jidao (1030–1106) to the tune of *Transcendent by the River:*

> After my dream, sealed away in my tower
>
> My drunkenness abated, blinds lowered,
>
> Last spring's grief returns again.
>
> Blossoms fading, she stands alone.
>
> Light rain falling, swallows fly in pairs
>
> I remember the first time I saw little *Pin*
>
> Two "hearts" embroidered on her silken garments,
>
> Strumming her *pipa*, she sang of our mutual desires.
>
> Now the same luminous moon shines
>
> That shone when the elegant clouds returned.

The writer's pain sets the lyric's tone, but we then have an image of his first encounter with "little Pin," a term of endearment for his lost lover. Strumming the *pipa*, exuding emotions that scholars would often not admit, she is the other side of the lyric's growth in the Song dynasty. One has to imagine the synergy, the connection, between a musically gifted woman and a deeply learned man who would never have such easy rapport within a traditional household. These entertainment quarters were places of escape, and the blending of word, image, and melody was its result.

Another literary form that has lasted into the present is the drama, which reached its height in the Southern Song and Yuan dynasties. Although Beijing opera has had its challenges in the twentieth century (as many readers will know from the film *Farewell My Concubine*), it has re-emerged as a popular entertainment in the capital and beyond. Some of the Yuan dynasty plays themselves have become literary texts of great distinction and have inspired remakes in the theater (and, more recently, on television dramas that go on for many weeks). Among these are the *Xixiang ji* (*Western Chamber Romance*), the *Mudan ting* (*Peony Pavilion*), and the *Taohua shan* (*Peach Blossom Fan*). Chinese audiences have been attuned to dramatic performances for centuries, and market towns on busy trading days were a popular place for the acting of dramas by local troupes. The larger cities were always places for staging more elaborate productions, and that is just as true today as it was five centuries ago. Just weeks before this writing, there were only scalped tickets available to Shanghai performances put on by a well-known Taiwan troupe of the *Western Chamber Romance* and the *Peach Blossom Fan*.

Any discussion of literature as it relates to the Chinese world today must deal with the fiction of the Ming and Qing dynasties. By the fifteenth century, literacy rates had expanded in China, and there were many more candidates for examinations who had studied classical texts and the poetic tradition we've discussed than would ever find employment. The development of printing over almost five centuries had contributed to this as well. There was a new readership that was open to a nuanced set of texts that told a good story (even "retold" it), with layers of philosophical meaning and literary crafting (even the "*aha!* effect" noted above). Written in a mix of classical and vernacular prose, but filled with allusions to all of the traditions that have been mentioned in this section (snatches of plays, quotations from poems, phrases from the classics), these novels and short stories "rewrote" tales that readers "knew" from their earlier studies for the examinations, with a far "less serious" subject matter. They are dense, and each runs either 100 or 120 chapters. In English translations (and virtually all have excellent ones now) they each run to well over a thousand pages.

The earliest, and still most famous, is the *Sanguo yanyi* (*The Romance of the Three Kingdoms*). Based on historical texts of that famous period, the novel retells a tale of intrigue and loyalty at the end of the Han dynasty. As noted in chapter 1, everyone today knows the major figures of these periods, and several are so famous as to figure into *chengyu* and other popular sayings. The "raciest" of the Ming novels also is the one least well-known. The *Jinping mei* (*The Plum in the Golden Vase*) is the tale of the rise and fall of a degenerate household. It is more than occasionally lewd, and sometimes it is downright raunchy. More often, it is beautifully evocative, even as it tells a tale of destruction in a flawed family. Although it is still difficult to obtain in China, the English translation is brilliant, and it was the inspiration for the author of China's greatest novel, the *Honglou meng* (*Dream of the Red Chamber; Story of the Stone*). That Qing dynasty novel is a more delicately told tale of the slow decline of a prominent family, and the love (and love lost) of one of the most tragic couples in all of Chinese literature. The *Rulin waishi* (*The Scholars*) is a satiric glimpse at traditional education, and makes entertaining reading for those interested in how some in China viewed their own educational system.

The tale that is most deeply filled with religious meaning is also the best-loved, since it has been the backdrop for countless storytelling sessions within families and the most breathtaking of opera scenes. These center on the Monkey King and the novel *Xiyou ji* (*The Journey to the West*). Many of my Chinese friends have told me about the ways their parents and grandparents related this story of the arduous journey taken by a monk and his companions (including "Monkey") to India to gather sacred scriptures (and tame the wild "Monkey Mind"). Finally, the *Shuihu zhuan* (*Outlaws of the Marsh*) is a long novel about a group of bandits and their Robin Hood-like quest for social and even economic justice in the face of government corruption. They are "good," even as they defy a government they regard as corrupt.

Writers of the twentieth century have struggled with all of the issues that we have encountered in this section. How important is the weight of tradition in the writing of contemporary literature? To what extent do classical allusions or phrases from poetry enhance a modern writer's work? One of the greatest questions has been the writing of fiction in the vernacular, drastically cutting the use of classical prose style in writing. It is important to note that some of the fiercest critics of traditional style were not connected in any significant way to the Communist movement that led to the establishment of the People's Republic of China. Writers such as Lu Xun and Ba Jin in the 1920s and 1930s were responding more to the calls for reform found in the late nineteenth century and the inspiration of the May Fourth Movement than any more fundamental change in the nature of ruling the Chinese people. Their stories are crisp and often incisive, with a critique of earlier culture that is in many ways far more withering than what would be found in the "People's Revolution" several decades later.

Although the writing of literature (not unlike religious practice and educational policy) has had a trying time in the twentieth century, it is important to note the power of tradition and the enormous possibilities for change. One sees it in writing today. In fact, not unlike open religious practice, one senses a wariness on the part of writers at the changes that took place in almost every decade of the past century. The literature that emerged in the late 1970s and the 1980s (before Tian'anmen) is an interesting case in point. It is as though writers were trying to find their voices while keeping a wary eye on the receptivity of both the public and the authorities. One can see in much of that literature a complex relationship between short stories, national political discussion, and a changing readership.

The writers who have gained fairly wide readership never strayed far from political issues. One Western critic stated in the foreword to a book on the subject that the "dull orthodoxy" of the material makes for challenging reading. Although this hardly seems to be strong motivation for readers, the point is well taken—such literature is worthy of careful consideration by students of Chinese society precisely because of its place in decades of profound change. Indeed, the stories themselves often represent elaborate literary dances in relation to "official" thought and popular opinion. Perhaps the most dramatic case is that of critic-turned-writer Li Jian, whose 1979 essay "'Praising Virtue' and 'Lacking Virtue'" provoked an overwhelmingly negative response from readers. Within six months, however, Li had written almost a dozen stories that were more sensational, more sexual, and more violent than anything he had criticized. Although many of Li's critics accused him of hypocrisy and "double think," is it really any surprise that writers might shift with the winds of political change in a turbulent century? Educational policies have shifted, religious sects have gone underground, and writers have changed opinions in the flow of continuity and abrupt change.

Popular Culture

The somewhat vague term *popular culture* is often used by writers to refer to "everything else" that is not covered by religion, literature, history, and other topics similar to those in this book. With the growing affluence found in many households within China today, many new forms of entertainment are now available. This is just one of the reasons why such pursuits as reading and composing poetry, attending operatic performances, and reading long, 100-chapter novels has been supplemented by television, radio, magazines, and that import from Japan, karaoke. Like our other topics, however, there is both great change and an impressive continuity at work. One recent evening walk starting from the area called the Bund along the Huangpu River in Shanghai revealed a great array of popular cultural activities, and certainly more than would have been found five centuries ago or, perhaps more significantly, even thirty years ago.

My walk began on Nanjing East Road, which is filled with the effects of globalization. The department stores are stocked with new fashions, and Western fast food restaurants are mixed with venerable Chinese establishments, some dating back to Shanghai's heyday in the 1920s and 1930s. It is also where I passed what can only be called a tribute to shopping—a bronze statue of a woman with a large purse and a child in tow, which is a popular photo spot for Chinese and Western tourists. I walked quickly through side streets filled with fruit stands, dumpling sellers, and little barber shops until I found Fuzhou Road. There, in front of a closed office complex, I saw perhaps forty men and women in their fifties, sixties, and seventies on folding lawn chairs, fanning themselves and watching passersby. When the skies opened for a brief shower, they hurried with their chairs under an overhang before moving them back into the open. Further down the road, I walked into a six-story bookstore, "Book City," filled with people reading guidebooks for travel within China and beyond, cookbooks, traditional literature (including at least a dozen different editions of the Ming novels mentioned above), English-language works, and how-to manuals. I was amazed by how many shoppers had large plastic grocery baskets of books at the checkout counters.

From there, I walked away from the major shopping networks and thoroughfares. I found Western-style, twenty-four-hour convenience stores (common throughout Asia) as well as small storefronts, open well into the night, selling an assortment of fruits, snacks, and liquor. As I passed by businesses that had been open just hours before, I saw half-closed sliding doors allowing glimpses of tables and people playing cards or mahjong. Many had televisions on, and some were watching intently. As I walked through trendier sections, I saw all-night bars, karaoke centers, and late-night noodle and dumpling counters.

In short, I found a similar range of activities to what I might find walking through any other major city in the world. Only the details were different. In rural locations, one sees less variety, perhaps, but the effect is the same. Ordinary people shape their days and structure their activities in ways that we too often take for granted in our studies. As discussed earlier in this chapter, there are rhythms built into the day, the week, the month, and the year in China that are little known to Westerners. The activities I have just mentioned are only the outer shell of these patterns. Readers will surely note the way that their own lives are "paced" through a weekday, a work week, or a weekend. More important, there are yearly patterns that we often take for granted, but have an enormous effect on the way we structure our personal and social lives.

Far from being a thing of the past that died with the arrival of a more "modern" China, there remains a style of life for many people that is tied to the cycles of the moon. This is certainly true in Hong Kong, Taiwan, Southeast Asia, and many cities in the West with large Chinese populations. What people tend not to realize is that this "lunar rhythm" is alive in both rural and urban China. Although it has become quite common for people in China to refer to the Western calendar dates, the cycles of the moon remain very important in the timing of family activities. One of the best known of these is the full moon on the eighth lunar month (this usually falls sometime in September). It is a day for enjoying the full moon, drinking tea, and eating "mooncakes" (*yuebing*). Other important lunar holidays include "Tomb-Sweeping" Day and the Dragon Boat Festival. Each has a long tradition that remains alive today.

I will touch upon a few major themes in Chinese popular culture that have remained continuous from early times all the way to the present, and then conclude with several examples that represent a marked break with the past. We will look at the calendar, lucky (or "auspicious") days, lucky directions and *fengshui,* as well as the concept of lucky numbers. The key points are these. Every single one of these practices has deep philosophical roots in early China and has been a part of studies by some of the greatest minds in Chinese history. Every one of the themes has also taken on more commonplace overtones over the centuries. Finally, every single one of them is alive today, and not only within the borders of the People's Republic of China. As the contributors to this book have repeated throughout these pages, the government one finds in China today represents both a break with the past and a powerful continuation of it. It is no different in popular culture than it is in politics, economics, or history.

Chinese almanacs and calendars have been published for centuries. Indeed, it is true that the calendars one can buy in Hong Kong, Singapore, or Chicago are similar in overall form to those printed during the Ming dynasty, five hundred years ago. Calendars available for purchase elsewhere in China or in Taiwan have a different appearance, but similar information within them. When examining a traditional Chinese calendar and almanac, what strikes the observer first is the initial section, printed in red characters, that contains a cowherd and the spring festival ox—giving a general picture of the coming year's weather, not unlike what one might see (without ox and cowherd) in an American *Farmer's Almanac*. This is followed by a geomancer's (*fengshui*) compass and details concerning important directions for the coming year. Further sections in red characters (a sign that the details change from year to year) are a series of calendar charts that organize astrological and even governmental information from the past two centuries. One has to turn to the back of the volume to find the actual calendar, with a separate column for each day of the year, and characters in red and black ink. Together, these pages represent the daily reference "bookends" of the almanac. These sections are the reason people need to buy new almanacs in the late months of the year, and it is still the work of calendar specialists to put together an accurate and, one might say, compelling calendar for personal and family reference. One can find them in the autumn and winter in any city's Chinatown, and I buy mine every year at an Asian grocery store in Madison, Wisconsin.

Complete with month-by-month and day-by-day breakdowns, current calendars are divided into as many as eight sections. The calendar has traditionally figured prominently in everything from family decisions and business negotiations to government activities and the planning of large events. For example, days on which one would get engaged, marry, or hold a funeral were almost always consulted, *even if a person felt that the book was "superstitious."* Why? Because so many others followed the practices, it was difficult (without appearing arrogant) for an individual to choose an "unlucky" day for an important event. It mattered to others, even if it did not for the individual. (Think of a similar situation in American society. Imagine an atheist among very devout Christians. How "easy" would it be to have a nondenominational funeral service for a beloved family member?) By no means did everyone accept such customs, even in earlier centuries. Social pressures helped perpetuate practices as much as the beliefs themselves.

The most important parts of the Chinese calendar for popular cultural practices are the items to avoid and items best-suited to any given day. There are several days a month on which it is unlucky to cut one's hair or clip one's nails. Mixing sauces or digging wells also have prohibitions. In fact, it is startling to see how popular the almanac and calendar remain in urban areas such as Hong Kong, Taipei, Singapore, Shanghai, and Beijing, when a large proportion of activities in these sections is clearly linked to life in an agricultural setting. The "activities to do" section on any given day might well include "study" (*ruxue*). In fact, after looking at every almanac for the past two decades, and many from much earlier periods, I have never seen a day in which the calendar notes that it is unlucky to study. There are good (and bad) days to move one's house, bury the dead, go on long (or short) trips, and put up beams in a shed. The activities give a fascinating perspective of daily life and its domestic rhythms.

Although the calendar is the reason people buy new almanacs every year, it is impossible, while paging through the more than forty sections that make up the larger versions of the book, to miss the rich array of cultural information embedded within it. These sections are of varying importance and historical distance from the present, but they provide a window on concerns for what I have already called "fate and future" in Chinese life. It is in these middle sections that one finds the most interesting illustrations in the almanac. Aside from the very first and last pages, the calendar information is not illustrated. These middle sections contain descriptions of dreams, omens, bad luck, small-business management, and numerous fortune-telling charts. There is even an English pronunciation guide. In these illustrations one sees a clear connection between text and picture, often in the *bantu* (half-picture) format that made the book at least somewhat accessible for a wide range of people in a household, even those who couldn't read well.

In addition to sections on charms, agricultural information, and the sections of folk wisdom mentioned above, one finds a series of divination sections of widely varying seriousness. Many of these sections are intended, from their own introductions, to give a small "glimpse" of the characteristics of future events in a person's life. These sections serve similar functions to the fortune-telling booths and popular divination activities that one can find virtually anywhere in the Chinese-speaking world (or the Western world, as well, with its telephone psychics). It is easy to mistake many of these activities (and their corresponding almanac sections) for extremely serious inquiry into the future. That, however, has always been the role of professional astrologers, who would go far beyond the sections of the almanac to link personal fate and future for their clients.

So why would anyone in China today buy a calendar or go to a fortune teller? Admittedly, it is easier to find fortune tellers in the trade centers of Hong Kong, Singapore, Taipei, or even large cities in the Western world than it is in Shanghai, Beijing, or much smaller cities. They exist, however, in spite of the protestations one might hear that these beliefs are dead. I offer three brief examples—one from Taiwan and two from the People's Republic of China. While working for a computer company fifteen years ago in Taiwan, I had a female colleague who had recently graduated from college. She was good at her job, yet (and this was before I started studying these matters for a living) she would come back from lunch quite often, with her latest "read" from a fortune teller. I asked her how someone so well-educated could believe such "nonsense."

I had no sense then of the subtlety of these issues. Her answer intrigued me, leading me to study what some people call "superstition" in Western and Chinese culture. She said that she liked being single, but she was being pressured to marry. She wanted to "get a feel" for what might come. That phrase, "to get a feel," seemed far away from questions of what might happen in one's life. How could one "get a feel" for the future? But that is entirely the point, and it is not the kind of thing that can be understood in ways many of us would call "logical." One must shift one's thinking. The best advice I could give is to think about it as I instruct my students in class. Do they walk under ladders? Do they know people who do? If they do, do they think about it, or is it "natural?" The questions go on and on, and in much more thorough fashion than we can cover here. The point is, however, that these are not "easy" questions of "gullibility" or "reason," as I, too, once believed they were. There is so much "culture" wrapped up in the middle that it is impossible to sort the "reason" from the rest.

These themes are alive in the People's Republic of China as well. People still talk of the ill-fated "double eight" year of 1976 (a common feature of the lunar calendar in which a month is "repeated" to bring it into line with the solar calendar). That year Mao Zedong died and there were major floods throughout China. Almost twenty years later people speculated that 1995 would be the year of Deng Xiaoping's death—it was the first "double eight" year since Mao died (Deng lived two more years, dying in 1997). Another very common example is the pictures taxi drivers in Beijing had of Mao in the 1980s and 1990s. He had become a minor god of taxi drivers because, it is said, a driver survived a horrific accident because he was one of the few at the time to have had a Mao picture on his dashboard.

Such ideas are also seen by the fact that businesses pay a great deal of money for "auspicious" phone numbers that play on the numerical symbolism of early Chinese thought, and that geomancy, known as *fengshui,* has become an international phenomenon. Although the social and political landscape has changed dramatically, and there is by no means a unified voice in these matters, the "language of fate" that I referred to earlier in this section is a vital part of everyday life in China (and in our own lives as well). This can be seen in cultural ideas about directions and numbers.

It seems that there are as many English-language books these days with *fengshui* in the title as *Dao (Tao).* It has become associated with what many call "Eastern" thought. What is *fengshui* and why has it captured so many imaginations?

It would be no exaggeration to say that the best thinkers in earlier Chinese society studied matters of *fengshui* and, at the same time, criticized nonscholars who used it. They often described the methods of determining burial directions as confusing and deceptive—a waste of the people's energy. Yet the Ming tombs just north of Beijing are laid out in exquisite geomantic (*fengshui*) fashion, with nothing left to chance. One of my friends has noted that party members always seem to have houses with excellent *fengshui* and lucky telephone numbers. Foolishness? Perhaps.

Numbers are, in fact, a powerful cultural issue in China (and are a larger part of Western life than many realize). As early as the third century B.C.E., several thinkers were articulating the power of numbers. The categories of *yin* and *yang* were at work in these conceptions, but they ran much deeper to include ideas contained in the challenging text, the *Yijing (I-Ching).* What we call "even" numbers were *yin,* and "odd" numbers were *yang.* Just as in the West (but for completely different reasons), the number three is a powerful symbol, in this case of *yang* strength. Numbers related to it carry even more power. Thus, the number nine is one that holds great symbolic value, because it is three squared. The number twenty-seven is also seen as one that is "more than counting," as I often tell my classes. Still, it is the number eighty-one (3^4) that packs an even more powerful punch in Chinese life. Some novels have eighty-one chapters, while others have eighty-one challenges that the hero must face. An example from more recent times comes from the nineteenth-century reformer Zeng Guofan, who wrote a treatise that was meant to help bridge the *tiyong,* or "Eastern Ethics, Western Science" gap, in the mid-nineteenth century. The title? *Eighty-one Loyal Admonitions.*

Advertisement for the 2008 Summer Olympics in Beijing (Bruce Connolly/ CORBIS)

An even more current example can be found in hotel rooms and phone numbers. The number four is a homonym for "death." The characters don't look anything at all alike, yet they are pronounced the same way. For that reason, saying or hearing "four" in most dialects can make people uncomfortable. The fourth floor is traditionally skipped (as some Western buildings do the thirteenth). Even more perplexing is the habit of putting Westerners on the fourth floor. My colleague on a recent trip to Beijing was put in room 20442. In some dialects, that sounds like "You dead, dead—you," and it is the reason why some hospitals change room number 244 ("you dead dead") to "2C4" or something similar.

When my colleague mentioned this to a Chinese friend (after hearing my explanation), she got a very interesting response. "True, but that's *our culture*. It's not *yours.*" The Chinese friend interpreted it not as an act of ill will but rather as a cultural anomaly that no Westerner would take seriously. Another example is the fascination in China with the "lucky" number 666, which in Western culture holds a Satanic reference that renders it unliked by some. I once had a waitress in Waterville, Maine, ring up my breakfast tab as "$6.66." She immediately changed color and said she was terribly, terribly sorry.

Beijing McDonald's restaurant (Julia Waterlow; Eye Ubiquitous/CORBIS)

Those numbers, however, are the essence of *yin* beauty in China, and it is an address or phone prefix to which companies aspire. They also pay big money for good numbers. No cab company wants "444," of course. A beautiful mix of *yin* and *yang* numbers is not just a "superstitious" way of "feeling good." There really is a bottom line to it. Companies pay very large amounts of money—today, in a China that has eschewed superstition—for phone numbers and even addresses that will be "good for business."

One final example should suffice. I have often asked students and colleagues in the West, particularly the United States, if they can think of one person who is so "bottom line," so obsessed with making a profit, that superstition would never enter his or her thoughts. The vast majority, even without prompting, say "Donald Trump." More than ten years ago, though, *CBS News* ran a feature on a Trump enterprise in New York's Chinatown. The apartment complex was, for the most part, empty. In the end, the practical, "hard-nosed," and "bottom-line" Donald Trump spent US $250,000 to call in *fengshui* experts to improve the buildings' directional influences, and the apartments started selling. If ever there was an example of popular culture overriding even the staunchest critic, this may be it.

With the awarding of the Olympics to Beijing in 2008, and the increasing affluence of many Chinese households, there are many new possibilities in Chinese popular culture. One of my students recently befriended a young man obsessed with "extreme sports" and ESPN. Skateboarders can be seen where there is pavement and relatively few people. For that matter, there have been more "Olympic" sports on television than have appeared in recent years. The internet, for all of its challenges in China (the Google Web site was shut down for a period by the government just days before I wrote this), remains an important wild card in popular culture and represents a very serious challenge to the government. Perhaps this is the place to tie together the themes of this section and to note the continuing interest in printed texts, the fact that the texts often come from abroad without license, and the extreme wariness of a government that is not in control of that medium. "Themes in Chinese Culture" may seem like a catch-all to round out more "practical" matters of history, economics, politics, and society, but education, religion, literature, and popular culture lie at the heart of a changing China. The themes are interwoven in ways that cannot easily be explained. Like Chinese boxes, each discovery brings with it a new opportunity. The past is dead, as many critics from the nineteenth century onward have claimed (or hoped). And the past is everywhere. The only constant is a flowing river of continuity and change.

References
Ahern, Emily. *The Cult of the Dead in a Chinese Village.* Stanford: Stanford University Press, 1973.

Ba Jin, *Family.* Hong Kong: Cheng and Tsui, 1992.

Barme, Geremie, and Linda Jarvin. *New Ghosts, Old Dreams* Chinese Rebel Voices. New York: Times Books, 1992.

Bodde, Derk, and M. L. C. Bogan. *Annual Customs and Festivals in Peking with Manchu Customs and Superstitions.* Taipei: SMC Publishing, 1986.

Cave, Roderick. *Chinese Paper Offerings.* Oxford: Oxford University Press, 1998.

Chan, Anita, Jonathan Unger, and Richard P. Madsen. *Chen Village under Mao and Deng.* Berkeley: University of California Press, 1984.

Cheng, Francois, *Chinese Poetic Writing.* Bloomington: Indiana University Press, 1982.

Chiang Yee. *Chinese Calligraphy.* Cambridge, Mass.: Harvard University Press, 1938.

Chow, Rey. *Primitive Passions.* New York: Columbia University Press, 1995.

Croll, Elisabeth. *Changing Identities of Chinese Women.* London: Zed Books, 1995.

Davis, Deborah, and Stevan Harrell, eds. *Chinese Families in the Post-Mao Era.* Berkeley: University of California Press, 1993.

De Glopper, Donald R. "Doing Business in Lukang," in Arthur P. Wolf (ed.), *Studies in Chinese Society.* Palo Alto: Stanford University Press, 1978, pp. 291–320.

Dean, Kenneth. *Taoist Ritual and Popular Cults of Southeast China.* Princeton: Princeton University Press, 1993.

DeFrancis, John. *The Chinese Language.* Honolulu: University of Hawaii Press, 1986.

Dikotter, Frank. *The Discourse of Race in Modern China.* Stanford: Stanford University Press, 1992.

Eberhard, Wolfram. *A Dictionary of Chinese Symbols.* London: Routledge, 1986.

Ebrey, Patricia. *The Inner Quarters: Marriage and the Lives of Chinese Women in the Sung Period.* Berkeley: University of California Press, 1993.

Fairbank, John K. *The United States and China.* Cambridge, Mass.: Harvard University Press, 1979.

Fei, Hsiao-tung. *Peasant Life in China.* London: Routledge, Kegan & Paul, 1939.

Feng, Menglong. *Stories Old and New: A Ming Dynasty Collection..* Seattle: University of Washington Press, 2000.

Gates, Hill. *China's Motor: A Thousand Years of Petty Capitalism.* Ithaca: Cornell University Press, 1996.

Gernet, Jacques. *Daily Life in China on the Eve of the Mongol Invasion, 1250–1276.* Stanford: Stanford University Press, 1962.

Gilmartin, Christina K., Gail Hershatter, Lisa Rofel, and Tyrene White (eds.). *Engendering China: Women, Culture, and the State.* Cambridge, Mass., Harvard University Press, 1994.

Granet, Marcel. *La pensée chinoise.* Paris: Gallimard, 1968.

Hinsch, Brett. *Women in Early Imperial China.* Oxford: Rowman and Littlefield, 2002.

Jordan, David K. *Gods, Ghosts, and Ancestors.* Berkeley: University of California Press, 1972.

Kwok Man Ho and Joanne O'Brien. *The Eight Immortals of Taoism*. New York: Penguin, 1990.

Liu, James J. Y., *The Art of Chinese Poetry*. Chicago: University of Chicago Press, 1962.

Louie, Kam. *Between Fact and Fiction: Essays on Post-Mao Chinese Literature & Society*. Sydney: Wild Peony, 1989.

Lowe, H. Y. *The Adventures of Wu: The Life Cycle of a Peking Man*. Princeton: Princeton University Press, 1983.

Lu Hsun. *Selected Stories of Lu Hsun*. New York: W. W. Norton, 1977.

Mackerras, Colin. *Peking Opera*. Oxford: Oxford University Press, 1997.

Mair, Victor. *The Columbia Anthology of Traditional Chinese Literature*. New York: Columbia University Press, 1994.

Norman, Jerry. *Chinese*. Cambridge, Cambridge University Press, 1988.

Owen, Stephen. *An Anthology of Chinese Literature: Beginnings to 1911*. New York: W.W. Norton & Company, 1996.

Plaks, Andrew. *Four Masterworks of the Ming Novel*. Princeton: Princeton University Press, 1986.

Roberts, Moss. *Three Kingdoms: A Historical Romance*. Berkeley: University of California Press, 1990.

Rolston, David. *How to Read the Chinese Novel*. Princeton: Princeton University Press, 1990.

Roy, David. *The Plum in the Golden Vase, Vols. 1–2*. Princeton: Princeton University Press, 1993, 1999.

Schipper, Kristofer. *The Taoist Body*. Berkeley: University of California Press, 1993.

Seybolt, Peter. *Throwing the Emperor from His Horse: Portrait of a Village Leader in China, 1923–1995*. Boulder: Westview Press, 1996.

Smith, Richard. *Chinese Almanacs*. New York: Oxford University Press, 1992.

———. *Fortune-Tellers and Philosophers: Divination in Traditional Chinese Society*. Boulder: Westview Press, 1993.

Spence, Jonathan D. *The Death of Woman Wang*. New York: Viking Press, 1978.

Stein, Rolf. *The World in Miniature: Container Gardens and Dwellings in Far Eastern Religious Thought*. Stanford: Stanford University Press, 1990.

Sullivan, Michael. *The Arts of China*. Berkeley: University of California Press, 2000.

Tyson, James, and Ann Tyson. *Chinese Awakenings: Life Stories from the Unofficial China*. Boulder: Westview Press, 1995.

Watson, James L. *Golden Arches East: McDonald's in East Asia*. Stanford: Stanford University Press, 1998.

Watson, Ruby. *Memory, History, and Opposition under State Socialism*. Santa Fe: School of American Research Press, 1994.

Whyte, Martin King. *Small Groups and Political Rituals in China*. Berkeley: University of California Press, 1974.

Wolf, Arthur P. (ed.). *Studies in Chinese Society*. Palo Alto: Stanford University Press, 1978.

———. "Gods, Ghosts, and Ancestors," in Arthur P. Wolf (ed.), *Studies in Chinese Society*. Palo Alto: Stanford University Press, 1978, pp. 131–183.

Wong, Yuen Ling (ed.). *Reflections and Resonances*. Beijing: Ford Foundation, 1995.

Yang, Mayfair Mei-hui. *Gifts, Favors, and Banquets: The Art of Social Relatioships in China.*. Ithaca: Cornell University Press, 1994.

Yu, Anthony. *The Journey to the West, Vols. 1–4.* Chicago: University of Chicago Press, 1977–1983.

Zhang Xudong. *Chinese Modernism in the Era of Reforms.* Durham: Duke University Press, 1997.

Zito, Angela, and T. E. Barlow (eds.). *Body, Subject, and Power in China.* Chicago: University of Chicago Press, 1994.

Films

Chen Kaige, director, *Farewell My Concubine,* 1993.

———, *King of the Children,* 1987.

———, *Yellow Earth,* 1984.

Hinton, Carma, director, *Small Happiness,* 1984.

Tian Zhuangzhuang, director, *Blue Kite,* 1992.

———, *Horse Thief,* 1985.

Zhang Yimou, director, *Ju Dou,* 1990.

———, *Raise the Red Lantern,* 1991.

———, *Red Sorghum,* 1987.

———, *The Story of Qiu Ju,* 1993.

———, *To Live,* 1994.

PART TWO
REFERENCE MATERIALS

Key Events in Chinese History

The dates given here in reference to events prior to China's Zhou period are traditional, and readers of Chinese history will observe that dates for certain periods have slight variations. These reflect the time required—after taking control of a region and declaring a new dynasty—to solidify power. For example, the date 206 B.C.E. is often used for the founding of the Han dynasty, even though full control was not achieved until 202 B.C.E., a date some historians use. Similarly, the Sui dynasty was declared in the north in C.E. 581, but the integration of southern territories was not complete until 589. Historians list the different dates depending on what they are choosing to emphasize. A guiding consideration is that to solidify rule took a long time—sometimes almost forty years, as in the Qing dynasty—and that to lose power took just as long—for example, the Han rulers tottered after the Yellow Turbans uprising for almost forty years. Note that references in the text of the history chapter (Chapter 1) follow the chronological order listed here.

c. 2850	Fu Xi
c. 2750	Sheng Nong
c. 2700	Huangdi (Yellow Emperor)
c. 2350	Yao, first "sage king"
c. 2250	Shun, second "sage king;" selected from among the people to rule

c. 2150–1750 B.C.E., Xia Period

c. 2150	Yu, third "sage king"; queller of floods, founder of Xia
1818	Jie, depraved last ruler of Xia

1766–1122 B.C.E., Shang Period

1766	King Tang, founder of Shang
1154	Zhou, depraved last ruler of Shang
1600–1100 c.	Archaeological finds show divination with oracle bones (ox scapulae and tortoise shells) and the development of a distinctive script and political culture centered on kings and scribes.

c. 1100–221 B.C.E., Zhou Period

1122–771	Western Zhou
c. 1050	Duke of Zhou, regent for a child king
770–221	Eastern Zhou
722–481	Spring and Autumn Period
c. 500–250	Hundred Schools of Thought
481–221	Warring States Period

221–206 B.C.E., Qin Dynasty—Capital: Xianyang

221–210	First Emperor, Legalism in practice
206–202	Struggles for supremacy after fall of Qin
206 B.C.E.–C.E. 220	Han Dynasty
206 B.C.E.–C.E. 9	Former Han—Capital: Chang'an
202	Liu Bang defeats rivals, declares the Han
141–87	Reign of Emperor Wu
81	Debates on Salt and Iron

C.E.—Common Era

9–23	Wang Mang, "Xin Dynasty," reviled as a usurper by later writers
c. 20	Red Eyebrows Rebellion
c. 50	Introduction of Buddhism (traditional date)
25–220	Later Han Dynasty—Capital: Luoyang
180s	Yellow Turbans uprising
190–220	Control (and protection) of imperial family by powerful generals

220–581 PERIOD OF DIVISION

220–280	Three Kingdoms Period
280–581	Northern and Southern Dynasties
300–500s	Buddhism takes root as a major doctrine, as does religious Daoism. Flourishing of literary culture—poetry, ghost stories.
581–604	Sui Wendi, first ruler of Sui
610	Grand Canal system completed

604–617	Sui Yangdi, second and last ruler of Sui
618–906	Tang Dynasty—Capital: Chang'an
626	Tang Taizu takes power from his father and cements Tang rule.
645	The monk Xuanzang returns from India with Buddhist texts.
690–705	Reign of Empress Wu and her Later Zhou dynasty
713–756	Emperor Xuanzong; peak of Tang rule
755–763	An Lushan Rebellion; Tang rule is weakened thereafter.
700–800s	Growing persecution of Buddhism and Daoism; reassertion of Confucian values
700–1000s	Called by some writers the "great divide" in Chinese history, a time of profound change in social organization, agriculture, and cultural patterns. A restructuring of earlier social patterns.
907–959	Five Dynasties Period

960–1279, SONG DYNASTY

960–1126	Northern Song—Capital: Kaifeng
1000s	Reform movements; civil government ideal. Growing conflict with northern groups to the northeast and northwest.
1127–1279	Southern Song—Capital: Hangzhou
1206	Chinggis (Genghis) Khan selected Mongol paramount leader
1279–1368	Yuan Dynasty—Capital: Beijing
1260–1294	Reign of Khubilai Khan; southern China conquered; height of Yuan
c. 1270s	Purported travels of Marco Polo. *Travels* printed in early 1300s.
1300s	Yuan-style drama
1368–1644	Ming Dynasty—Capitals: Nanjing, then Beijing in 15th century
1405–1433	Voyages of Zheng He
1400–1600s	Rise of the vernacular novel and shorter fiction
Late 16th c.	Growing Manchu power in the northeast
1644	Last Ming emperor hangs himself in Beijing.
1630s–1680s	Ming loyalist resistance, also known as "Southern Ming"

1644–1911, QING DYNASTY— CAPITAL: BEIJING

1661–1722	Kangxi Emperor; longest official reign in Chinese history
1683	Qing gains control of contested territories
1736–1796	Qianlong Emperor; peak of Qing rule
1796–1804	White Lotus Rebellion
1838–1841	Opium War
1851–1864	Taiping Rebellion
1862–1874	Restoration attempts ("Tongzhi Restoration")
1894–1895	First Sino-Japanese War; Treaty of Shimonoseki
1898	Reform Movement
1900	Boxer Rebellion
1908	Death of Cixi, empress dowager
1911	End of Qing rule

1912–1949, REPUBLICAN PERIOD

1912	Yuan Shikai declares the Republic of China
1921	Chinese Communist Party founded. Alliance between Nationalists and Communists.
1937–1945	Second Sino-Japanese War
1945–1949	Civil War between Nationalists and Communists
1947–1949	Nationalists flee to Taiwan

1949–PRESENT, PEOPLE'S REPUBLIC OF CHINA—CAPITAL: BEIJING

1949	Mao Zedong declares the founding of the People's Republic of China
1950–1953	Korean War
1953–1957	First Five Year Plan: Soviet-style economic system adopted
1958–1960	Great Leap Forward: communes established; economic decision making highly politicized
1959–1961	Severe famine; twenty million die
1959	Rebellion in Tibet crushed; Dalai Lama flees to India.
1960	Sino-Soviet split; Soviet Union withdraws engineers and other experts from China, crippling Soviet-designed projects.
1962	Sino-Indian War

1964	China explodes its first nuclear bomb.
1962–1965	Recovery from Great Leap Forward
1964–1971	Third Front industrialization program in hinterland, preparing for invasion
1966–1976	Cultural Revolution—Mao Zedong's attack on top Communist Party leaders
1969	Armed clashes with Soviet Union
1971	Mysterious death of Lin Biao, designated successor to Mao Zedong
1972	U.S. president Richard Nixon's trip to China
1976	Deaths of Zhou Enlai and Mao Zedong; great Tangshan earthquake; arrest of the Gang of Four
1978	Deng Xiaoping becomes paramount leader.
1979	Normalization of relations between United States and China; economic reforms begin; Special Economic Zones are created.
1983	China and Great Britain sign accord on return of Hong Kong to China in 1997.
1984	Expanded reform initiatives focus on state-owned enterprises.
1979–1984	Communes abandoned; switch to household responsibility system
1986	Shanghai stock exchange reopens, first stock exchange in China since 1949.
1988	Acceleration of inflation in summer leads to slowdown in economic reform.
1989	Tian'anmen Square demonstrations and crackdown; state control of economy reemphasized, but major economic problems result.
1992	Deng Xiaoping visits Shenzhen and calls for resumption of economic reforms; Communist Party calls for establishing market economy in China
1993–	Successive reforms initiated to support market economy; China becomes major recipient of foreign direct investment.
1997	Death of Deng Xiaoping
2001	China is awarded the 2008 Olympic Games; joins World Trade Organization.
2002	Jiang Zemin begins the transfer of power as Hu Jintao prepares to take control. Shanghai is awarded the 2010 World Expo.

2003   Outbreak of Severe Acute Respiratory Syndrome
                (SARS) in China, Hong Kong, and Taiwan.

Significant People and Events

Boxer Rebellion (1900) The Qing dynasty's last major event, the Boxer Rebellion combined the nineteenth-century themes of internal rebellion and foreign influence. Known somewhat misleadingly to Westerners in China as the Righteous and Harmonious Fists (*yihequan*), the Boxers resented missionary and convert "privileges" in the treaty ports and the harsh social and economic conditions affecting China. Holding a deep belief in charms and supernatural powers, the Boxers gained recognition from the Qing court as an official military organization to support the court against foreign influence. On June 13, 1900, they laid siege to the foreign legation in Beijing. Eight days later, the Qing court declared war on the treaty powers. Almost five hundred foreign civilians and three thousand Chinese Christians were held that summer until a force of Japanese, Russian, British, American, French, Austrian, and Italian troops lifted the siege on August 14, 1900. The empress dowager and the court fled to Xi'an, and the resulting defeat, international condemnation, and sizable reparations were a major blow to the Qing and China's reputation in the international community.

Chiang Kai-shek (1887–1975) Leader of the Nationalist (Guomindang) party and president of the Republic of China, Chiang Kai-shek received an education that mixed classical, military, and Japanese influences. He joined Sun Yat-sen's army in Guangdong in 1924 and solidified his power in the Nationalist Party after Sun's death in 1925. Chiang had rapid success, and by the end of 1926 the Nationalist Army controlled half of the country. By 1927 Chiang had engineered a bloody break with a tenuous Chinese Communist Party alliance, and by 1928 he had completed the unification of the north, finally achieving recognition by Western powers. Chiang formed a government in Nanjing that ruled until the Japanese invasion, when he was forced into an uneasy alliance with a resurgent Communist presence. After the Japanese defeat in 1945, Chiang's forces were defeated by the CCP's People's Liberation Army during China's four-year civil war. Nationalist forces retreated to Taiwan, where Chiang served as leader of a Nationalist government in exile, with the goal of developing a model state and flourishing economy. His ultimate aim of recovering and reuniting the mainland under Nationalist rule was never achieved, and the Republic of China on Taiwan has moved away from such rhetoric in recent years.

Chinggis (Genghis) Khan (d. 1227) Paramount leader of the Mongols during their rise to power in the thirteenth century, Genghis Khan was one of the world's great military organizers. Although the Southern Song would not fall to the Mongols until fifty years after his death, his planning for conquest was felt throughout Asia and Europe. Several years ago, *Life* magazine in its edition on the hundred greatest events of the millennium listed the Mongol conquests among them. It could be argued that they were ranked too low (eighty-third), but the Mongols failed to hold power for very long either in China or other parts of the world. In spite of the glowing success of Khubilai Khan's reign, Mongol power in China would wither quickly. Their success, it seems, came in conquest, and not particularly in ruling. By the 1340s, rebellions and natural disasters helped to shake the dynasty, and within three decades, their rule ended.

Confucius (551–479 B.C.E.) A native of the small state of Lu, Confucius taught groups of disciples who eventually compiled his sayings into a slender volume known as the *Lunyu,* or *Analects.* He spent the better part of a decade in middle age traveling throughout northern China in hopes of persuading territorial lords to put his teachings into practice. Confucius cast himself as a transmitter of the old ways that had been practiced by the Duke of Zhou, and he argued that states of his day were corrupting key ritual practices and usurping the authority of the Zhou dynasty. His teachings were, from his perspective, merely a restatement of the core ideals practiced by the three sages—Yao, Shun, and Yu—and the early Zhou leaders. He deplored the deterioration of his society and sought to reassert the core values that would revitalize the human order. Confucius was traditionally believed to have written or edited many classical works, including the *Book of History,* the *Book of Poetry,* and the *Spring and Autumn Annals,* a history of his own state of Lu.

Cultural Revolution (1966–1976) A social and political movement with roots in Communist Party leadership factional struggles that spread to a much wider scale of conflict, even affecting individuals on a local level. Mao Zedong's role was muted in the later years, but the movement, with its echoes from Red Guards of "continuing revolution," affected China for more than a decade. The Red Guards often dealt harshly with those suspected of "rightist" tendencies, and demonstrations with thousands of students and other young people were frequent at its height. Virtually the entire Chinese leadership was affected in some way by the changing political climate.

Decentralized Power Another overarching theme in Chinese history, this can be seen from even mythical origins all the way down to the twentieth century. In brief, there is a complex relationship between central power (the kind so important to Chinese dynastic leaders) and those who have firm knowledge of the resources and people in a given territory. Throughout Chinese history, when rule has been threatened by uprisings, central governments have given troops and financial resources to commanders who would be tempted to keep themselves in control of the defeated areas. Classic tales in Chinese history often describe commanders and the complex interplay between loyalty to the court and desire to rule that followed their military victories. From the epics of the Three Kingdoms period to the An Lushan and Taiping rebellions—indeed, well into the twentieth century—central power was never secure when "the center could not hold" and rulers gambled by using talented men of questionable loyalty to subdue rebels.

Democracy Wall Movement (1978–1979) In the years after the Cultural Revolution, Mao's death, and the incarceration of the Gang of Four, a number of cities saw the growth of what has become known as the Democracy Wall Movement. The most prominent of these movements was in Xidan, just west of the Forbidden City in Beijing, where posters and magazines became notice boards for people dealing with the effects of the Cultural Revolution and striving to articulate a future for the country. The movement prompted the kind of public discussion of political events that had been lauded in theory but often punished in practice.

People who had been forced to leave cities during the Cultural Revolution were returning, and many former Red Guards were seeking to articulate their feelings about the previous decade. Most early posters supported Deng Xiaoping and the kinds of reforms that he espoused. They also questioned why China was a poor nation with little standing with its global neighbors. A former Red Guard, Wei Jingsheng, put up a poster declaring that China's Four Modernizations would fail with a fifth—democracy. His later writings made clear that he sought a fundamental break with the political system he saw.

The initial months of the movement were useful for Deng and his allies. It could be argued that the people supported the kinds of reforms that Deng envisioned. Once Deng had solidified his position, however, he and his followers started to view the movement as disruptive and as echoing the chaos of the early Cultural Revolution, during which Deng and many senior leaders were purged and even brutalized. Deng called a halt to Democracy Wall Movement in early 1979, stating that there would remain four modernizations, not five, and requiring people to keep all criticism with the limits of the "Four Upholds"—Socialism, The People's Democratic Dictatorship, Marxism–Leninism–Mao Zedong thought, and the leadership of the Communist Party—a policy that remains in effect. Wei Jingsheng responded to the halt by publicly calling Deng a dictator. Wei was subsequently arrested on trumped up charges of revealing state secrets (in this case the publicly known name of the commander of China's troops invading Vietnam) and sentenced to fifteen years in prison. Despite Wei's arrest, posters continued to appear until the National People's Congress removed the clause in the constitution that allowed people to place posters and engage in "great debates."

Wei Jingsheng became one of the most prominent of China's political prisoners, especially after Tian'anmen; several international human rights groups advocated his release. He was released in 1993 as part of China's efforts to win the 2000 Olympic Games but arrested and jailed soon afterward, only to be released again and sent into exile in the United States in 1997 after Deng's death. The Democracy Wall Movement ended in late 1979 and early 1980, with many of its leading members arrested and exiled, though not before some of them attempted to run in local elections, prefiguring the limited political reforms of the late 1990s.

Deng Xiaoping (1904–1997) The People's Republic of China's second powerful leader, Deng Xiaoping never held positions that reflected his formidable power in the Chinese government. Born to a prominent land-owning family in Sichuan near the end of the Qing dynasty, Deng left at the age of sixteen to study and work in France. There he met a number of figures who would achieve prominence in the coming decades, including Zhou Enlai. After joining the Chinese Communist Party in 1924 and training in Moscow, Deng returned to China in 1927 and served in Jiangxi before taking part in the Long March. Deng experienced several reversals of fortune in the 1960s and 1970s but rose to his greatest influence in the period following Mao's death in 1976, emerging from the power vacuum that followed to secure control in 1978. He led a series of reforms of economic policy that transformed China in the 1980s, with an effect that is still being felt today. Agriculture was decollectivized, and farmers were allowed to use their surpluses as they wanted. Industrial controls were also decentralized, and more power was given to local plant managers. Deng also encouraged foreign investment and set up Special Economic Zones (SEZ) in which capitalist-style reforms could take place in the pursuit of "socialism with Chinese characteristics." Deng's later career also reflects the tensions built into PRC rule, in which maintaining power is all-important, even as reforms might take root. In June 1989, Deng ordered troops to attack demonstrators in Tian'anmen Square, and many regard this as a black mark on his leadership. He continued to wield power behind the scenes even in his nineties, despite the fact that he had no formal appointment.

Du Fu, Li Bo, and Tang Poetry These two poets, as well as the rich poetic tradition of the Tang, are famous to this day in China. Du Fu and Li Bo represent the poles of Chinese scholarly and poetic life for many, and that is one reason (along with the fact that they wrote poems about each other) that they are read, even memorized, to this day. Du Fu chose a government career. When he encountered the problems of the An Lushan Rebellion in the mid-eighth century, his sadness and frustration poured forth in such poems as "The Ballad of the Army Carts," which describes the destruction wrought by the rebellion, even as it hearkens back to an earlier, more vibrant time. Li Bo comes across in his poetry as a lover of life, whose easy nature wouldn't be troubled as intensely as Du Fu's, even in the face of an exile that cut him off from the life of the court. One of Li Bo's famous poems describes drinking by the light of the moon, in which he shares his enjoyment with the shadow cast by the moon. Together, these poets are responsible for one of the world's great poetical traditions.

Education and the Examination System Education was, early in Chinese history, the exclusive domain of wealthy families who were able to gain access to appropriate texts, tutors, and government positions. By the Song dynasty, however, an examination system had taken root that was to become the prime determinant of position in political life in the later imperial period. Although there were quotas under the Mongols and, to a lesser extent, the Manchus, the system was meant to evaluate prospects solely on the basis of their abilities. The curriculum became standardized as early as the Southern Song, with students beginning with simple texts such as the *Classic of Filial Piety* and advancing to memorization of the "Four Books" (Confucius's *Analects,* Mencius's philosophical works, and two shorter pieces entitled *The Doctrine of the Mean* and *The Great Learning*). Several authors have noted that students would have to memorize a half-million characters before they were done with even the preliminary years of their education. The examinations themselves were a grueling series of tests that began at the local level and eventually moved the most talented (or the best test-takers) to the imperial level. Those who pay attention to issues in contemporary China will surely recognize some of the broad themes of this early system still at work. Memorization and competitive examinations remain key to scholarly success, even though the subject matter has widened enormously since the last imperial examination was given early in the twentieth century.

Five Dynasties (907–959) Following the Tang dynasty, China was again divided between north and south. What traditionally are termed the Ten Kingdoms rose in succession in the south, largely unhindered by the more powerful northern states. Each state lacked the strength to consolidate the south or to approach unification of the empire. Each also modeled itself on Tang-style imperial institutions but generally enjoyed relative peace and the dimming splendor of late Tang culture. In the north, five dynasties rose and fell, each lasting only a matter of years, as military influence passed from one set of rulers to another. These northern regimes had little time for cultural pursuits and little inclination to support them. Far more than the dynasties in the south, they single-mindedly concentrated on maintaining what was, in fact, a very fragile military supremacy over other northern leaders and frontier groups who were building great strength on China's northern borders.

Great Leap Forward (1958–1960) In 1958, China embarked on the Great Leap Forward—Mao's plan to propel the economy to a new level of development by arousing the socialist enthusiasm of the people. The plan sought an unprecedented rise in industrial production and reflected Mao's frustration with Soviet-style five-year plans and his growing distrust of the bureaucracy that handled them. Production goals were raised dramatically, and the entire population was urged to help with steel production. The quality of steel produced in household and community furnaces was so poor, however, that much of it was unusable. Collectivization of agriculture also rapidly advanced as the countryside was organized into rural communes that combined political and economic power in a single entity. The intention was to use the agricultural labor force to transform the rural economy, with large-scale heavy industry as the main focus of development. Although the planning and control system was partially decentralized, the goal of rapid industrialization remained paramount. Leaders at multiple levels reported inflated production figures, and these combined with heavy floods and droughts to create one of the greatest disasters in modern Chinese history. The Great Leap Forward continued on through 1959 and 1960. Peasants continued to be diverted from agriculture and to work at a pace far beyond available food rations. Bad weather hampered agriculture and aggravated the problem. China's leadership reacted slowly to the developing disaster. By the time the Great Leap was officially abandoned, the damage was done. Famine swept the country, and China lost twenty to thirty million people.

Han Dynasty (206 B.C.E.–C.E. 220) Corresponding roughly to the height of the Roman empire, the Han effectively controlled significant territory within the Yellow and Yangzi River valleys and was able, for much of the dynasty, to hold off threats from the Xiongnu tribes to the north. Beyond its more than four hundred years of rule, the Han dynasty is notable for cementing an administrative system that began in the Qin but was given a new philosophical dimension by its own thinkers. Avoiding Qin's excesses, the Han emperors were able to rule the people effectively. The period saw several rises and falls of its authority, however, and the most important of these was the usurpation of Wang Mang at the very beginning of the common era (C.E. 9–23).

Han Wudi; Emperor Wu (141–87 B.C.E.) One of the most effective rulers in Chinese history, Emperor Wu made major changes in Han policy with its neighbors and within its borders. He strove to eliminate the growing "regionalizing" tendencies of territorial lords, and he asserted Han control over the Xiongnu tribes to the north. Emperor Wu's reforms would not be carried through by his successors, and the dynasty was lost in the early years of the common era, during the "interregnum" of Wang Mang.

Hongwu Emperor (r. 1368–1398) The founder of the Ming dynasty was the second emperor to rise from commoner status to occupy the imperial throne. An orphan, Zhu Yuanzhang was raised in a Buddhist monastery. During the tumultuous last decades of Mongol rule, with the countryside in confusion, Zhu effectively gained control of the Yangzi River valley region near Nanjing and was able to solidify power by the late 1360s. The Hongwu emperor's reign was marked by a reassertion of Chinese cultural values (including a revived examination system) and measures taken to check the activities of landowning families as well as merchants in large coastal cities. The later years of his reign cast a negative shadow, with violent purges that affected a large number of officials and their families.

Hu Jintao (1942–) Hu Jintao, the recently named head of the Communist Party and president of the People's Republic of China, was born in Anhui province and was a highly regarded student of hydraulic engineering at Beijing's prestigious Qinghua University before beginning his work for the Ministry of Water Resources and Electrical Power after his graduation. Hu's experience is different from many of his contemporaries because he spent a significant amount of his early career in Western China, including Gansu, Guizhou, and Tibet, where he served when authorities declared martial law in Lhasa in 1989 in the face of anti-Chinese protest.

Hu Jintao made his appearance on the national stage in 1992, when Deng Xiaoping arranged his appointment to the Politburo's Standing Committee. His selection as vice president in 1998 gave him an even greater role in government policy, and in late 2002 he became the General Secretary of the Communist Party. In early 2003, Hu was elected president of the People's Republic of China, giving him the top posts in both the government and the Communist Party.

Jiang Zemin (1926–) The third major leader of the People's Republic of China, Jiang Zemin was the first in almost a century to come from a nonmilitary background. Jiang's legacy may be the transition he helped create from the "great leaders" Mao and Deng to a more collective and consensus-building government. His continuing pursuit of economic growth has also brought China to the world stage in the early twenty-first century. Born in Jiangsu province and the adopted son of a "revolutionary martyr," Jiang came of age during the tumultuous changes in China during the 1940s and 1950s and survived the Cultural Revolution with few of the difficulties felt by many of his peers. Jiang served as mayor of Shanghai from 1985 to 1987 and rose to a position of prominence during the 1989 Tian'anmen Square demonstrations and government crackdown. Having handled student protests in Shanghai and embraced the kinds of economic reforms championed by Deng Xiaoping, he was enlisted by the senior leadership of the Chinese Communist Party. Deng lived for eight years after appointing Jiang as his successor, which allowed Jiang to consolidate power in a way that might have been impossible during more tumultuous times, especially for a leader without a military background. Jiang's tenure has not been without incident, with world concern over human rights issues, the American spy plane incident, and tensions with Taiwan. Still, his economic reforms and continuous opening to the international community—with the awarding of membership in the World Trade Organization, the Beijing Olympics (2008), and the Shanghai Expo (2010) as hallmarks—represent a rapidly changing China.

Jie and Zhou (second century B.C.E., traditional) Known to later readers as degenerate rulers who brought their dynasties to terrible ends, Jie and Zhou became synonymous in Chinese political writings with self-gratification with no thought of the people's problems. They form the very model of "bad last rulers" in the traditional interpretation—those who worried more about their own comforts and lost control of the empire.

Kangxi Emperor (r. 1661–1722) The second ruler of the Qing dynasty, the Kangxi emperor reigned longer than any emperor in Chinese history. Exercising full power on his own by the age of fifteen, the Kangxi emperor solidified Manchu rule in China and oversaw the full north-south integration of Chinese territory, including the island of Taiwan. He was thoroughly Manchu in his tastes for the outdoors—from battle to travel and hunting—but a refined Son of Heaven at court, who became increasingly comfortable with not only the daily demands of officialdom, but the arts of Chinese literature, philosophy, and letters. The last years of his reign saw a bitter factional struggle among his sons as they sought to succeed him.

Li Bo. *See* **Du Fu.**

Liu Bang (r. 202–195 B.C.E.) Also known as Han Gaozu ("Lofty Ancestor of Han"), Liu Bang was the first emperor to come from among the people. He established central rule after only fifteen years of Qin rule threatened to return the territory to a system of territorial leaders vying for power amongst themselves. The first emperor of the Han dynasty was said to have been a coarse individual (it was written that he urinated into the official cap of a minister of government when he grew impatient with his speech), but one who knew how to accept critical advice from members of his government.

Liu Shaoqi (1898–1969) A senior official in the Chinese Communist Party, Liu Shaoqi succeeded to the office of State President after Mao Zedong relinquished some of his control during the Great Leap Forward in 1959. Liu is often contrasted with Mao for his pragmatic approach to government, and growing conflict between his policies and those espoused by Mao contributed to the Cultural Revolution. Liu, along with Deng Xiaoping, favored economic incentives as a boost to production, but such an approach quickly fell afoul of Mao. In 1968, in the throes of the Cultural Revolution, Liu was dismissed from all of his posts and imprisoned until his death the next year. He was rehabilitated in 1980, and his former "transgressions" were attributed to framing by his political enemies, without mention of Mao or any role he might have played in the matter.

Mandate of Heaven This concept, which dates back to at least the Zhou period, was used to legitimize ruling dynasties by noting the connection of rule to the will of heaven. Heaven was said to grace rulers who were able, through the combined force of power and virtue, to bring order to "all under heaven," as the territory we now call China was called. As a concept, the mandate was used to call into question government practices in times of confusion. The mandate was also used by conquering armies, who often noted that governments in power had lost their connection to heaven's will. One illuminating case is the Manchu conquerors of the Ming dynasty in the seventeenth century, who claimed that the Ming rulers had squandered their mandate and proposed that they themselves were the restorers of legitimate rule.

Mao Zedong (1893–1976) The top leader of the People's Republic of China at its founding, Mao set his imprint on China with a new kind of rule—one that acknowledged the wider populace of laborers, farmers, and other traditionally neglected groups. Born in 1893, as calls for reform of the traditional order were growing more intense, Mao was one of the original members of the Chinese Communist Party in 1921. Through three decades of struggle with the Nationalist army and (as uneasy allies) against the Japanese, the Communist Party won the civil war with the Nationalists and founded the People's Republic in 1949. Mao's rule during the 1950s and 1960s saw both the consolidation of Communist power and the seeds of difficulty with his numerous campaigns to solidify power. Although he retained power until his death in 1976, his leadership contained the disasters of the Great Leap Forward, in which 20–30 million people lost their lives, and the Cultural Revolution, which had an enormous negative effect on the Chinese people.

May Fourth Movement (May 1919) Following their defeat in the Sino-Japanese War (1894–1895) and the humbling Treaty of Shimonoseki, Chinese intellectuals spoke out against internal corruption and external domination. After the Paris Peace Conference, in which the fact that the Chinese warlord government acceded to Japanese demands became known, demonstrations of students and workers spread throughout China, sparking a New Culture Movement, which led to calls for wholesale change in Chinese policy. In a broader sense, the New Culture and May Fourth movements represent a rethinking of traditional culture, from the influence of prominent thinkers such as Confucius to family organization and the Chinese writing system.

Mencius (372–289 B.C.E.) A Warring States period political thinker, Mencius gave advice to the kings of several states that were pursuing unification of the fractured Zhou dynasty order. Whereas Confucius's teachings were set down in the form of pithy moral maxims, often no more than a few sentences long, Mencius expanded these concepts with full historical and cultural examples that ran to many pages. He promoted the concept that people are basically good, and through paying attention to what he saw as the core ideals in human nature—not the flawed realities of what people actually did—leaders could create order in their domains and assert their dominance peacefully throughout the empire. More than any other early thinker, Mencius asserted that the heart of rule lay in promoting the welfare of the people. This can best be summarized by his statements that a ruler merely needed to exude goodness to succeed. If the good ruler did that, the people from other states would take notice and flock to him. Mencius's writings achieved enormous prominence in the last millennium, after they were included as part of the "Four Books" fundamental to later imperial education and memorized by every student who studied for the traditional examinations.

Ming Dynasty (1368–1644) Led by the Hongwu emperor, the Ming was established as a thoroughly Chinese dynasty after a period of Mongol rule. The Ming saw the growth of imperial power and government punishments on a scale that would have shocked its predecessors in the Song. It also saw the great flourishing of vernacular literature and printing on a scale the world had never seen before. Although most young scholars aspired to be government officials, the intellectual world was changing, and there were far more examination candidates than positions. Both employment opportunities and literature reflected this theme, with positions for "failed" candidates in teaching and low-level government service, as well as a rich literature that dealt with aspects of life that were rarely treated in earlier works. The last decades of the Ming saw the presence of Westerners at court, the most famous of whom was the Jesuit Matteo Ricci.

North-South Cultural Division Early in Chinese history, what we refer to as "Chinese civilization" developed in the north, in the area surrounding the Yellow River valley. What we today call southern China was perceived as a marshy land of barbarian tribes. The famous *Song of Chu* is a long dreamlike poem with rich imagery of the southlands—precisely of the kind that struck northerners as coming from a different land. Even during the first integration of the empire during the Qin and Han dynasties, the north and south were lands apart. Over the course of two millennia of imperial history, however, there were several periods during which northerners were compelled to move southward from their native homes and begin new lives. Southerners, especially those who traveled for scholarly or economic purposes, often made lives in the north during times of relative peace. There is a vast literature and storehouse of anecdotes in China on the cultures of north and south. It is one of the most important themes in the study of China, and the experienced reader learns to treat it seriously without being overtaken by some of the "interpretive excesses" of northerners and southerners. These range from observations today about the relative health of diets with rice as a staple (the south) and those with wheat products such as noodles and dumplings (the north). They can be more extreme, though, as is apparent in several exchanges between northerners and southerners during the Song dynasty (960–1279). There, northerners refer to southerners as hailing from a land of fish and turtles (referring to the marshy southland), and southerners retort that their land doesn't smell like livestock (a thinly veiled reference to the "barbarian" groups who had taken over the northern homeland).

Opium War (1839–1842) Although ostensibly about the illegal traffic in opium that was a part of British attempts at trade with China, the latter's defeat in the Opium War had far broader consequences for the Qing government. China was forced to open five "treaty ports" to the British forces (other Western powers would soon follow) and pay Great Britain more than $20 million in silver. The Opium War is a fascinating study of cultural misunderstanding, as well as a rich source of thought about the intersection of cultural practice and market forces (both domestic and international). Above all, however, China's relationship with the rest of the outside world would never be the same.

Period of Division (220–589) From the long crumbling of the Han to the beginning of the Sui almost four hundred years later, no single state or ruler was able to regain control of what was called *tianxia,* "all under heaven." Although the political history of the period is dizzying, with minor states rising and falling in rapid succession, it is one of the richest in all of Chinese history for the development of intellectual traditions and religious practices. Buddhism was established as a major religious force in the small states of north and south that sought to define themselves in opposition to an older order. Daoist "religious" practice also became an important force in the medieval Chinese world. Indeed, it was during this period that we can first see a truly *syncretic* merging of Daoism, Confucianism, and Buddhism in political and social life.

Qin Dynasty (221–206 B.C.E.) This was the first period that can legitimately be called a "dynasty," and that is only because the First Emperor saw his rule continuing on to his sons and grandsons over numerous generations. The Qin saw the implementation of Legalist philosophy and the repression of "heterodox" teachings. One of the primary themes of this period is standardization. After thousands of years of regional fragmentation, the Qin sought to standardize everything from writing scripts to weights and measures—even axle widths were standardized, allowing for smoother travel between regions.

Qing Dynasty (1644–1911) The last imperial Chinese dynasty, the Qing was an "alien" dynasty controlled by the Manchus. Although 150 years of strong rule at the beginning of the dynasty set a strong tone for Manchu rule, undercurrents of resentment were a part of the Chinese reaction throughout its almost three hundred years of rule. The Qing also shows the remarkable resiliency of the Chinese political system. Over several generations, Manchu rulers became increasingly "Sinified," as they were influenced by Chinese culture. Although there were internal seeds of real change as early as the seventeenth century, the nineteenth century and the successive shocks of the Opium War, the Taiping Rebellion, and last-ditch efforts at reform shook the Qing to its foundation.

Regency—the Ideal of the Duke of Zhou (c. 1050 B.C.E.) The very model for the ideal of *regency* in Chinese history, the Duke of Zhou was said to have served little King Cheng, still a minor, as he ruled in his stead until the king came of age. Although the duke's motives were questioned and his rule contested, even among ministers of government in the fledgling house of Zhou, later texts attest to his resolve in creating effective rule as well as his selflessness in turning over government to the young king once he came of age. As hazy as the documents might be as a historical record, they speak to the important ideal of governing on behalf of the dynasty until a legitimate heir can rule. Regents in Chinese history who were often criticized for failing to restore the heirs to power include Wang Mang (first century C.E.), Empress Wu (seventh–eighth centuries C.E.), and the Empress Dowager, Cixi (nineteenth–twentieth centuries C.E.).

Republican China (1912–1949) After the fall of the Qing dynasty, there was a power vacuum that could only be filled by a political figure with significant military power. Yuan Shikai (d. 1916) became president of the Republic of China in 1912 but quickly sought to assert his power in imperial terms. He died in 1916, and the republic degenerated into a fragmented array of warlord power. In the 1920s, two leaders, Mao Zedong (d. 1976) and Chiang Kai-shek (d. 1975), emerged from the Communist and Nationalist camps, respectively, and they would figure prominently in Chinese politics for the next half century. After combining to defeat invading Japanese forces in the late 1930s and early 1940s, both groups faced off in a civil war that saw the Communists take control of the Chinese mainland in 1949. Chiang Kai-shek and his Nationalist forces fled to the island of Taiwan in the late 1940s, where they remain, at least in official terms, in a state of war with the Chinese government.

Restoration Restoration is the key idea that a dynasty, once it has begun to spiral toward failure, can be propped up and set aright by a few talented ministers of government who act solely on behalf of the best interests of "all under heaven." When the Han dynasty tottered during the short usurpation of Wang Mang, it could have been lost, according to political thinkers of the time. That it wasn't, and went on to thrive for almost two more centuries, is due to the determination of talented emperors and ministers to return to the basics of good rule—compassion for the people, proper attention to education, and firm control of the government both within and beyond the capital. Although this may seem to be a dusty old notion of earlier centuries, it is vitally important in contemporary Chinese politics. Indeed, following the Cultural Revolution and the death of Mao, China's leadership was forced to face the same kinds of challenges that faced earlier leaders. If one follows Chinese politics today, this concept will become very clear.

Shang (1766–1122 B.C.E.) Growing evidence exists for political and religious practices during this period, although it is impossible to equate names in texts with individual actions. Archaeological evidence shows the use of oracle-bone divination (short prophecies that were read in the cracks created in tortoise shells and ox scapulae, or shoulder blades) after asking a question and sticking a red-hot iron into them. It is only with the end of the Shang that a written record begins to emerge in Chinese history, but traditional historians spoke of both the Shang and the Xia as periods with real ruling figures.

Sima Guang (1019–1085) A major Song dynasty official and writer of history, Sima Guang is still known for his role in one of the great bureaucratic debates of Chinese history—that with Wang Anshi over the use of government resources in aiding the people and dealing with northern threats. Sima was a talented writer of history who, during a long period of self-imposed exile after his political defeat by Wang, completed one of the richest works of history in the Chinese tradition. His *Zizhi tongjian* ("Comprehensive Mirror for Aid in Ruling") is a thorough, chronological account of China's past from 403 B.C.E. to C.E. 959 and covers, in recent editions, almost ten thousand pages of text.

Sima Qian (c. 145–86 B.C.E.) Arguably China's most innovative historian, his works are still read by many, as much for their literary qualities as their portrayals. The best way to contrast the "Two Simas" (see above) to a Western audience would be to call to mind Herodotus and Thucydides. The former was known for his fantastical, but deeply memorable, accounts of the lands in present-day Greece and beyond. So, too, is Sima Qian an author who brings vivid accounts to the page, even twenty-one centuries after he wrote the works. The 130 chapters of his history are filled with portrayals of sage kings, emperors, and even quite ordinary people such as money-lenders and fortune-tellers.

Song Dynasty (960–1279) After the Five Dynasties period, when the Chinese territory was divided between north and south, the Song founder integrated the domestic structure of the dynasty and moved its capital to Kaifeng to check encroachment of the northern Liao and Xi Xia states. The Song's first 150 years of rule saw perhaps the height of the "civilian ideal" in government, with some of the most talented scholar-officials China would ever see exercising power. The Song dynasty was never as strong militarily as the Tang dynasty before it, however, and it was beset by constant problems in dealing with northern groups. By the twelfth century, the rapidly growing Jin state captured Kaifeng and forced the imperial family to flee southward, where the capital would remain in Hangzhou. Thus, Song is divided into "Northern" (960–1127) and "Southern" (1127–1279) periods, reflecting the move of the capitals. The Southern Song was finally defeated by Mongol forces in 1276 and was thoroughly eliminated by 1279.

Southern Ming (c. 1640–c.1685) With Manchu power growing in China, and many northern territories already taken, some families fled to the south and southeast. The resistance movement figured prominently in the far southern provinces, in Taiwan, and in areas of Southeast Asia including Vietnam. It took almost forty years for Manchu forces to subdue the "rebels," and the loyalist movement lived on during the Qing dynasty in subtle but often deep-seated resistance to the Manchus. Even to this day, many contemporary citizens of the Republic of China on Taiwan see themselves as "resisting" an oppressive rule, in much the way their countrymen did over three centuries earlier.

Sui Dynasty (581–617) "Short-lived" is the phrase that is often connected with descriptions of the Sui. The Sui dynasty had only two rulers—father and son. The first, Sui Wendi, took control of a northern state and established control of north and south between 581 and 589. He started the Grand Canal and solidified power throughout the kingdom. His son, at least in the traditional histories, was said to have undone it all. He built large palaces and engaged in questionable sexual practices. He also prepared a number of ill-advised invasions of Korea. After fewer than fifteen years, he was deposed.

Sun Yat-sen (1866–1925) Sun Yat-sen is claimed by both Communists and Nationalists as the founder of the new post-imperial Chinese order, and he is to this day revered in Taiwan and the mainland of China. Sun was born to a farming family in Guangdong but emigrated to Honolulu, Hawaii, in his early teens. He was educated at various English schools, culminating in medical studies in Hong Kong and a brief practice of medicine in Macao. He took an increasing interest in late-Qing political affairs and was forced to flee to Japan, the United States, and, finally, London after he took part in a failed uprising in Guangdong. He returned to Japan in 1897, where in the next decade he further developed his political ideas and wrote his influential text, *Three People's Principles.* He fled to Japan during Yuan Shikai's parliamentary crackdown in 1913, returned to China in 1917, and the next year founded the Military Government of the Republic of China based in Guangzhou. In 1920 Sun Yat-sen was elected president of the republic, but his government remained regional and without the recognition of foreign powers. In 1923 he became the leader of a new coalition government—the National Revolutionary Government, again based in Guangzhou. Sun realized that no central power would be possible without strong military backing and so founded a Revolutionary Army and the Whampoa Military Academy to train officers for war against the northern warlords. Before these plans came to fruition, Sun died of cancer in 1925; he was succeeded by Chiang Kai-shek.

Taiping Rebellion (1850–1864) Although it had humble beginnings, with the "conversion" of a young ethnically Hakka examination student to Christianity, the Taiping Rebellion would take on a special power that would foreshadow the people's movements of the twentieth century in China. Part religion, part social movement, and part political force, the Taiping rebels moved north from their southern roots to capture the city of Nanjing in 1853. Although they were eventually subdued by government forces, the challenge they had posed to both the traditional political and social orders was profound. Mao Zedong was heavily influenced by the Taiping rebels and incorporated some of their strategies into his campaigns. The human cost was enormous, with more than twenty million lives lost during the rebellion.

Tang Dynasty (618–906) The Tang is known to students in Chinese history classes as one of the high points (along with the Han) of Chinese civilization. Led by strong founders, most notably Tang Taizong, who solidified power after the shady dispatch of his brothers and abdication of his father, the Tang dynasty rose to new heights in its first 150 years of rule. Even with the "usurpation" by the third emperor's wife (Empress Wu), who ruled for fifteen years and controlled the government for at least that many more, the Tang saw the widest stretch of territory to date in Chinese history. After a long reign by Emperor Xuanzong (r. 713–756), the Tang was shaken by the revolt of a Central Asian general, An Lushan, who, although himself killed early in the conflict, created a level of instability that would have the Tang ruling in a much-weakened state for the next 150 years. Some of the most exquisite poetry, painting, and essay writing in the Chinese tradition came from this period.

Three Kingdoms (220–280) The period in Chinese history best known to students, the Three Kingdoms is, to this day, the stuff of legend. From at least the year 180 onward, the Han was crumbling, and several men, including Dong Zhuo and Cao Cao, sought either to control or solidify the dying empire. The territories that emerged were centered in the north (Wei), the west (Shu Han), and the south (Wu). Much of the literary tradition surrounding the period centers on the struggle to defend the Han, even as rulers were tempted to take over rule for themselves. Still, for almost a century, three territories stood, "like three legs of a tripod," while the Han dynasty took forty years to reach its end.

Tian'anmen Square Democracy Movement (1989) The Democracy Movement that led to the Tian'anmen Square massacre owes much to the reform policies of Deng Xiaoping in the 1980s and the relatively successful demonstrations in major cities during that time, focusing on issues ranging from Japanese "economic aggression" to demands for free speech. The Chinese Communist Party leadership was at odds over how best to handle such protests, and the mid-April 1989 gatherings at Tian'anmen Square were in fact meant to mark the death of Hu Yaobang, a popular party general secretary who had been dismissed in 1987 for his "soft" stance on student protest. Hu had fallen victim to hardliners arguing for strict reactions to protest. By the middle of May, the demonstrators had reached two million, and Deng was confronted with a serious threat to Communist Party rule. On May 16, Mikhail Gorbachev, on a state visit meant to heal rifts between the Soviet Union and China, was unable to enter the Great Hall of the People by the front doors, which deeply embarrassed China's leaders. Zhao Ziyang argued for leniency; Li Peng argued for a hard line. On May 20, martial law was declared. On May 30, students erected a replica of the Statue of Liberty, which quickly became known as the Goddess of Democracy. After days of debating within the Politburo, Deng Xiaoping ordered a crackdown on the students and, in the early-morning hours of June 4, 1989, government troops and tanks expelled the demonstrators, with casualties numbering in the hundreds. The aftermath of Tian'anmen was no brighter, with mass arrests and reprisals among prodemocracy groups.

Treaty of Shimonoseki (1895) In the peace treaty that marked the end of the 1894–1895 Sino-Japanese war, the Chinese government ceded its influence over Korea and its control of Taiwan to Japan, while agreeing to pay Japan's cost of waging the war. Other nations took advantage of China's weakened state to occupy or claim expanded spheres of influence in China. Chinese have regarded their defeat and the subsequent treaty as a low point in their modern history, and an example of how fragile the imperial order and traditional methods in education, military, and government had become.

Xia (c. 2357–c. 1766 B.C.E.) Although very little evidence exists for this period, Chinese texts speak of it as a dynasty established by the sage king Xia, after the terrible floods that had plagued his reign. Xia was said to quell the floods by toiling so hard on behalf of the people that he developed a lameness in his legs and neglected even his own family. Traditional texts describe the dynasty's end with the follies of the depraved king Jie, who was overthrown by the Shang.

Yao, Shun, and Yu (third century B.C.E., traditional) Known as the "three sages," and the time of their rule the "three dynasties," Yao, Shun, and Yu figure prominently in writing about government in Chinese history. They provided a model for later interpreters as rulers devoted to their people, to such an extent that Yao and Shun chose talented successors who weren't their own sons, and Yu was said to have toiled during great floods without any thought of his own family, only the fate of "all under heaven."

Yuan Dynasty (1279–1368) Mongol rule of China saw a number of great changes to the Song dynasty pattern. The examination system, although it was continued, had heavy quotas built in to reflect the political power of the Mongols and their allies. It also saw an administrative system that is quite interesting when compared to other dynasties. The upper level of control was reserved for Mongol generals and ministers of government. The middle and lower rungs (as well as a few high posts), however, were peopled by Chinese officials. The decision to serve "outsiders" was often a difficult one for Chinese scholars, but many made the decision to do so. Many were reviled for it in later centuries, none more so than the brilliant painter and Yuan official Zhao Mengfu.

Zhao Mengfu (1257–1322) A scholar-official and painter during the transition from Southern Song to Yuan, Zhao was a descendant of the Song dynasty's first emperor. He served the Mongol-ruled Yuan dynasty as a writer of memorials and proclamations and is an example of the key to effective ruling on the part of outside peoples in China. Without the collaboration of Chinese administrators, negotiating the bureaucracy and managing the empire would have been impossible for the Mongols. Zhao came to regret his decision to aid the Mongols, and he was vilified by many historians for it. He excelled at landscape painting and was a skilled calligrapher. He is well known for his paintings of bamboo, often perceived as being resilient in the face of the elements—a none-too-subtle allusion to a Chinese spirit that would bend but not break in the face of outside pressures.

Zhou (1122–221 B.C.E.) A wildly diverse period that has been divided in numerous ways by both traditional and modern Chinese historians, the Zhou began as a loose alliance of ruling families with a Zhou king, to whom they paid allegiance in rituals. The nine hundred years of Zhou history saw an increasingly bloody set of conflicts in its territories surrounding the Yellow River, especially in the last five hundred years, often called "Eastern Zhou." Confucius, teaching in the fifth century B.C.E., bemoaned the growing warfare, but it would increase until what were originally over a hundred small states were absorbed into seven, then two, and, finally, one integrated empire.

Chinese Language, Food, and Etiquette

CHINESE LANGUAGE

Shin Yong Robson

To the Western eye the appearance of the Chinese language is altogether novel: instead of neat rows of alphabetic letters, there are thousands of unique characters, many that seem incredibly intricate. Fascinating also is the diversity of these characters, visually and aurally. For example, the word *China* requires two characters (figure 1, a and b). But one may also render the word *China* with the two characters in figure 1, c and d using the simplified version of character 1b (character 1d). Cantonese Chinese pronounce this word junggok; people from Shanghai pronounce it zonggoh; and Mandarin speakers say zhōngguó or chūngkuó. Which is the correct form and pronunciation for the word *China*? In fact, all of them are right. Chinese is not as "simple" as English, which has a five-letter word representing the name of the largest country in Asia. Variety is what the Chinese language is about, and all aspects of this variety have evolved through China's long history. The respective pronunciations for the word *China*—junggok in Cantonese, zonggoh in Shanghaiese, and zhōngguó in Mandarin—represent three of the eight major dialects of China.

Figure 1: The word *China* in Chinese writing

a. b.   c. d.

The History of Written Chinese

The legendary Cang Jie (c. 25 B.C.E.), the official historian of the Yellow Emperor, is often credited with the invention of the earliest Chinese characters. According to folklore, Cang Jie had an extra pair of

231

eyes that brought him extraordinary discernment. Inspired by the natural objects around him, particularly by the footprints of birds and animals, he ostensibly created the pictographic symbols that marked the beginning of the Chinese written language.

The actual origin of such a sophisticated writing system is, of course, less simple. The early pictographs were reflections of daily life, and they developed gradually and from various sources. Thus Cang Jie could be considered the collector and organizer of existing signs and symbols rather than as the genius who successfully created an intricate communication method single-handedly. Still, the legend surrounding his contribution remains—the first computer program for building characters not yet in the vocabulary pool (developed in the 1980s) was named after Cang Jie.

The oldest form of the Chinese written language is found in the oracle bone inscriptions called jiǎgǔwén. Carved on tortoise shells and mammal bones during the Shang dynasty (c. 1600–1100 B.C.), these inscriptions recorded royal events and documented divinations. Each symbol represented a concrete image: a number, an animal, a tree, a mountain, the sunrise, etc. These early inscriptions demonstrate the inconsistencies found in primitive writing: an idea can be carved with many strokes or with just a few. Likewise, character size varies, and character positioning can be upright, sideways, or reversed.

During the late Shang dynasty and throughout the Zhou dynasty (c. 1100–256 B.C.) inscription on bronze, zhōngdǐngwén, prevailed. This form refined oracle bone inscription. Although its earliest characters resembled the oracle bone inscriptions, bronze inscription contained characters that were more regular in size and mainly upright. The number of characters was also greater: Zhou dynasty texts contained as many as 500 characters.

Standardization of Chinese characters began under the First Emperor of the Qin dynasty (221–206 B.C.), who founded the first unified Chinese empire and ordered the unification of the written language. This standardized writing, called the Small Seal script (*xiǎozhuàn*), was the official national script designed by the court of the Qin. The characters in the Small Seal script are highly stylized, each confined to a vertically oblong shape. The lines are even, thin, and wiry; the space is carefully regulated, and pictorial elements from earlier writing forms are not apparent (see figure 2).

Although the Small Seal script was crisply distinctive, its composition required patience and skill, so it was inconvenient for daily use.

The Clerical script (lìshū, figure 2) began to appear at the end of the Qin dynasty and was adapted as the formal writing form in the Han dynasty (206 B.C.–A.D. 220). As its name suggests, the Clerical script was initially used by clerks for daily documentation of government records in the early Han. Reaching its height of popularity in the Later Han period (A.D. 200), it simplified the complicated curves of the Small Seal style and replaced them with sharp angles, for clarity in reading and ease of writing. The Clerical script marked an important change in Chinese writing, for hereafter Chinese characters progressed from ancient symbols to their modern form.

Following the Clerical script was the Regular styled script (kǎishū, figure 2), which came into use at the end of the Han dynasty (A.D. 220). It is an austere script that eventually replaced the Clerical for daily official functions. The Regular has been the formal script and remains the standard printing type in China today. Its major features are clarity and legibility—every character has a definite form, a square shape, and only minor variations are allowed. Each character in the Regular script clearly displays the basic strokes of Chinese writing that Chinese schoolchildren learn and practice.

Figure 2: Evolution of Written Chinese

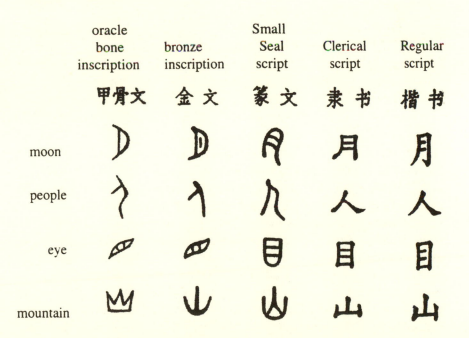

It is technically true to say that Chinese writing reached its modern form as early as A.D. 200, because the basic principles of Chinese writing have remained unaltered for more than 1,800 years. A Chinese schoolchild today can read and write the characters written by a clerk in the Han court because the contemporary Chinese script (Regular script) is so closely related to its literary past (see figure 2).

Formation of the Characters

To an untrained Western eye, Chinese characters may look like many small, square-shaped pictures. Chinese characters in fact are written with strokes (see figure 3. Some of the basic strokes—dot, hook, and turn strokes—allow variations. The number of strokes for a character may range from one such as for the word *one* to seventeen (or more) as for the word *dragon* (figure 3).

Figure 3: Eight Basic Strokes of the Chinese Charactors

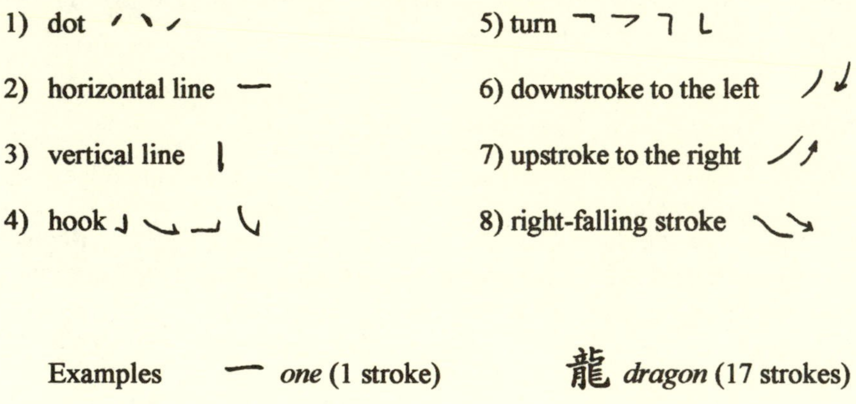

1) dot ＜ ＞ ／

2) horizontal line ─

3) vertical line |

4) hook ⌐ ⌐ ⌐ ⌐

5) turn ⌐ ⌐ ⌐ ∟

6) downstroke to the left ／ ↓

7) upstroke to the right ／ ／

8) right-falling stroke ＼ ↘

Examples ─ *one* (1 stroke) 龍 *dragon* (17 strokes)

Contemporary Chinese dictionaries commonly arrange characters by recurrent parts, called radicals. For example, the characters for *juice, pond, river, sea,* and *soup* all have a radical called "three drops of water" on the left side of the character. The "three drops of water" radical derives its name from the three dot strokes that resemble water drops. Similarly, the characters for *snow, cloud, thunder, frost,* and *dew* share a "rain" radical (on the top). This radical is the miniature of the pictographic character for the word *rain*, which illustrates raining under the sky. A dictionary normally begins with a section that lists categories according to 214 radicals. The radicals are arranged in ascending order of stroke numbers. In this arrangement, the "three drops of water" radical, which contains three dot strokes, comes before the "rain" radical, which has eight strokes. The characters under each category of the radicals are arranged in ascending order of the number of the remaining strokes (that is, the strokes other than those of the radical). For example, in the section for the "three drops of water" radical, the five characters listed in figure 4 would appear in this order: *juice,* whose remaining part (on the right) contains two strokes; *pond,* with three strokes in its remaining part; *river,* with five; *sea,* with seven; and finally *soup,* which has nine strokes in its remaining part.

Figure 4: Examples of the Character Arrangement

RADICAL NAME	RADICAL	CHARACTERS				
three drops of water	氵	汁	池	河	海	湯
		juice	*pond*	*river*	*sea*	*soup*
rain	雨	雪	雲	雷	霜	露
		snow	*cloud*	*thunder*	*frost*	*dew*

The number of Chinese characters has increased over time. The first dictionary, compiled by Xu Shen in the late Han dynasty (c. A.D. 100), *Explanations of Graphs and Analysis of Characters* (Shuō Wén Jiĕ Zì), contains 9,353 characters. *Kangxi* (Kang-hsi) *Dictionary,* the largest dictionary compiled in Chinese imperial history, was completed in 1716 at the request of the Emperor Kangxi and lists 47,035 characters. *The Grand Chinese Dictionary* published in 1986 lists 56,000 characters. The increased numbers of characters in the later dictionaries (after the Han dynasty) arose from an attempt to capture dialects, geographical names, colloquial expressions, and variant forms. The most commonly used characters, around 8,000, however, are mainly collected in Xu Shen's *Explanations of Graphs and Analysis of Characters.* In modern times, a person who knows 3,000 characters is able to read a newspaper and handle the ordinary events of the day.

Chinese characters generally originated in four ways (see figure 5). The first group contains image shapes (xiàngxíng). These are imitative symbols, that is, each character resembles an object's shape. The character for *mountain* shows three mountain peaks (figure 5a). The character for *door* shows a door with two swinging panels (figure 5b). *Eye* is a vertically standing eye (figure 5c). *Sun* and *moon* characters are also in this category (figures 5d and e). *Wood* shows branches and roots of a tree (figure 5f).

The second group of the characters, "pointing to matters" (zhǐshì), is used to indicate abstract meanings. The characters for *one, two,* and *three* are simply one, two, and three lines. The meanings of *up* and *down* are clearly indicated by their characters, as are the meanings of the characters for *convex* and *concave*. The character for *dawn* shows the sun rising above the horizon.

The third group of characters, the "meeting of ideas" (huìyì), includes logical compounds. Two or three ideographic symbols are joined to form a new character that reflects the compounded meaning. For example, *wood* is originally an imitative symbol (figure 5f). Two *wood* characters are combined to make *grove* (figure 5g) and three of them combined would make the character for *forest* (figure 5h). Similarly, the character for *bright* is formed by the combination of *sun* and *moon*. The original form of *sun* shows the sun with an added short line, and it has changed to the modern script (figure 5d). The character for

Figure 5: Formations of the Characters

FORMATION CATEGORY	EXAMPLES
Image shapes (*xiàngxíng*)	a. b. c. d. e. f. 山 門 目 日 月 木 *mountain door eye sun moon wood*
Pointing to matters (*zhǐshì*)	一 二 三 上 下 凸 凹 旦 *one two three up down convex concave dawn*
Meeting of ideas (*huìyì*)	木 + 木 → g. 林 *grove* 木 + 木 + 木 → h. 森 *forest* 日 + 月 → i. 明 *bright*
Shape-sound (*xíngshēng*)	j. [qīng] 青 *green* 氵 (*water* radical) + 青 → k. [qīng] 清 *clear, unmixed* 日 (*sun* radical) + 青 → l. [qíng] 晴 *fine, sunny (day)* 言 (*speech* radical) + 青 → m. [qǐng] 請 *to request* 忄 (*vertical heart* radical) + 青 → n. [qíng] 情 *feeling, sentiment* 魚 (*fish* radical) + 青 → o. [qīng] 鯖 *mackerel*

moon has changed from its original form, which is easily recognized as a crescent moon, to the script used today (figure 5e). The combination of (figure 5d) and (figure 5e) is (figure 5i), the character for *bright.*

The fourth and largest group of characters is "shape-sound" (xíng-shēng). These characters are formed of two parts: a radical that indicates the meaning of the character and another character (usually on the right) that represents the pronunciation. For example, the character for *green* is pronounced qīng (figure 5j). The five other characters (figures 5k–o) that are written with additional strokes, but share the same character *green* (on their right), are also pronounced qīng. While the right-hand character *green* identifies the pronunciation of these five characters, their meanings are indicated by their left-hand radicals, as shown in figure 5.

Simplified Characters

The Mainland Chinese write certain characters differently than the standard form established more than 1,800 years ago, using fewer strokes for some characters. For example, they use the simplified second character in the word *China* (figure 1d). Characters with reduced strokes are known as simplified characters (jiǎntǐzì), as opposed to complex characters (fántǐzì), or traditional characters.

The simplified characters are the products of the script reform begun in 1956 in the PRC to promote universal literacy and to increase the efficiency of writing. The second edition of *A Comprehensive List of Simplified Characters,* published in 1964, is the official guide for the simplified characters used in the PRC today. This list contains 2,236 simplified characters, which account for about one-third of the 8,000 most commonly used characters in modern Chinese. In other words, about one-third of the total number of characters commonly used in modern Chinese have two written versions—the traditional form and a corresponding simplified form. In the case of the two characters for *China,* the first character does not have a simplified version, whereas the second character (figure 1b) does have a simplified equivalent (figure 1d).

Simplifying the traditional characters usually means reducing the number of the strokes in complex radicals or side components. For example, although the character *door* (figure 6a) is simplified, it is also simplified when it serves as a radical or side component. Consider the three characters that follow *door* in figure 6, in which *door* serves as a radical (figures 6b and c) and as a side component (in figure 6d). Sometimes only one part of a traditional character remains and the rest of the character is simply deleted as in the characters in figures 6e and f. When the shorthand forms replace the traditional forms, the simplified characters look entirely different, such as the character *ten thousand* (figure 6g). And when this simplified character *ten thousand* appears in other characters as a side component, those characters also look very different from their traditional counterparts. (see figures 6h–k).

Figure 6: Traditional and Simplified Characters

TYPE	EXAMPLES					
	a.	b.	c.	d.	e.	f.
Traditional	門	問	閑	們	習	飛
Simplified	门	问	闲	们	习	飞
	door	to ask	not busy	*suffix that turns single pronouns plural*	*practice; exercise*	*to fly*
	g.		h.	i.	j.	k.
Traditional	萬		厲	礪	勵	邁
Simplified	万		厉	砺	励	迈
	ten thousand		*strict*	*whetstone*	*to encourage*	*to stride*

This set of simplified characters was officially adopted in 1964 as the standard writing in the PRC. Although publications aimed at overseas Chinese are often in traditional characters, since the 1960s almost all books and newspapers in Mainland China have been printed with simplified characters, as are textbooks for schoolchildren. Chinese educated before the 1960s using the traditional characters have added the simplified forms to their visual repertory, whereas those educated thereafter have only learned the simplified characters.

Problems of Simplification

The simplification of characters has not, however, yielded a "the simpler, the better" consensus among Chinese, and simplification remains controversial. Despite its original intention of making writing simpler, this reform, in practice, has complicated matters. Although China's simplification of characters is acknowledged worldwide, it is habitually avoided outside of the PRC. Traditional characters are common-

place for street signs and for printing in Chinese communities overseas. Taiwan and Hong Kong allow simplified characters for informal
communications but use traditional characters in virtually all printed
matter. In Singapore newspapers print simplified characters, but traditional characters dominate most other communications. *People's
Daily,* the official newspaper of the PRC, regularly provides an overseas edition in traditional characters.

The simplified characters may take less time to write, but their use
causes difficulties for nonnatives. Certain radicals and characters, for
example, are hard to distinguish in the simplified form. One such problem is the resemblance between the two simplified radicals—*metal*
and *food.* The traditional radical *metal* is the miniature of the character for *gold* (figure 7a). Characters sharing the *metal* radical (on
their left) refer to objects made of metals such as *needle, nail,* and
pliers, or to natural elements such as *silver* (see figure 7). When the
radical *metal* is simplified (figure 7b), the characters that contain this
radical also change. Similarly, another traditional radical *food,* which
is the miniature of the character for *food* or *to eat* (figure 7c), is also
simplified (figure 7d). Characters sharing the *food* radical, normally
related to food names or matters relevant to eating, are correspondingly simplified. Consider the contrast between the traditional and
simplified versions for the characters *dumpling, pancake, restaurant,*
and *be hungry* in figure 7. To many nonnatives the two radicals *metal*
and *food* are very similar in appearance after they are simplified (figures 7b and d). In writing, students often erroneously substitute the
simplified radical *metal* for the characters related to food or vice versa.
For them, these two simplified radicals seem like entirely new symbols that are no longer related to their origins—the characters for *gold*
and *food.*

Figure 7: Radicals for Metal and Food

TYPE	RADICAL NAME	RADICAL	EXAMPLES			
Traditional	*metal*	a. 金	針	釘	鉗	銀
Simplified		b. 钅	针	钉	钳	银
			needle	*nail*	*pliers*	*silver*
Traditional	*food*	c. 食	餃	餅	飯館	餓
Simplified		d. 饣	饺	饼	饭馆	饿
			dumpling	*pancake*	*restaurant*	*be hungry*

Another illustration of simplified characters cut from their historical roots is the simplified version of *country*, which is the second character of the word *China* (see figure 1) The ancient pictogram in the bronze inscription for the idea *country* is a character representing an ancient weapon defending a town surrounded by a fence (see figure 8a). In the Small Seal script this character is enclosed in a larger square that indicates the surrounding boundary of a state. From this conception the traditional character for *country* evolved (figure 8b), and later the character in Regular script (figure 8c). Another character for *territory/region* (figure 8d) also derived from the ancient pictogram for *country* (figure 8a), in which a radical representing *earth/dirt* is added to its left. In other words, the ancient pictogram (figure 8a) is the origin for two characters: *country* (figure 8c) and *territory/region* (figure 8d). Just as one easily relates the meanings of *country* and of *territory*, so also one connects the characters that represent them. There is a simplified form for *country* (figure 8e), which replaces the ancient pictogram for *country* (figure 8a) with the character *jade* inside a large square. Ideology replaced history in this case. The reasoning behind this simplified character (figure 8e) is that *jade* here represents the jade imperial seal, the representation of a state. And when it is enclosed by a large square, the meaning of *state* is expressed. This equation of *jade* and *country*, however, is far from obvious. The character for *territory* (figure 8d), on the other hand, does not have a simplified version. Breaking the historical and linguistic link that has existed for centuries, the simplified character for *country* has no connection to the character *territory*.

Figure 8: The Characters for Country

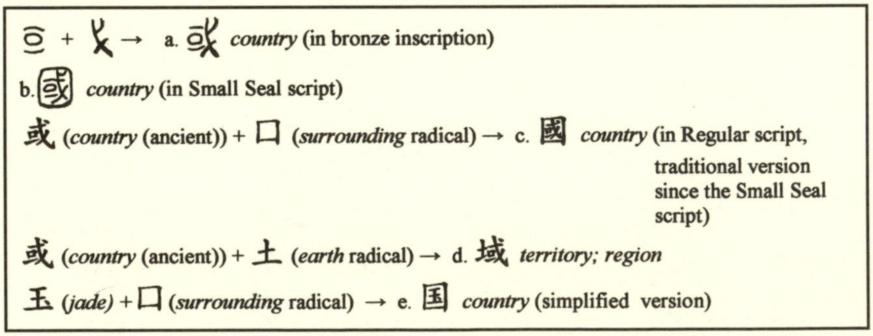

回 + 弋 → a. 或 *country* (in bronze inscription)

b. 國 *country* (in Small Seal script)

或 (*country* (ancient)) + 囗 (*surrounding* radical) → c. 國 *country* (in Regular script, traditional version since the Small Seal script)

或 (*country* (ancient)) + 土 (*earth* radical) → d. 域 *territory; region*

玉 (*jade*) + 囗 (*surrounding* radical) → e. 国 *country* (simplified version)

In many cases, by recreating the characters, the reform has broken the logic behind the structure of the traditional characters. For instance, many characters related to trading share the character *shell*, the valuable item used in trading in ancient China before money was invented. The character *shell* (see figure 9a) is originally an imitative symbol. Some of the characters containing the "shell" radical have an obvious semantic connection to its ancient origin (see figure 9c–i). When the character *shell* is simplified (figure 9b), the other characters with the "shell" radical are correspondingly changed (figure 9c–g). But two of the most important characters in this sequence, *buy* and *sell*, lose both historical and logical contexts in their simplified versions (figures 9h and i). These two characters have no connections to other members of their philological family. People who learn only simplified versions of these two characters may never relate them to other characters that share the "shell" radical.

Figure 9: Characters Related to Trading

TYPE	EXAMPLES						
	a. Evolution of the character for *shell*. 𝕏 (oracle bone) → 𝕎 (bronze) → 目 (Small Seal) → 貝 (Regular) 貝 (traditional) → b. 贝 (simplified)						
	c.	d.	e.	f.	g.	h.	i.
Traditional	財	貴	費	資	貸	買	賣
Simplified	财	贵	费	资	货	买	卖
	wealth	*expensive*	*fee*	*capital*	*loan*	*buy*	*sell*

Although the simplified characters are the official written language of the PRC, they have not completely replaced the traditional characters in Mainland China. The traditional characters are still preferred for such activities as the printing of historical documents and of classical literary works.

For highly educated Chinese residents of the PRC switching gears between the simplified characters and the traditional characters is a common practice; the average citizen masters traditional characters by reading classical literature. On the other hand, this mixed use is difficult for those who know only one type of character. Unlike the people inside the PRC who are mainly exposed to simplified characters, nonnatives who live outside the PRC routinely encounter publications in traditional characters from outside the PRC and publications in simplified characters from the PRC. They consequently must learn both traditional characters and simplified characters to accommodate the constant encounter with publications in both versions. To most readers outside the PRC, learning a large set of characters in addition to an already existing and familiar written language has been burdensome. Hence publications in the simplified characters from the PRC are not popular among Chinese communities overseas.

There is hope, however, that this confusion will end. In recent years, more and more scholars in the PRC have addressed problems caused by the simplification of characters. Some point out that in the time of modern technology, Chinese may achieve another era of shū-tóng-wén, "to write in the same language." For Chinese, that will mean writing (typing in the computer) in one version of characters—the standardization of characters that the First Emperor of the Qin envisioned 2,000 years ago.

Pronunciation

Throughout their long history of language, the Chinese have used ideographic writing, using characters rather than phonetic symbols (alphabetical letters). To native Chinese, the idea *he is Chinese* is conveyed by a five-character sentence. This sentence is pronounced tā shì zhōng guó rén. A listener who wishes to write Chinese but is unable to write the characters must use a phonetic script to represent this phrase. Using the Roman alphabet, the phonetic script can record Chinese pronunciations, but this phonetic writing is difficult for native Chinese and nonnatives to read. So, let us explore the system of Chinese pronunciation.

Every Chinese character represents a syllable made up of three parts: an initial consonant, a single or a compound vowel, and a tone (which indicates inflection). For example, in mài the *m* represents the initial consonant, *ai* the compound vowel, and [`] the tone. In chéng the *ch* is the initial consonant, *eng* is the compound vowel, and [´] is the tone. If any one of these three parts changes, the sound and meaning of the syllable change.

Tones are a distinctive feature of Chinese, as important as the other two parts of a syllable. They represent one of the chief differences between Chinese and English. In English a speaker expresses affirmation with "Yes!"; a question with "Yes?"; and a reluctant agreement with "Y-e-s." Unlike the expressive intonation of English, Chinese tones are used to distinguish word meanings. Thus Chinese mǎi means buy, but mài means sell. Consider another example. The English word *fee* has the same meaning in the question "Do they charge a fee?" with a rising intonation and in the statement "We need to pay the fee" with a falling intonation. The meaning of the Chinese fei, however, depends on the tone that is used. Spoken with a high, level tone it means to fly [fēi]; with a rising tone it means fat [féi]; with a very low tone it means bandit [fěi]; and with a falling inflection it means fee [fèi].

Tone is the movement or the holding of the pitch of the voice within the time span of the syllable. Every syllable in Mandarin belongs to one of four tones: high and level, rising, low, and falling.

To further complicate things, there are hundreds of homonyms in Chinese, that is, characters that are written differently and have different meanings have the same sound and the same tone. For instance, the sound *fēi* with the high, level tone can mean to fly, but it can also mean imperial concubine, wrong, door leaf, or Pacific herring. The sound *qián* can mean money, front, or pliers. If one considers full words rather than single syllables, the problem is certainly compounded. For example, without tones it is rather difficult to determine, even from context, whether the two-syllable word *shiyan,* is *shíyán* (salt), *shìyàn* (test), *shìyàn* (rehearsal), *shíyàn* (experiment), or *shìyán* (oath, pledge). Because most Chinese words have two or more syllable combinations, pronunciation without tones produces chaos. On the other hand, even though the tones provide the words with a distinguishing feature, to native Chinese, only the characters represent the language in pronunciation and in meaning.

Phonetic Writing (Romanizational) Systems: Peking or Beijing?

The phonetic system for Chinese using the Roman alphabet is called Romanization. Of the several alphabetical systems for transliterating Chinese to English, the Wade-Giles system was the most widely used internationally until 1979. After 1979 the pinyin system gradually replaced Wade-Giles for Chinese pronunciation in matters pertaining to China. This switch has puzzled some Westerners. For example, does one say Peking or Beijing? The latter. Was Guangzhou once Canton? Yes. Do Chiang Kai-shek and Jiang Jieshi refer to the same person? Yes. Many Chinese names and terms once familiar to Westerners now are transliterated to pinyin and may no longer look familiar.

The Wade-Giles system originated in 1859 with Sir Thomas Wade (1818–1895), a British military and diplomatic official in China in the mid-nineteenth century and later a scholar of Sinology (Chinese Studies) at Cambridge University. His system of Romanization was revised by Herbert Giles (1845–1939), a prolific writer and a translator of Chinese literature at Cambridge, in his *Chinese-English Dictionary* published in 1892.

For many years the Wade-Giles system was used in publications including newspapers and maps. What made Wade-Giles widely acceptable to Westerners was its ease of use. Supposedly any English speaker could pronounce a Chinese syllable without serious inaccuracy and without extensive study. For example, a Westerner would probably find *t'a shih chung kuo jen* easier to capture than *tā shì zhōng guó rén* and *Chiang Tse-min* less exotic than *Jiang Zemin*. In both cases, the earlier transliteration is Wade-Giles; the latter is pinyin. To Chinese speakers, however, the latter transliteration in each case more accurately represents the standard pronunciation.

Pinyin was officially adopted in the PRC in 1958 and has had a growing number of uses: teaching character pronunciation, transliterating proper names in the press, transcribing some minority languages, and teaching people to speak Mandarin. It is also used in dictionaries and textbooks. In 1979, the government of the PRC began to replace Wade-Giles with pinyin in its publications for foreign distribution.

Although the same linguistic principles apply to Wade-Giles and pinyin, Westerners may find it more difficult to pronounce pinyin script because some consonants in the system are pronounced quite differently from what Westerners would expect. For instance, the *Q* in *Qing* is pronounced like the English *ch,* and *xiao* is pronounced hsiao. To some Westerners, many of the familiar names become unfamiliar under the pinyin system. But to Chinese ears, pinyin produces a more accurate pronunciation of the language. Pinyin was quickly accepted as the standard transliteration for Chinese terms in linguistics, science, and in textbooks. Since the 1980s, pinyin has been gradually adapted in all fields of humanities and has become the dominant transliterational system. Nowadays readers are more familiar with the term *Daoism* (which used to be *Taoism*) and understand that *tofu* is actually pronounced dòufù.

Most sounds in Mandarin are not difficult to pronounce. Those that might be unfamiliar to Westerners include the pronunciation of some consonants such as *j, q, x, z, c, zh* and *r,* which, although they may appear puzzling to a Western eye, are not impossible to manage. *J* is a tight sound somewhat close to the first three letters in *jeep; q* is sounded as *chee* in *cheer; x* is sounded as the English *c* pronounced with a smile and with the teeth almost closed; *z* is pronounced dz; *c* is pronounced ts; *zh* is as the *G* in *Gerry;* and *r* is as the *r* in *run.* To

A Comparative Table of Pinyin and Wade-Giles

Pinyin	W-G	Pinyin	W-G	Pinyin	W-G	Pinyin	W-G
b	p	r	j	**a**	a	iong	iung
c	ts'	ri	jih	ai	ai	iu	iu
ch	ch'	s	s	an	an		
chi	ch'ih	sh	sh	ang	ang	**o**	o
ci	tz'u	shi	shih	ao	ao	ong	ung
		si	ssu; szu			ou	ou
d	t			**e**	e; o		
f	f			ei	ei	**u**	u
g	k	t	t'	en	en	ua	ua
h	h	w	w	eng	eng	uai	uai
j	ch	x	hs	er	erh	uan	uan
k	k'	y	y			uang	uang
		ye	yeh	**i**	i	ui	uei; ui
		yi	yi; i	ia	ia	ueng	ueng
l	l			ian	ien	un	un
m	m	z	ts	iang	iang	uo	uo
n	n	zh	ch	iao	iao		
p	p'	zhi	chih	ie	ieh	**ü**	ü
q	ch'	zi	tzu	in	in	üan	yüan
				ing	ing	üe	üeh
						ün	ün

say "the Chinese speak Chinese" in Mandarin: zhōng-guó-rén shuō zhōng-wén.

Mandarin versus Dialects

When people talk about the Chinese language they are usually referring to the language used by the Han people who make up more than 95 percent of the Chinese population. Correspondingly the term for Chinese characters is *hànzì*, "the Han characters." Other Chinese languages used by China's minority ethnic groups, such as Mongolians and Manchus, are entirely different from that used by the Han.

Although all Han Chinese read and write the same characters, some Chinese speak Cantonese, Taiwanese, or Shanghaiese, etc. The Chinese language possesses eight major dialect systems, most of which developed because the country was divided by natural barriers. These so-called dialects are all Han languages that differ from one another in pronunciation, much as French differs from other Romance languages. Named for the main areas in which they are spoken, the dialects are Northern division, Wú (in regions of Jiāngsū-Zhéjiāng provinces), Yüè (Cantonese dialect), Xiāng (Húnán dialect), Hakka (spoken by the descendants of northern immigrants widely scattering from Sìchuān to southeastern China), Gàn (Jiāngxī dialect), Northern Mǐn (Northern Fukienese), and Southern Mǐn.

To standardize communication, the government of the PRC decided in 1955 that the northern dialect based on the Beijing pronunciation would be the official means of communication. It is known by Western people as Modern Standard Chinese or Mandarin.

Mandarin was originally a term used by Europeans to refer to a public official in imperial China; its Chinese equivalent is *guān*. The original term for the Mandarin language was *guānhuà,* which means "speech of the official class." After the fall of the Manchu regime in 1911, the term *guóyǔ,* meaning "national language," was used to refer to Mandarin until 1949, when the PRC was established in Mainland China. The term *guóyǔ* is still used in Taiwan. In the PRC today the term referring to Mandarin is *pǔtōnghuà* or "common (people's) speech." So when a Chinese friend says "I speak *guóyǔ*" and another one says "I speak *pǔtōnghuà,*" these two are actually telling you the same thing, that is, "I speak Mandarin." From the term they use to identify Mandarin, you know that the first person is from Taiwan and the second is from Mainland China.

The most obvious difference between the dialects and Mandarin is pronunciation. For instance, the numbers one through five in Mandarin are pronounced yī, èr, sān, sì, wǔ; in Cantonese, they are yah, yee, sam, say, hmm. "How are you?" in Mandarin is nǐ hǎo, which in Cantonese is lay hoe. Such differences exist between all of the dialects.

Chinese people who speak any one of the dialects ordinarily cannot be understood by those speaking other dialects, or by people using Mandarin. Mandarin remains the standard language taught in schools and used in all the media in the PRC. Educated Chinese usually learn Mandarin in addition to their native dialect. Although Mandarin is also the official language in Taiwan and in Singapore, most people in Hong Kong speak Cantonese, which was long the dominant dialect of Chinese communities in the United States and Canada. In the 1980s and 1990s, and especially since 1997 when control of Hong Kong was taken over by the PRC, Mandarin became more and more common in these previously Cantonese-speaking communities.

Useful Chinese Expressions

Hello!	Hǎo a!
Bye!	Zài jiàn!
Good morning!	Zǎo!
How do you do? Pleased to meet you.	Nǐ hǎo!
May I ask what your name is?	Qǐngwèn, nín guì xìng?
What is your name (to a young person/child)?	Nǐ jiào shénme míngzi?
I am Mary.	Wǒ shì Mary.
Thank you. You are welcome.	Xièxiè. / Bú xiè.
Excuse me! Sorry!	Duì bù qǐ!
OK!	Hǎo!
That is fine. There is no problem.	Méi wèntí.
Is that so?	Shì ma?
Excuse me, where is the bathroom?	Duì bù qǐ, Cèsuǒ zài nǎr?
Is there a cafe around here?	Zhè fùjìn yǒu méiyǒu kāfēi guǎnr?
Please, no MSG.	Duì bù qǐ, bú yào wèijīng.
Delicious food!	Zhēn hǎo chī!
Cheers!	Gān bēi!
Bill, please.	Duì bù qǐ, zhàngdān.
How much does it cost?	Duōshǎo qián?
Can you help me?	Néng bù néng bāngbāng máng?
I understand a little Chinese.	Wǒ dǒng yìdiǎnr zhōngwén.
Sorry, I do not speak Chinese.	Duì bù qǐ, wǒ bù shuō zhōngwén.
Does anyone here speak English?	Zhèr yǒurén shuō yīngwén ma?
Please speak more slowly.	Qǐng nǐ shuō de màn yìdiǎnr.
I do not understand.	Wǒ bù dǒng.
I do not know.	Wǒ bù zhīdào.
What time is it?	Xiànzài jǐ diǎn?
What did you say?	Nǐ shuō shénme?

CHINESE CUISINE AND CULINARY HABITS

Food in Chinese Culture

Although food is rarely a subject of scholarly study in China, it constitutes a central element of Chinese culture—suggested in part by the standard greeting "Have you eaten yet?" (The proper response is a perfunctory "Yes"—any other response will result in extensive efforts to feed you!)

Outside of China, the sweet tastes of Guangzhou ("Cantonese") and the spicy flavors of Sichuan (Szechwan) are familiar—but there the differences are far greater between regions. Some of those differences depend upon the availability of certain kinds of foodstuffs. Contrary to popular belief, not all Chinese survive on rice. In the arid northern plains, wheat is a staple, and noodles, steamed buns, and other wheat products are the standard fare. In the south, where both rice and labor are plentiful, one finds elaborately produced dim sum. Southern cuisines have a reputation for being more adventurous than Northern ones, with a broader range of ingredients that include delicacies such as snake or rat. Northerners enjoy lamb, and they also appreciate strong flavors in a wide variety of wheat-based dishes, including dumplings, wontons, pancakes, and steamed, boiled, baked, or fried buns. Deservedly famous is Beijing (Peking) duck, as well as mu shu pork and Mongolian beef.

Cooking methods also vary across China. Although electric and gas ovens are virtually unknown in China, there is a broad range of possibilities for cooking over an open wood or coal fire. Breads, as well as other foods including dumplings and some noodles, are often steamed in wooden or metal baskets that sit atop a stove. Foods are also fried—from deep fried (in the south) to lightly sautéed (in the north). Sweets, other than manufactured candy or fresh fruit, are not often part of a Chinese meal. Instead the focus is on providing a balance of flavors that comes from both the primary ingredient and the spices that are used. Like the art of calligraphy, cooking takes place in one single motion. Cooking happens quickly, over a hot fire, with little room for contemplation or for error.

Although in national Chinese cuisine, stir-fried dishes routinely accompany the staple food, the cooking styles of these dishes vary by region. Chinese roughly divide the cuisine into four regions: the northern region above the Yellow River, the coastal region, which features fish dishes and fresh vegetables, the inland region, which includes the Hunan and Sichuan provinces, and the southern region, which is best known for the cooking varieties of Guangdong province. Cultural consensus is that coastal cuisine is relatively sweet, for native residents like to put a bit of sugar in the dishes; that northerners favor salty dishes; and that Hunan and Sichuan dishes are very spicy.

Three meals a day is Chinese custom. The breakfast is relatively simple: a steamed bun, a sesame-seed pancake, or a pair of deep-fried dough sticks (*youtiao*) with a bowl of soymilk for a northerner, or rice porridge with pickled vegetables for a southerner. Far more elaborate, however, is the Cantonese restaurant breakfast of dim sum, a veritable feast of perhaps fifty dishes from which a group of friends will choose perhaps a dozen. These possibilities include braised Chinese mushrooms stuffed with pork and water chestnuts, egg rolls with shrimp and pork, and steamed buns with roast pork fillings or steamed crabmeat dumplings. Major meals are lunch and dinner in China. A typical major meal for a family consists of a staple such as rice plus three or four stir-fried dishes.

Feasts and family banquets are a different story. The hospitable Chinese habitually invite friends home for a meal. For a planned family treat, the feast starts with various alcoholic beverages, often quite refined, and a few cold appetizer dishes, such as roast pork, thousand-year-old eggs (exquisitely cured duck eggs), jellyfish, asparagus salad, and fried peanuts, which accompany the varied beverages. After the cold appetizers are consumed, ten to twelve hot courses are served, followed by a final soup course.

During the banquet, Chinese hosts constantly encourage guests to eat more and drink more. They continually add food to a guest's plate and bowl, and the complement to this hospitality by the host is the guest's obligation to accept the endless supplements. It is a custom that Chinese hosts would never want to see a guest's plate become empty. During a typical two-hour meal, course after course of food is served. Visitors to China are sometimes surprised by the "impossible" amount of food—always sampled but rarely finished—on the table at the end of a banquet-style meal.

The liquid complement to any meal in China is tea. With some 250 varieties of tea from which to pick, there is a tea for every regional cuisine or individual preference. Everyday tea is like *vin ordinaire,* or table wine, and fine tea (like fine wine) is expensive. In a Cantonese restaurant, tea boys carry on each arm a huge kettle with a long spout. When they notice a teapot with the lid upright, they refill it with fresh boiling water. The tea boy usually stands a foot away from the table. As he raises a kettle, the hot water with steam travels gracefully through the air in a two or three foot arc into the open tea pot before him. When the pot is nearly full, the tea boy withdraws his arm, and the pouring ceases without a drop spilled. For the visitor, trust, just like the concept learned in Chapter 1 dealing with early Chinese philosophy, is necessary.

The Chinese believe that food reflects multiple forms of balance, all in pursuit of the ultimate form of balance, *yin* and *yang.* Balance is achieved by matching hot dishes to cold weather, and vice versa, and by the proper proportion of *fan* and *cai*—the staple food (rice or noodles, for example) and all other dishes. Within *cai* (other dishes) one must also have balance. Thus neither meats nor vegetables are cooked whole but cut appropriately and blended carefully. Depending on the mode of cooking—steaming, braising, stir-frying, or boiling—certain ingredients should be cut thinner or thicker, in slices or cubes. Ultimately, every dish should satisfy three standards: good appearance, good scent, and good taste. The best food strikes a perfect balance.

Chinese Regional Cuisines

Northern Cuisine

As touched upon earlier, wheat products prevail over rice in China's northern provinces. Many varieties of noodles and dumplings make up the northern diet, and Westerners will likely recognize *jiaozi* (steamed dumplings) and *chunjuan* (spring rolls), as well as a variety of roasted meats, the most famous of which is *Beijing kaoya* (Peking duck). The duck should be ordered whole, unless the party is very small indeed, and (in contrast to some Western restaurant customs), the diners should pay attention to the slicing of the duck at the table. The first cuts will be the most tender (and somewhat greasy) skin, which should be dipped lightly in sauce and eaten without accoutrements. After that, plates will emerge to accommodate virtually every part of the duck (some of which skittish travelers may find challenging). The more mundane parts of the duck should be wrapped "pancake style" and eaten with sauce and scallions. There will be at least one (and usually more) soups made from the duck, and a wide array of dishes on the menu that can accompany the meal.

Other northern cooking relies less on seafood than freshwater fish, and poultry dishes are also quite prevalent. Those from China's south and west tend to think of northern cuisine as bland, but the combination of dumplings, vegetables (especially cabbage), and meats make it a good fit for the hardy northern conditions, where winds blow all year round and the chill of winter is fierce. In fact, many Northerners pride themselves on the enormous possibilities afforded by the use of wheat in their diets and consider rice a bit one-dimensional for a meal. The possibilities for noodles and dumplings are seemingly endless, and the only way to begin to grasp the wonders of wheat is to order these foods at every opportunity.

Southeastern (Coastal) Cuisine

The bountiful coastal areas of China's southeast provide a rich array of culinary opportunities. The farmlands are subtropical, so the Southeastern cook has a range of vegetables far richer than those to the north or west. The cuisine from Fujian, Jiangsu, and Zhejiang provinces tends to be too oily for the tastes of northerners, but is a rich blend of steamed, deep-fried, boiled, and braised vegetables and meats. The balance of fish, meats, and vegetables is impressive, as are the soups that blend the same ingredients in innovative ways. A southeastern cab driver recently admitted that he pitied the northerners, with their predictable array of foods and endless cabbage dishes. On the coast, he said, he could sample not only fish from the sea, but the rich variety of fish from the Yangzi River.

He went on to say that the oil in southern cooking was "healthier" than the "dry" diet of the north, and that a little bit of oil in the diet was good. Indeed, the coastal cuisine is exciting, and not only in terms of the wide array of ingredients. Vegetables are plentiful, and one can sample *doumiao* and *bocai* (tasty bean sprouts and leafy spinach) in ways that have only recently become available to northern residents, thanks to improvements in produce trucking. Shrimp, prawns, and crabs are plentiful as well, and it is only the experienced diner who is able to eat all of the tasty parts of a very large crab.

Western Cuisine

Most Westerners are familiar with Sichuan (Szechwan) and Hunan cooking, and many think of them (along with some Americanized dishes of the south) as "Chinese food." Even those familiar with such restaurants in the United States will be amazed by the rich possibilities in the hot, spicy dishes of the west. For quite obvious geographic reasons, one will not find seafood as often as one will encounter poultry, freshwater fish, soybeans, legumes, and a wide variety of vegetables cooked together in heavy seasonings. Tiny dumplings in hot, spicy sauce (*chaoshou*), hot pepper dishes with chicken or other meats (*gongbao; kung-pao*), and spicy beancurd and pork (*mapo doufu*) are among the dishes most familiar to foreigners, but they only scratch the surface of culinary possibilities.

In recent meals in China, I should not have been surprised to see very fine Sichuan restaurants in all of the major cities I visited. It is not unlike finding a good Sichuan or Hunan restaurant in New York, Chicago, London, or Berlin. Smaller towns are unlikely to stray quite as far from regional specialties, but it is interesting to note how much China itself is blending restaurants that serve its major cuisines, at least in the largest cities. For those readers who have only sampled kung-pao chicken or ma-po beancurd, there is a world of possibility available. One famous dish in Sichuan is fried string beans. They are cooked over a hot flame and served in what looks to be a withered form but are quite tasty. Even the more familiar Sichuan and Hunan dishes are likely to arrive at the table much spicier than those found in any but the most authentic and hardy restaurants in the West.

In Beijing recently, I had the hottest dish I have ever eaten. It was a fish stew, with a whole fish, cooked in hot, red oil and a large bowl full of peppercorns. One dipped one's chopsticks into a stew of oil, peppercorns, and red peppers to find the tender pieces of whole fish. The only reason the fish could even be found, however, is because the server, using a large ladle, removed at least three cups of red peppers from the serving bowl. Hunan cuisine has a slightly different range of spices, but the dishes are equally spicy, and the array of vegetables and meats used also vary somewhat. This is not bland food, though, and (as several of my companions have learned) one must work very hard to choose dishes that will allow more sensitive palates to survive the meal. One student of mine ordered milk or yogurt before every Sichuan or Hunan meal, with generally favorable results.

Southern Cuisine

This style of Chinese cooking is the most familiar to the Western world, since most immigrants before the 1970s had ties to Guangdong or neighboring southern provinces. The weather in Guangdong is hot in the summer and still warm in the winter. It is humid, and there is a great deal of rainfall (unlike the western and northern regions of China). The possibilities for combining vegetables and meats are enormous in this climate, and they tend to be stir-fried or steamed so that they keep their taste as much as possible. Southern cuisine is justly famous for dim sum and its seemingly endless variety of dishes that subtly echo the cuisines of the various regions of China. The dim sum meal is more than a time to eat, though. The Chinese characters for dim sum represent "a spot on the heart," meaning that one talks, eats, enjoys one's companions, and eats some more. It is a festive occasion that has become a weekend ritual for many Chinese and Westerners in restaurants throughout the world.

A regular dinner of Guangdong cuisine, though, can include some of the following dishes. It can be a bland cuisine (according to some tastes) if one sticks to sweet and sour dishes and the array of menu items found in many Western restaurants. In many ways, however, Guangdong cuisine is the most daring in China. In addition to an enormous variety of green vegetables, often combined with mushrooms, one will find both river and sea fish, including eel backs with eggplant, prawns prepared in multiple ways, stewed pigeon (with meat that only emerges for the most determined diner), and even camel (a culinary stretch if one thinks of the improbability of such sources in southern China). I will not even try to give a sample of the truly most exotic southern cuisine (some of which has persisted in the West as almost "urban legends" of dining). Suffice it to say that the cuisine of the south has wonders that can only be sampled by repeated dining.

PRACTICAL ETIQUETTE FOR THE TRAVELER TO CHINA

Though by now the reader's understanding of Chinese culture is surely improved, there remains the challenge of traveling in China without giving offense through blunders in etiquette or needlessly taking offense at behavior rooted in cultural differences. The following advice will serve you well as you make your way in your travels. It represents a beginning "cultural grammar" that you can build on as you get to know China better.

First, let us start by comparing and contrasting China and the United States. As we have seen in this book, China has a very long history and an ancient culture that has evolved over thousands of years, and of which the Chinese are very proud. The United States has a very short history by Chinese standards and has a constantly changing and evolving culture born of immigrant interaction. Chinese society is strongly based on hierarchical relationships—fifty years of Communist rule has not eliminated the importance attached to knowing one's place in the family, in personal networks, and in the larger society.

U.S. society is relatively egalitarian, in principle, where economic and social mobility based on ability is believed to be both possible and desirable. Chinese society relies on personal relationships and networks to achieve personal ends to a much greater extent than does U.S. society, which relies much more, in both theory and practice, on rules and laws, ideally applied impersonally and fairly to all people. Finally, communication in China is much more indirect and face saving, whereas frank, direct speech is more highly valued in the United States.

Considering these contrasts, we can easily imagine the unintended insult that typical behavior in the United States might produce in China, and vice versa. A business person from the United States, who is well respected at home for frankness and for being "a straight shooter," might well be considered rude, overbearing, and uncultured in China. Polite, circumspect, "face saving" behavior in China might seem indecisive or even dishonest in an American context. Chinese and Americans both have distinctive patterns of communication, and interaction, with many layers of experience and memory that make for vast cultural differences. An awareness and appreciation of differences in each nation's cultural norms and communication can help decrease misunderstanding and promote a richer set of interactions than would have otherwise been possible.

"Saving Face"

The key to good relationships and good communication in China is respect. People in China place great weight upon "face"—attaining and maintaining self-respect and the respect of others. "Saving face" is of paramount importance in China, and in the East Asian world in general. "Face" consists of reputation, trust, and influence—how one appears and wants to appear to others. It depends upon social position, personal ability, economic status, and social ties. But, above all, "face" depends upon how others treat you. Also, if you cause someone to lose face, then you have behaved rudely and have lost face as well.

The following activities or gestures threaten a person's "face" and may provoke embarrassment and defensive reactions:

- being openly challenged
- being openly disagreed with
- being openly criticized
- being openly denied

When communicating a "no" to someone in China, you should be less direct than is normal in the United States. How do you say "no" or even know when a request of yours has been denied? The following phrases avoid a blunt denial, saving face while leaving open future possibilities. They will blend so nicely into the flow of your interactions in China that they will soon become second nature.

- We'll see what we can do.
- We'll do our best.
- Let us think about it.
- It may be difficult.

- We'll try.
- Let us talk about that later.
- We need to discuss this with my supervisor.

If a conflict does arise, avoid reactions that cause the loss of face. In particular, avoid finger pointing or assigning blame. Also avoid "losing your cool," no matter how angry you feel. This is not just a matter of being polite in another cultural context; it is a practical issue as well. Americans in particular have a reputation (fair or not) for becoming quite heated in their interactions. We authors have all seen the effect—the official taking abuse from a foreigner becomes embarrassed, then shuts down, and sometimes becomes defiant, making all wrath completely counterproductive. Instead, a good strategy is to focus on common ground and seek a resolution without an absolute winner or loser. Particularly if you are involved in a conflict where you feel you are clearly in the right, diligently seek a face-saving way to allow your counterpart to correct the mistake.

Names and Titles

The first name is usually the family name, followed by the given name of one or two syllables. For instance, in the name Li Jianguo, Li is the family name that you would normally use with a title—Mr. Li, for example. In the United States we address people by their given names much more often and much more casually than is done in China. For the U.S. traveler in China, the best rule is to address a person by family name plus a title, and to resist using first names until one becomes very familiar with an individual. Even in a friendship, it is better to err on the side of formality. In a business setting, it is a good idea always to use formality. One does not create a more fluid working relationship in China (as we often assume in the United States) by being "on a first-name basis." Doing so is, in fact, often quite counterproductive.

Gifts

The giving and receiving of small gifts is much more common in China than in the United States. When visiting China, small items distinctive to your region of the United States make good gifts. Do not give knives or other sharp objects, clocks, or handkerchiefs. There is, in fact, a set of customs surrounding gift-giving in China that is so complex that it can bewilder a foreigner. Chinese gift recipients certainly understand that you won't know all of the "rules" of gift giving, but do pay attention to the clues you receive. Here are the three most basic rules: First, give and receive gifts with both hands. Second, do not unwrap or ask the recipient to unwrap the gift in your presence. Third, if you later give a gift in return for a gift you have received, reciprocate with a gift of equal or less value.

Eating and Drinking

Dining is a social occasion that builds relationships. Drinking is a social activity as well. Learn to use chopsticks well, and do not eat food with your hands. Western rules, however, apply in Western-style fast-food restaurants such as Kentucky Fried Chicken or McDonalds. Expect your host or hostess to put food into your bowl (often reversing the chopsticks to the "clean side" for this purpose) or to fill your glass. You should not drink "on your own," the way people often do in the West. Drinking is seen as a time for toasting; if you pay attention, you will quickly develop a sense of the rhythms of a Chinese meal. Eat with a hearty appetite, but beware of cleaning your plate or emptying your glass, for each is a sign of continuing hunger and thirst. When you have had enough, leave food in your bowl and beverage in your glass. If in doubt, follow the lead of your host and other guests. Finally, never stick your chopsticks into your rice bowl, even if you don't know where else to put them. A rice bowl with chopsticks in it is a way of making an offering and conjures up ideas surrounding death and family rituals. It does not fit well with the festivities of a meal.

Conversation

Because meals are social occasions, not simply times to "fill up the tank" or "strap on the ol' feed bag," good conversation is a necessary part of a good meal. Conversation topics that are always suitable include family, the meal, food in general, shopping, and other topics of general interest. Open-ended questions that allow people to speak about their lives or their country are a good way to learn more and allow your hosts to show themselves in a good light. Avoid initiating conversations on politics and religion, in particular, and don't ask questions, even if well-intended, that might put a person on the spot. For example, many Americans may desire to tell about their country, but might be embarrassed to be asked about particular details of history and geography. Seek a balance with your questions and answers that is not unlike the balance found in a fine meal, as described above. Finally, you should expect an atmosphere in a restaurant that is *renao*. This translates to something like "hot and noisy," which sounds strange, but you'll recognize it when you see large tables filled with festive conversation and toasts, as well as children playing between tables and a busy atmosphere filled with movement, noise, and tables full of food.

Respectful Behavior

The norms of respectful behavior in China sometimes seem to be the exact opposite of those in the United States. As we have discussed, the frank and straightforward talk so often praised (at least in theory) in the United States can seem rude and disrespectful in China. For example, a Chinese host will not praise a meal when he or she serves it, as we might do in the United States (for example, "I think you will love this dish"). Rather, the host would apologize for serving such plain food. Further, you should respond to a compliment not with a simple "Thank you," as in the United States, but with counter compliments that the host would then defer.

Compliments are greatly appreciated in China, even possibly more than in the United States, and are used much more frequently in polite speech. However, Western visitors to China (and most other part of East Asia) will quickly realize that no compliment received should ever be allowed to rest without self-effacement. To wit, if you compliment a host or hostess in China for an excellent meal, the response will be "Oh, not at all, I am sorry I could not serve you a better meal." You, of course, would repeat your praise a time or two more to communicate your thanks, while your host or hostess would say, "don't thank me," or "it was nothing," or similar deprecating remarks. Be sure though that you are giving and gaining face by trying to fit your behavior to Chinese standards, and do not be like the American boyfriend in *The Joy Luck Club* who agrees with his girlfriend's mother that her cooking was "too salty."

The Chinese Art of Apology

In China, the apology is used frequently. Sometimes an "apology" may simply be part of a ritual—"Please excuse my poor English," a translator may say to you in perfect English. In Chinese, a request or question often is preceded by *duibuqi*—please excuse me, serving merely as a polite sound. Other times the apology may be quite sincere. You can use both types in order to follow local custom or to cover your ignorance and lapses in Chinese etiquette. No rule book can describe all of the nuances of proper behavior in any culture, and even if it could, who could remember all of the details? Any traveler in a foreign land is bound to make mistakes. When you blunder in China, apologize.

- "Please excuse me for not speaking Chinese, do you speak English?"
- "Pardon me for bothering you, but do you know how I can find ____?"

China-Related Organizations

BUSINESS AND ECONOMIC RESOURCES

United States–China Business Council
Suite 200
1818 N Street NW
Washington, DC 20036
Phone:(202) 429-0340
Fax: (202) 775-2476
Web site: http://www.uschina.org

The U.S.-China Business Council is the principal organization of U.S. companies engaged in trade and investment in the People's Republic of China. Founded in 1973, the council serves more than 250 corporate members through offices in Beijing, Shanghai, and Washington, D.C.

World Trade Organization (WTO)
rue de Lausanne 154, CH-1211
Geneva 21, Switzerland
Phone: (41-22) 739-51-11
Fax: (41-22) 731-42-06
Web site: http://www.wto.org
E-mail: enquiries@wto.org

The WTO is the only international organization that deals with the global rules of trade between nations. It encourages free trade throughout the member nations, including—since December 11, 2001—China.

CULTURAL EXCHANGE AND EDUCATIONAL RESOURCES

American Field Services–U.S.A (AFS–USA)
Web site: http://usa.afs.org
American Field Services–U.S.A Regional AFS–USA Centers
AFS Central States
2356 University Avenue West, Suite # 424
St. Paul, MN 55114

Phone: (651) 647–6337
Fax: (651) 647–6628

AFS Northeastern States
32 Hampden Street
Springfield, MA 01103–1263
Phone: (413) 733–4242
Fax: (413) 732–3317

AFS Southeastern States
1610 West Street, Suite 202
Annapolis, MD 21401–4054
Phone: (410) 280–3000
Fax: (410) 280–3001

AFS Western States
310 SW 4th Avenue, Suite 630
Portland, OR 97204–2608
Phone: (503) 241–1578
Fax: (503) 241–1653

For more than fifty years, the American Field Services–U.S.A has provided individuals, families, schools, and communities with international and intercultural learning experiences through a global volunteer partnership. With an impressive international exchange program, AFS sponsors more than ten thousand students internationally. Each year, AFS-USA makes it possible for more than 1,700 American students to live, study, and volunteer in one of forty-four countries, including China.

Asia Society
725 Park Avenue
New York, NY 10021
Phone: (212) 288–6400
Fax: (212) 517–8315

Web site: http://www.asiasociety.org
The Asia Society works to foster understanding of Asia and communication between Americans and the peoples of Asia and the Pacific. A national nonprofit, nonpartisan educational organization, the Asia Society provides a forum for building awareness of all countries in the Asia-Pacific region. The society sponsors films, art exhibitions and performances, publications and materials for various groups, and lectures, seminars, and conferences designed to help Americans appreciate the uniqueness and diversity of Asia.

AsiaNetwork Freeman Foundation Program
Professor Madeline Chu
ASIANetwork Freeman Programs Director
Kalamazoo College
1200 Academy Street
Kalamazoo, MI 49006
Phone: (616) 337–7325
E-mail: chu@kzoo.edu

Made possible by a generous grant from the Freeman Foundation, the ASIANetwork promotes study at fifteen colleges and universities in East Asia. The overall goal of the program is to increase the number of American students (from a wide range of disciplines) who are familiar with Asian cultures.

Fulbright Memorial Fund Teacher Program
Institute of International Education
1400 K Street NW, Suite 650
Washington, DC 20005–2403
Phone: 1–888-CHINA-FMF
Fax: (202) 326–7698
E-mail: fmf@iie.org
Web site: http://www.iie.org/pgms/fmf

The Fulbright Memorial Fund Teacher Program is designed to provide American primary and secondary teachers and administrators with opportunities to participate in fully-funded, short-term study programs abroad, including China. Its goal is to increase Americans' understanding of other cultures through its educators, who will help shape the next generation of leaders.

GOVERNMENT RESOURCES

**Embassy of the People's Republic of China
in the United States of America**
2300 Connecticut Ave NW
Washington, DC 20008
Phone:(202) 328–2500
Fax:(202) 588–0032
E-mail: chinaembassy_us@fmprc.gov.cn
Web site: http://www.china-embassy.org

The Chinese Embassy's Web site is a good place to learn the official

Chinese government view on events in China and around the world. It also is helpful when planning a trip to China. See "Visas and Passports" at the Web site. The site also links to the five Chinese consulates in the United States.

**Embassy of the People's Republic of China
in the United States of America**
Visa Office
2201 Wisconsin Avenue NW, Room 110
Washington, DC 20007
Phone: (202) 338–6688
Fax: (202) 588-9760
E-mail: chnvisa@bellatlantic.net

A visa application for visiting China can be obtained on-line or by writing to the embassy or to the consulate assigned to process visa requests from your state. You probably should heed this warning from the Chinese embassy: "Please be advised that sending your visa application or document(s) to the incorrect office may result in complication or delay in processing or even denial of application."

All visa requests from the following states are handled by the Chinese embassy in Washington: Delaware, Idaho, Kentucky, Maryland, Montana, Nebraska, North Carolina, North Dakota, South Carolina, South Dakota, Tennessee, Utah, Virginia, West Virginia, and Wyoming. Residents of other states should contact the appropriate consulate office listed below.

Chinese Consulate General in Chicago
100 West Erie Street
Chicago, IL 60610
Phone: (312) 803–0095
Fax: (312) 803–0110
Web site: http://www.chinaconsulatechicago.org

Consular District: Colorado, Illinois, Indiana, Iowa, Kansas, Michigan, Minnesota, Missouri, Wisconsin

Chinese Consulate General in Houston
3417 Montrose Boulevard
Houston, TX 77006
Phone: (713) 524–0780
Fax: (713) 524–7656
E-mail: info@chinahouston.org

E-mail for Visa and Passport: visa@chinahouston.org
Web site: http://www.chinahouston.org

Consular District: Arkansas, Alabama, Florida, Georgia, Louisiana, Mississippi, Oklahoma, Texas

Chinese Consulate General in Los Angeles
443 Shatto Place
Los Angeles, CA 90020
Phone: (213) 807–8088
Fax: (213)–265–9809
Web site: http://www.chinaconsulatela.org

Consular District: Arizona, Hawaii, New Mexico, and Southern California

Chinese Consulate General in New York
520 12th Avenue
New York, NY 10036
Phone: (212) 736–9301 (24 hours); (212) 502–0271 (Monday–Friday 2:00–4:30 p.m.)
Fax: (212) 736–9084
Web site: http://www.nyconsulate.prchina.org

Consular District: Connecticut, Maine, Massachusetts, New Hampshire, New Jersey, New York, Ohio, Pennsylvania, Rhode Island, Vermont

Chinese Consulate General in San Francisco
1450 Laguna Street
San Francisco, CA 94115
Phone: (415) 674–2900
Fax: (415) 563–0494
Web site: http://www.chinaconsulatesf.org

Consular District: Alaska, Nevada, Northern California, Washington, Oregon

United States Embassy in China
3 Xiu Shui Bei Jie
Beijing, PRC 100600
Phone: (86–10) 6532–3431 (embassy switchboard)
Web site: http://www.usembassy-china.org.cn

American Consulate General, Chengdu
No. 4 Lingshiguan Road
Chengdu, Sichuan PRC 610041
Phone: (86–28) 558–3992
Fax: (86–28) 558–9221
Web site: http://www.usembassy-china.org.cn

American Consulate General, Guangzhou
1 Shamian Nanjie
Shamian Island, Guangzhou, PRC 510133
Phone: (86–20) 8188–8911
Fax: (86–20) 8186–4001
Web site: http://www.usembassy-china.org.cn

American Consulate General, Hong Kong and Macau
26 Garden Road
Hong Kong
Phone: (852) 2523–9011
Fax: (852) 2845–1598
Web site: http://www.usconsulate.org.hk

American Consulate General, Shanghai
1469 Huaihai Road (M).
Shanghai, PRC 200031
Phone: (86–21) 6433–1681 (direct); (86–21) 6433–6880 (consulate switchboard)
Fax: (86–21) 6433–1576
Web site: http://www.usembassy-china.org.cn

American Consulate General, Shenyang
52 Shi Si Wei Lu, Heping District
Shenyang, PRC 110003
Phone: (86–24) 2322–1198
Fax: (86–24) 2322–2374
Web site: http://www.usembassy-china.org.cn

The United States Embassy in China represents the United States government in China, provides services to Americans traveling and doing business in China, and processes visa applications for Chinese traveling to the United States. In addition to handling passports and birth registrations, the embassy provides information and assistance about notaries and tax and voting information. The United States also maintains five consulates in China: in Chengdu, Sichuan province; Guangzhou (Canton), Guangdong province; Hong Kong; Shanghai; and Shenyang, Liaoning province.

NEWS RESOURCES

China Business World includes information on Asian markets as well as educational and internship opportunities. The tourism link is also very useful. Available at http://www.cbw.com.

China Daily on the Web gives access to the *China Daily,* China's official English-language newspaper. Includes a searchable archive of past issues. Available at http://www.chinadaily.com.

China World Factbook from the CIA provides current economic and political facts about China along with maps. Available at http://www.odci.gov.

South China Morning Post is Hong Kong's largest circulation, English language newspaper. Available at http://www.scmp.com.

Virtual China offers financial information as well as general news and features dealing with contemporary China. Available at http://www.virtualchina.com.

TOURISM RESOURCES

Fodor's
Web site: http://www.fodors.com

Fodor's Web site provides mini-guides for several major cities in China. Each mini-guide gives travel tips, provides an overview of the city and a map, and recommends sights, activities, restaurants, hotels, shopping, nightlife, and more. A resource section includes more maps, Web links, and information on purchasing Fodor's extensive and well-respected guidebooks.

Lonely Planet
150 Linden Street
Oakland, CA 94607
Phone: 1–800–275–8555 or (510) 893–8555
Fax: (510) 893–8563
E-mail: info@lonelyplanet.com
Web site: http://www.lonelyplanet.com

Lonely Planet's Web site provides a thorough guide to travel in China, including when to visit, how to get there and how to get around, money and costs, events and attractions, and activities (including some off-the-beaten-track ones). Overviews of the history, culture, and environment of the region are available, as is a resource section with Web links, information on purchasing Lonely Planet guidebooks, and access to traveler's postcards with tips and useful current information.

Annotated Bibliography of Recommended Readings

The books and, where applicable, CD-ROMs, periodicals, and Web sites below are organized according to the chapters in this book, as well as the section on language, food, and etiquette. Every effort has been made to include accurate and readable sources that should assist readers who want to know more about China. The resources included in this section are, for the most part, general works on China. The contributors to this volume are happy to say that we have tested the vast majority of these books in our own classrooms, and have a good sense from our students that they are effective. For more specialized titles, please check either the References section at the end of each chapter or the bibliographies in the works listed here. Readers are encouraged to check the Beloit College Asian Studies Web site (see below) for updates of recommendations, as well as those from our colleagues in religion, literature, and philosophy.

GENERAL WORKS

For all of the subjects of this book, the award-winning interactive CD-ROM *Contemporary Chinese Societies,* produced by the University of Pittsburgh's Asian Studies Program with grants from the Chiang Ching-kuo Foundation and the Henry Luce Foundation, is indispensable. Includes maps, charts, graphs, and much basic information on Chinese history, society, culture, economics, language, and politics.

Beloit College Asian Studies Web Site, www.beloit.edu/~asianstudies. The contributors to this volume and our colleagues in areas of Asian Studies that could not be covered in the structure of the present volume have created an expansion and series of updates to the list below. The site also contains illustrations, translations, and informative charts.

Ellington, Lucien, ed. *Education about Asia.* Ann Arbor: Association for Asian Studies. This eighty-page illustrated magazine, published three times a year, includes articles on China that are relevant for both teachers and general readers.

Spence, Jonathan D. *The Search for Modern China.* New York: W. W. Norton, 1990. This is an excellent, lively history of China since 1600 written by a top historian. Although the book is long, it is a wonderful introduction to China's social, political, and economic development over the past four hundred years.

GEOGRAPHY AND HISTORY

Ebrey, Patricia. *The Cambridge Illustrated History of China.* Cambridge: Cambridge University Press, 1999. A well-written and beautifully illustrated history of China that balances political history nicely with social, cultural, intellectual, literary, and artistic approaches.

————. *Chinese Civilization: A Sourcebook.* New York: Free Press, 1993. This is the book that our students almost never sell back after our courses are over. In one-hundred nicely chosen and well-translated texts, Ebrey gives a wonderful overview of Chinese civilization that has the kind of depth that beginning or even experienced readers will find satisfying. Ebrey has also now produced a Web-based version entitled *A Visual Sourcebook of Chinese Civilization* (http://www.depts.washington.edu/chinaciv/), under a grant from the NEH, the Freeman Foundation, and the Chiang Ching-kuo Foundation of Taiwan.

Hansen, Valerie. *The Open Empire: A History of China to 1600.* New York: W. W. Norton, 2000. This is the best general book on Chinese history before the modern period. Some previous background study is helpful before reading this work, because Hansen has given a tremendous sense of historical sources from archaeology to literature. It is the rare overview that includes as profound a sense of both primary and secondary sources of Chinese history.

Shaughnessy, Edward, ed. *China: Empire and Civilization.* New York: Oxford University Press, 2000. This edited volume is a useful introduction to Chinese history and culture. Nicely illustrated, the book provides well-written two-page layouts dealing with more than a hundred key themes. No other book we know of introduces as many important cultural themes.

Smith, Richard J. *China's Cultural Heritage: The Qing Dynasty, 1644–1912.* 2d ed. Boulder: Westview Press, 1994 (available in paperback). This book goes far beyond its subtitle in its range. It should not be the first book in this list that you read, but it is a fine companion for Valerie Hansen's history of China to 1600. Richard Smith provides one of the best portrayals of a "total" world of Chinese history, politics, society, and thought that we have seen, and in a text that is accessible for most readers.

Wills, John. *Mountain of Fame: Portraits in Chinese History.* Princeton: Princeton University Press, 1992. This book might have been a mere collection of "takes" on Chinese history through its major figures were it not for an author as skilled as Wills, who gives a historical narrative at the same time that he is creating a picture of individual lives. It is both accessible to generalists and appreciated by specialists, who enjoy the subtle, but not intimidating, depth.

THE ECONOMY

Books

Dunung, Sanjyot P. *Doing Business in Asia: The Complete Guide.* Lanham, MD: Lexington Books, 1995. This is a useful country-by-country introduction that briefly covers history, political structure, economy, customs, and business-specific topics.

Eastman, Lloyd E. *Family, Fields, and Ancestors: Constancy and Change in China's Social and Economic History, 1550–1949.* Oxford: Oxford University Press, 1988. This book's subtitle precisely describes the contents of the book. Eastman's account is excellent, readable, and accessible to a general audience.

Engholm, Christopher. *Doing Business in Asia's Booming "China Triangle."* Upper Saddle River, NJ: Prentice Hall, 1994. A good book that focuses on China, Taiwan, and Hong Kong in much more depth than is found in the general books noted here on business in Asia.

Lardy, Nicholas R. *Agriculture in China's Modern Economic Development.* Cambridge: Cambridge University Press, 1983. To gain a deeper understanding of the Chinese economy, you cannot go wrong by reading anything written by Nicholas Lardy. This volume is an excellent study of agriculture in the People's Republic of China during the Mao years and in the first years of economic reform.

———. *Foreign Trade and Economic Reform in China, 1978–1990.* Cambridge: Cambridge University Press, 1992. An excellent study of the connections between economic reform and expanding foreign trade during the early years of China's economic reform.

———. *China's Unfinished Economic Revolution.* Washington, DC: Brookings Institution Press, 1998. Lardy emphasizes the downside to China's program of gradual reform, warning that China's economic momentum will be halted without timely reform of the banking sector.

Lin, Justin Yifu, Fang Cai, and Zhou Li. *The China Miracle Development Strategy and Economic Reform.* Hong Kong: The Chinese University Press, 1996. Written by three Chinese economists, this volume is an excellent discussion of why China's economic reforms have been so successful. The analysis is rooted in the authors' training at top graduate programs in the United States and informed by their perspective as practicing economists in China.

Macleod, Roderick. *China, Inc.: How to do Business with the Chinese.* New York: Bantam Books, 1988. Although an older book and focused on doing business in China, this book is well researched, well written, and well rooted in the author's own experience working in China. It provides good, general insights into cross-cultural communication and into Chinese culture.

Naughton, Barry. *Growing Out of the Plan: Chinese Economic Reform, 1978–1993.* Cambridge: Cambridge University Press, 1996. This is the single best discussion of economic reforms in China between 1978 and 1993.

Rawski, Thomas G. *Economic Growth in Pre-war China.* Berkeley: University of California Press, 1989. In this innovative look at China's economic history before World War II, Rawski argues that China experienced more modern economic growth than had been previously described and that the growth resulted in a growth in average output per person.

World Bank. *China 2020: Development Challenges in the New Century.* Washington, DC: World Bank, 1997. This book and many others on China from the World Bank can be downloaded as a PDF file or purchased at www.worldbank.org. This is an excellent overview of a multivolume study of major development challenges facing China.

On-line Journals

Asian Wall Street Journal, http://www.online.wsj.com/asian. This is a valuable resource for Asian markets as well as changing political and economic news.

China Business Review, www.chinabusinessreview.com. Published by the U.S. China Business Council, this outstanding journal focuses on U.S. firms doing business in China. Although not intended as a scholarly publication, top scholars contribute articles to it. Other articles are written by a staff of resident expert journalists.

China News Digest, www.cnd.org. Provides timely and balanced news coverage on China and China-related affairs, as well as information services to Chinese communities around the world.

Far Eastern Economic Review, www.feer.com. Published weekly in Hong Kong (and owned by Dow Jones & Company), this journal calls itself "Asia's premier business magazine." It contains articles on politics, business, economics, technology, and social and cultural issues throughout Asia, with a particular emphasis on both Southeast Asia and China.

See also the newspapers listed in the "News Resources" heading in the China-Related Organizations section of this volume.

POLITICS AND INSTITUTIONS

Dreyer, June Teufel. *China's Political System: Modernization and Tradition.* New York: Addison Wesley Longman, 2000. The best short introductory text on Chinese politics and foreign policy.

Ogden, Suzanne. *Global Studies: China.* Ninth ed. Guilford, CT: McGraw-Hill/Dushkin, 2001. The first half of this book contains a nice overview of recent Chinese history and its political system; the second half presents a good selection of longer recent magazine articles on all aspects of Chinese culture and society. A new edition is published every two years or so.

White, Tyrene, ed. *China Briefing 2000: The Continuing Transformation.* New York: M. E. Sharpe, 2001. Published in cooperation with the Asia Society and updated every few years, this edited volume includes articles by leading experts on China's history, politics, economics, foreign policy, and related subjects.

In addition, those with an interest in current affairs related to China should consult the excellent Asia section of the weekly British news magazine *The Economist,* plus the Asia-based *Far Eastern Economic Review,* as well as the *Asian Wall Street Journal Weekly* and the web-based news journal *China News Digest* (at www.cnd.org). Also, the magazine *Current History* has an annual issue devoted to China, usually published in September.

SOCIETY AND CULTURE

A book that provides a comprehensive overview of Chinese culture and society has not yet been written—a testimony to the complexity of this topic. Listed below are books and films that provide insights into contemporary cultural and social issues from a variety of perspectives—literature, linguistics, ethnography. Depending on the reader's interests, each can serve as the starting point for a more in-depth understanding of present-day Chinese society and culture.

Barme, Geremie, and Linda Jarvin. *New Ghosts, Old Dreams.* New York: Times Books, 1992. An excellent collection of short stories, poems, and personal essays by contemporary Chinese artists and intellectuals. Contrasted with much of what is translated and published by the state, the pieces in this book provide keen insights into the frustrations, and freedoms, of Chinese politics and culture at the end of the twentieth century.

Croll, Elisabeth. *Changing Identities of Chinese Women.* London: Zed Books, 1995. Some of the most interesting research on Chinese cultural and social issues in recent years has been research on women. Croll's book helps readers realize the importance of women's issues throughout the political changes of the past century and to see the impact of political change on women's daily lives.

Davis, Deborah, and Stevan Harrell, eds. *Chinese Families in the Post-Mao Era.* Berkeley: University of California Press, 1993. A collection of essays that looks at family life in contemporary China. The essays cover household structure, marriage, childbearing, and modern hardships.

DeFrancis, John. *The Chinese Language.* Honolulu: University of Hawaii Press, 1986. An introduction to Chinese language that is both entertaining and thorough. DeFrancis debunks many of the myths about both spoken and written Chinese, as well as giving readers a solid understanding of how the language works.

Gao, Minglu, ed. *Inside Out: New Chinese Art.* San Francisco: Museum of Modern Art and the Asia Society Galleries, 1998. This is an exhibition catalog for one of the first major exhibits of contemporary Chinese art in the United States. It includes essays from specialists in Chinese art, as well as full-color plates of the vivid images that are being produced by Chinese artists today.

Yang, Mayfair Mei-hui. *Gifts, Favors, and Banquets: The Art of Social Relationships in China.* Ithaca: Cornell University Press, 1994. An excellent ethnography that describes "the art of social relationships in China." Yang describes the importance of *guanxi,* with detailed discussion of how it works and accounts of her experiences over the course of ten years of research in China.

EDUCATION, RELIGION, LITERATURE, AND POPULAR CULTURE

Bodde, Derk, and M. L. C. Bogan. *Annual Customs and Festivals in Peking with Manchu Customs and Superstitions.* Taipei: SMC Publishing, 1986. Although this book can make for dense reading, it is one of the two most detailed works that allow readers a "nonspecialist" access to the rhythms of daily life in urban China early in the twentieth century (and with hints about cultural practices that have persisted for centuries).

Eberhard, Wolfram. *A Dictionary of Chinese Symbols.* London: Routledge, 1986. This book is just plain fun. Eberhard has created a list of important concepts in Chinese art, literature, and popular culture, many of which have persisted into the present. The many layers of meaning will surprise those who aren't used to multiple "readings" of symbols, but the book is sure to make readers think about symbols in Western societies in new ways.

Feng Menglong. *Stories Old and New: A Ming Dynasty Collection*. Seattle: University of Washington Press, 2000. We recommend these stories as a balance to the texts that describe festivals and customs in isolation. Although those books are of tremendous value for the reader eager to master details, Feng's stories give rich (and often ironic) perspectives on life in seventeenth-century China that provide both slight parallels and stark contrasts with contemporary Chinese life.

Lowe, H. Y. *The Adventures of Wu: The Life Cycle of a Peking Man*. Princeton: Princeton University Press, 1983. This is the other excellent book for learning details of traditional Chinese culture. Readers who are overwhelmed by detail will have a hard time with it, and might be encouraged to read just a few pages at a time. Those who love learning about cultural practices in great detail find this to be one of the most satisfying accounts they have read. The text is organized as the fictional, but culturally realistic, life of a little boy who grows into a young man in China in the early twentieth century. It was originally written by a Chinese author in the 1930s for Westerners in Beijing.

Mair, Victor. *The Columbia Anthology of Traditional Chinese Literature*. New York: Columbia University Press, 1994; and

Owen, Stephen. *An Anthology of Chinese Literature: Beginnings to 1911*. New York: W. W. Norton, 1996. These two anthologies are superb collections of traditional Chinese literature—among the world's most diverse, and a foundation for much modern Chinese literature (even when it was being "attacked" as reactionary or embraced as forward-looking during the tumultuous events of the twentieth century). Mair's work is organized by genre, with all of the major genres represented. We recommend mulling over the poetry, which contains wonderfully effective images, before proceeding to longer pieces. It is also worth reading the "jokes" at the end of the volume, just to see how different cultural categories of humor can be. Owen's anthology is organized chronologically, which makes it a wonderful companion to historical studies. This anthology makes it easier to see the development of literary ideas during important periods of Chinese history. The translations (like Mair's) are fresh and memorable.

Sullivan, Michael. *The Arts of China.* Berkeley: University of California Press, 2000. Sullivan's history of Chinese art is arranged chronologically and is nicely illustrated. Like the literary materials mentioned above, this work is useful even to readers who are most interested in contemporary society. The book nicely balances historical and contemporary art traditions and is a highly readable account.

LANGUAGE

Chang, Raymond, and Margaret Scrogin Chang. *Speaking of Chinese.* New York: W. W. Norton, updated edition, 2001. This is a pleasant book for a general audience who, as stated on the book's back cover, "wants to know more about Chinese [language] without learning to speak or write it." It offers a breezy overview of basic characteristics of the Chinese language, its history, and Chinese culture.

DeFrancis, John. *The Chinese Language: Fact and Fantasy.* Honolulu: University of Hawaii Press, 1986. With more than twenty illustrations and tables, this richly endowed volume provides careful scholarship to the informed nonspecialist. It discusses in depth such topics as Chinese dialects, the formation of the characters in relation to their phonetic representation, and the language reforms in both speaking and writing.

Go, Ping-gam. *Understanding Chinese Characters by Their Ancestral Forms.* San Francisco: Simplex Publications, 3d ed., 1995. Equipped with color photographs by the author, this delightful little book takes the reader on a walking tour through San Francisco's Chinatown, observing the Chinese characters on store signs. It explains the formative principles of the characters discovered and their evolution. The book also provides flash cards for learning the characters.

Li, Leyi. *Tracing the Roots of Chinese Characters: 500 Cases.* Beijing: Language and Culture University Press, 1993. For both intermediate and advanced readers, this informative and carefully structured study traces the evolution and calligraphic styles of Chinese characters. Detailed illustrations by the author complement the intent of the text to posit the original idea of each character. Seven calligraphic styles, which also represent the stages in the evolution of each character—oracle bone inscription, bronze inscription, small seal script, clerical script, regular script, cursive writing, and freehand cursive—historically ground each explanation.

Lindqvist, Cecilia. *China: Empire of Living Symbols.* New York: Addison-Wesley, 1991. This book explains the origins of the characters and explores aspects of Chinese civilization through both art history and archaeology. Numerous photos, illustrations, and sketches enrich a thoughtful and challenging text.

Moore, Oliver. *Chinese.* Berkeley: University of California Press, 2000. For those interested in the history and evolution of Chinese writing, this is a brief and easily understood introductory book. Well-written, with more than fifty illustrations, it describes the major Chinese scripts, the formation of Chinese characters, and how these shapes developed, as well as the art of Chinese calligraphy.

Ramsey, S. Robert. *The Languages of China.* Princeton: Princeton University Press, 1989. A book for linguistic students, concentrating on spoken Chinese. It provides a comprehensive linguistic history of all Chinese dialects, including the languages of the ethnic minorities. Both scholarly and comprehensive, the book benefits from the author's ability to analyze sophisticated structures in comparative terms.

Schneiter, Fred. *Getting Along with the Chinese.* Hong Kong: Asia 2000 Limited, 1998. Pure fun: a charming book full of wit, humor, and insights about how to understand subtle details of Chinese culture. Accompanied by clever cartoons, the book offers many helpful anecdotes that illustrate both the bridges and the chasms that link and separate East and West.

Yin, Binyong, and John S. Rohsenow. *Modern Chinese Characters.* Beijing: Sinolingua, 1997. Coauthored by two linguists, this thorough exploration of Chinese characters addresses itself to readers who write Chinese at an introductory or intermediate level and seek a richer grasp of its printed forms. In a readily comprehensible way, the book covers every aspect of Chinese characters such as their origin, evolution, shapes, formations, total numbers, pronunciation, and calligraphy styles, as well as dictionary ordering.

Index

About the Authors

Robert André LaFleur is associate professor of history and anthropology at Beloit College, where he served as chair of the Asian studies program from 1998–2002. He received his doctorate from the University of Chicago's Committee on Social Thought, where he specialized in Chinese literature and historiography. He has published or given papers on such topics as medieval Chinese historical writing, utopian images in early Chinese thought, the Chinese calendar, and Chinese management techniques during the later imperial period. Over the past decade he has taught a wide range of courses on East Asian history and culture at Colby College, Beloit College, and Waseda University.

Warren Bruce Palmer is an assistant professor in the Department of Economics and Management, Beloit College. Trained in the field of comparative economic systems, his research interests include the study of the electric power system and environmental problems in China. At Beloit College he teaches two China-related courses: Economic Reform and the Chinese Economy and Students and Revolution in China. He received his Ph. D. from the University of Wisconsin, Madison.

John A. Rapp is professor of political science at Beloit College and founder and current chair of its Asian studies program. He received his Ph.D. in political science, with a minor in East Asian studies, from the University of Wisconsin-Madison. His scholarly work has focused on political ideology in ancient and contemporary China, including the works of Daoist anarchists in the Warring States and Wei-Jin eras and Marxist dissidents in the Mao and Deng eras. He is coauthor of *Autocracy and China's Rebel Founding Emperors: Comparing Chairman Mao and Ming Taizu*. At Beloit his courses include Chinese Politics, Democracy in East Asia, Chinese Dissent, Communist and Post-Communist Systems, Daoism, and China: The Long Revolution.

Shin Yong Robson, a native of Beijing, received her Ph.D. in Chinese linguistics from the University of Wisconsin at Madison. She is adjunct associate professor in the Department of Modern Languages and Literatures at Beloit College. Dr. Robson teaches all levels of Chinese language studies and calligraphy. She has published papers in the areas of modern Chinese morphology, syntax, and semantics. Her current research interests include the history of Chinese writing and Chinese historical phonology. She is a member of the International Association of Chinese Linguistics and of the Chinese Language Teachers Association.

Tamara Hamlish is a cultural anthropologist in the field of user-centered design, where she uses ethnographic research to provide insights into innovative product design and technologies. Her research focuses on consumer culture, especially the culture of museums, and visual arts. She served as associate professor of anthropology and Mouat Junior Professor of International Studies at Beloit College. Her research on women artists in China, contemporary Chinese art, and China's museums has appeared in volumes from Stanford University Press, Routledge, and the Shanghai Fine Arts Press, as well as numerous journals. Tamara received her Ph.D. from the University of Chicago.